UNDONE

BREAKING MY BODY TO SAVE MY SOUL

MEGAN WOHLER

Eryn,
I myself have a rather large extended
family and I was glad to have
garned a lot more when I
married Mike. Cousin Eryn, I
hope you enjoy reading my
story. ☺
Love,
Meg

UNDONE

Breaking My Body To Save My Soul

MEGAN WOHLER

Undone
Breaking My Body to Save My Soul

Cover Design: Ken Raney, Raney Day Creative LLC

Cover Photo: Natalie Wohler

❀ Created with Vellum

Written for and Dedicated to
Luke and Natalie

M onday, December eleventh, 2000, 7:40 A.M. It's a very nasty, bitterly cold day today. The strong north wind burns my face and leaves me covered in goose bumps. My legs and arms are stiff from the freezing wind that seems to blow right through me. The walk up to my high school seems longer now that there are two inches of thick solid ice covering the sidewalk. I'm carefully shuffling along with my backpack draped just across my right shoulder and carrying an armful of books in the crook of my left arm. As I approach the door, all my books slip out of my arm into a heap of snow. Imagining everyone looking at me, I curse because I'm embarrassed and pick up my wet, snow-covered books. The bell rings for class before I get to my locker; I'm late, and so starts another cold miserable day in high school hell.

Considering the bullies, the peer pressure, the social cliques, the foolish juvenile mistakes we make, the unreasonable teachers, the busy work and full days of classes, I don't know anyone that misses high school. We may have some fond memories of friends and football games; however, I would venture to guess that once graduated, many are glad that part of their life is over. But I thought middle school was especially awful and no one could pay me any amount of money to repeat it. When it was finally over, I was glad to be out of middle school and I wanted high school to be different. I began high school with high hopes for a fresh start and expectations for new friends and new adventures. But, by my sophomore year, I'd sadly discovered high school wasn't much different than my miserable middle school years. I blended in with the crowd and was pushed aside. I felt devalued and unwanted, sometimes even in my own small group of friends. After many months of being in class with the same group of students, a common response I overheard when my name was called by a teacher for roll call was, "Megan who? Megan Mitchell? Who's that?" Their sneering, mocking tone and snickering made me angry; they knew perfectly well who I was. I said under my breath as I raised my hand for the teacher, "It's me, you jerks." But being as shy as I was, I felt helpless and didn't do much to try and make myself more memorable. I instead put all my effort into being a good student and tried not to care about what other people thought and said or *didn't* think and *didn't* say about me. As far as I was concerned, I might as well have been invisible. So, I put my focus not on popularity but on getting not just "good" grades, but nothing short of a 4.0 grade point average. I was especially good at math and I took great satisfaction in knowing I was the best in my class. My math teacher boasted about me and often used my papers as examples to teach the rest of the class, and I reveled in it.

This sophomore year's math curriculum is geometry and is my first class of the day. I walk back outside to get to my classroom. Mrs. Kline is demonstrating how to solve angles of different triangles. I'm trying to pay very close attention because I won't settle for anything less than 100% on my assignment and the upcoming test. My geometry class is held in an annex outside the main school building this year. I dislike annexes terribly; they're sweltering hot in the summer and bitterly cold in the winter. It is *very* cold in the annex today. My left hand is so frightfully cold that I put on a glove from my coat pocket. My left foot is also bitterly cold. I momentarily take my shoe off to rub it with my right hand in hopes of creating some friction and warmth. I'm sitting in the front of the class, hoping I'm not distracting Mrs. Kline or any of the other students while I try to make myself more comfortable. But I'm so uncomfortable and unnerved that I can't begin to concentrate on Mrs. Kline's teaching. All I can think about is how strangely cold I am. Once back in the main building, my icy hand and foot have become, if not warm, at least no longer a distraction. I feel frustrated that I missed out on Mrs. Kline's lesson and most likely will have difficulty completing the assignment. But, I trust Dad will help me sort through it at home, as he often helps me when I feel a little stuck. I have had two math teachers all through school: the teacher the school hired to teach me, and my father.

Unfortunately, I feel sick at lunch and can't stomach much. I force a third of my turkey sandwich down and drink some water. I'm saving my apple for later in case my appetite picks up. On the way to my next class, photography, I trip, nearly falling face first on the thin carpet beneath me. Embarrassed again, I look around to see if anyone saw and if it is necessary to try to act cool and play it off, but there is no one in sight. Good, no one saw. I also look for a possible fold or hole in the carpet that my foot could have caught on; I don't see a fold or hole either. I slow my pace slightly and barely make it into the classroom before the bell rings. Photography is my favorite class. For an hour I can forget about my mundane life and crappy classmates, hide in the darkroom and create pieces I'm proud of. My favored photographic subject is my youngest sister, Angie. She has a very natural beauty even at ten years old, and she enjoys being photographed. I'm developing a photo of my sister and anxiously wait for the picture to appear as the photo paper sits in the developer. Did I expose it for the proper amount of time? Was fifteen seconds two seconds too long? The developing process is simple: I lay the photo in the developer for a few minutes until the image appears, put it in the "stop" solution for thirty seconds to stop the developing process, and allow it to sit in the fixer for a few minutes before tossing it into the bath to wash. Although the process is short, today I have to sit down while I wait because I feel tired and dizzy.

Next and final class of the day is orchestra. I play violin and sit first chair (concert mistress) ahead of all the other sophomores, juniors and seniors in orchestra. Although good and known in orchestra, I am not well liked because I surpass all the older violinists and have held first chair nearly every year since I started playing violin in the third grade. It's not surprising that I'm skilled in music. Both Mama and Dad played instruments all through high school and college and became very good. Mama still plays in several musical groups across Wichita, but Dad had a throat injury right after college that leaves him unable to play his trombone. Dad grieved his loss, for it was something he was really good at and enjoyed. On New Year's Eve we occasionally had the privilege of hearing him ring in the New Year. It was the only time I heard him play. Mama and Dad's joint interest in music was one of the things that drew them together. Although music is something my parents find great joy in, I don't like it. I enjoyed playing and learning the violin when I started in third grade; but coming into the fourth grade, Mama took notice of my natural (inherited) talent and enrolled me in private lessons. Before I knew it, I was a part of the youth symphony as well. Mama "encourages" me to practice for an hour daily. What was once fun, now feels like a chore.

Anyway, today in orchestra we're on the stage in the school's auditorium practicing for our upcoming winter concert. I have been assigned a short solo. As we're running through my solo, my left hand feels cold again, and each time we run through my solo my fingers move slower and slower; I can't keep up with the tempo. My brain is keeping time, but my fingers aren't moving in sync. Our director furrows his brow and waves us on to continue. After class he visits with me about what may have happened to me on stage. I explain that I am just as confused as he is, but my hand feels stiff and cold. He grabs my left hand and says "Wow, your hand *is* cold." We agree that the stage is certainly much colder than the orchestra room and that my fingers struggled to move simply because they are cold and stiff from the cooler temperatures on stage; nothing to worry about. I need to remember to warm up my hand before the concert so my fingers will be ready to move swiftly across the strings on the neck of my violin.

Once home, I feel so exhausted. It's my duty to practice violin before dinner, but I plead with Mama that I take the day off today because I am so tired. She says, "Nice try; go." So, I sigh, laboriously pull my violin out of its case, put rosin on my bow, tune the strings on my violin and put my cassette tape from my private teacher into our player to play along with the scale exercises she has assigned. Each repetition of the scale gets faster. As I am playing through the scales along with the tape, my fingers move slower rather than faster at each repetition of the scale. I have been able to brush off dropping my books in the snow this morning, being cold in geometry, feeling sick at lunch, having to sit down in the darkroom, but now that I'm struggling to play my violin, I realize something seems to be seriously wrong. I run upstairs frantically to Mama, pale as a ghost and anxious. I show her on my violin that I can't play, and my fingers still struggle to move. She consoles me as I sob into her blouse and she quickly calls our dear doctor and friend, Kim.

Kim fortunately is able to get me in to her office right away. She looks me over as I walk across the tight exam room, tests my mental math skills, and checks my eyes–she says, "Follow my finger up, down, and side to side." Then finally I'm asked to touch each of my fingers on both hands to my thumbs. I don't notice anything alarming or different, and I'm wondering why she looks so serious and maybe even concerned? I can't tell. She pulls Mama out of the room to talk privately. I'm left alone in the exam room for what seems like thirty minutes or more. Now I'm beginning to wonder if they have forgotten that I'm still waiting. I cautiously open the door and leave the exam room. I feel the tension in the area as I search the office for Mama or for Kim. My legs feel heavy, my arms feel heavy, the *air* feels heavy. I struggle to breathe, I feel weighted down and my body drags as I take steps across the hall.

Relieved, I finally spot Mama and smile, but she's crying. She's visiting with a woman who looks very serious and almost sad. Mama has a brochure in hand and keeps nodding as the woman talks to her, and she occasionally glances my way with an expression of deep sorrow. Am I in a dream? Am I dying, or already dead? I don't ask Mama any questions until we both get to the car. Mama sits down in the driver's seat, stares out the windshield and says "Dr. Kim suspects that there is something wrong with your brain." Oh, that is kind of serious. Mama said, "Kim set an appointment for you to have an MRI first thing tomorrow morning." "Ok, Mama." I'm a little confused and don't know whether I should be angry or scared. Before such emotions sweep over me, I pray for Mama and try to console her. Mama is in shock and can't start the car. Her hands are shaking and tears are clouding her vision. As I pray for God's help, I suddenly see a vision of an angel above our car. I smile to myself and feel at peace. Although Mama doesn't see the beautiful angel that I do, I see her shoulders and hands relax. She wipes her tears, starts the car and the anguish and fear I sensed in Mama left her. The angel surrounded us and protected us, and for the drive home, we were at peace.

Neither of us uttered a single word on the drive home, but just as we walked inside the house, Mama said, "I think you ought to call Adam." "Why?" I asked, "Because I think he would like to know," Mama prompted. So, although I think it's not really a big deal, I call my boyfriend, Adam. Like Mama had been, he seems sorrowful when I tell him what's happening. I have a strange inexplicable peace about all of this. Although Adam is not a Christian himself, I say to him, "Will you pray for me?" He quickly responds, "Yes, yes I will."

I get a good night's sleep, but I still really hate to wake up early to undergo an MRI (whatever that may entail). The brochure Mama brought home from the doctor's office explicitly explained that I should not wear ANY metal in my clothing or hair during the test. I can't find anything in my closet that doesn't have metal. Even my comfortable sweat pants have zippers on the bottom. I can't wear a bra because they have metal clasps, my sweatshirts all have zippers, and all my hair ties have metal too. I don't have the option of going naked so I'll have to borrow Mama's sweats and go without a bra, for even my sports bra has a metal clasp. Mama's sweats are so uncomfortably big and unflattering that I would almost rather go naked. Mama rolls her eyes as I whine. "Megan, stop being ridiculous, no one's going to see you." Uh oh, Mama sounds a little impatient.

We are all yawning as we get set for the MRI. Both Mama and Daddy have come to the exam with me to hold my hands. The technician who prepares me for the MRI sets my head into a helmet and tries not to get my hair caught in it (he is not success-ful) and he reeks like cigarette smoke. I almost gag as he leans over me. Both the stench of cigarettes and my nervousness are making me feel very queasy. I feel "Ok" until he positions me on the table and straps me down. Daddy gently lays his hand on my left leg and Mama on my right. The team don't know what it is exactly that they are searching for, so they were instructed to take several images of both my brain and neck. The machine is so loud. I'm doing anything I can to make time seem to pass by quicker. I run through songs that our worship leaders, Meme and Ralph, have taught us at church. I count, and repeat the alphabet all to myself. I'm instructed to sit very still. Should I move, "We'll have to redo the entire scan." After an hour of bumps and thumps pounding in my head, Dan, the technician, says, "Now we need to reposition you to take images of your neck; try not to swallow too much." I look at Mama frantically; we're not done? Mama tears up again and I feel like doing so myself, but I'm instructed not to move.

I bite my lower lip, and just as soon as anxiety comes over me, it leaves, for the LORD again reveals to me the same angel I'd seen at the doctor's office the afternoon before. He was beside Mama. God made it clear that He was with me in the beginning and with

7

the angel's second appearance He seems to confirm that He'd be alongside me in everything hereafter.

Mama and I return home and anxiously wait for Dr. Kim's call with the results. We try to go about our day as we normally would, but there's so much tension in the air that we can't possibly relax. When we got home, Mama said they told her they were scanning me for tumors. Yikes! No wonder Mama is freaking out; my poor Mama. What will happen to me if I *do* have tumors? The only person I've known to have had cancer did not survive. I don't want to die.

Finally, Dr. Kim calls the house at two in the afternoon. Mama answers the phone in the kitchen. I very quietly sit close by on the stairs trying to make sense of what is being said by Mama's reaction and response. She sounds neither pleased nor displeased, but her legs are shaking. "Thank you, Kim, goodbye. Yes, we will" Mama says, and hangs up the phone. With her head down and a piece of paper in hand that she'd taken notes on, she sits down next to me on the stairs, and says "You have hemangiomas; two of them." "What's that, Mama?" "Well," she says, "Kim sounded pleased to report that they are not cancerous or malignant; they're benign tumors." "I still don't follow, Mama." Mama says, "I'm not really sure what they are either, but the good news is that they're not cancer. Our next step is to go see a neurologist (a brain doctor) that Kim recommends."

The doctor that Kim recommended was a pediatric neurologist, Dr. Shah. Dr. Shah is Indian and short. He's not terribly friendly but rather seems very quiet, reserved, and thoughtful. Dr. Shah is familiar with my condition and has dealt with similar cases in other children and young adults. He is very helpful in further explaining what hemangiomas are. He tells us that hemangiomas are masses made of tangled broken blood vessels. Dad had also done his research on hemangiomas and cavernous malformations (which they are more commonly called) and confirmed his findings with Dr. Shah: "Cavernous malformations are abnormal clusters of blood vessels embedded in normal brain tissue. Because they are low-pressure lesions, cavernous malformations can leach blood into the surrounding brain, causing the acute onset of neurological deficits. These lesions compose about 5% of all vascular lesions of the brain. However, they are only found in about 0.1% of the general population." I really wasn't too happy to hear that I was in this small 0.1%; lucky me! And Dr. Shah adds, "Many people who have them may never know they do; in other words, they can be asymptomatic. Your hemangioma, Megan, in the right hemisphere of your brain has bled. That's what explains the paralysis in your left arm and leg." And just as Dr. Kim had done, Dr. Shah watches me walk, asks me to follow his finger with my eyes, tests my mental capacity to do math, and does a reflex test. He further explains that the images from the MRI reveal that I have not just the one hemangioma on the right, but a second on the left. The more dangerous of the two seems to be the one on the right that has recently bled simply because of its location. The mass on my right is located deep in my brain, threatening the hypothalamus, and it appears that part of it may be *in* the hypothalamus. The hypothalamus is no larger than an almond, but of course it has very vital functions. The hypothalamus produces hormones for the posterior of the pituitary gland, maintains body temperature, blood pressure, fluid and electrolyte balance, and it regulates appetite, thirst, sleep, arousal and general reproductive behaviors. As Dr. Shah points to my mass on the MRI images, he asks me a peculiar question, "It looks as though this mass has bled before. Megan, do you recall having an incident in which you temporarily experienced symptoms similar to the ones you're having now?" I thought to myself, don't you think I would remember and have mentioned such an incident and reported it to my parents *then*?! Instead, I very calmly and politely say, "No sir."

However, many years later I recall the trip I'd taken with the school orchestra to Washington, D.C. the year prior to 2000. It was my first time flying, and I was so nervous. I got horribly plane sick and couldn't seem to recover from the trauma through the rest of the trip. I distinctly remember when showering and trying to lather the shampoo into my hair, how strange my hair felt on my hand and how sensitive my hand was to the warm water. I also remembered how my hand and foot were very cold and stiff as we played on the Capitol steps; I could scarcely get my fingers to move. My appetite was amiss and I missed out on an entire free day because my head and stomach felt so awful. Perhaps on that experience I'd had my first bleed and was none the wiser. Had I not gone, maybe I would never have had a bleed, or at least not so early in my life. Maybe I caused it!

After Dr. Shah's question he makes no other mention of the previous bleeding and moves on. He shows us where my additional mass is; in the left hemisphere of my brain in a much less problematic area and thus far asymptomatic. In regard to the mass on the right that has bled and left me crippled on the left, Dr. Shah says, "Surgery would be very risky, but worth looking into." He keeps using words like rare, unusual and unknown, which are words Dad found over and over in his research. He says "Unfortunately, there is not enough information about these cavernous malformations to know why they are there, or what causes them to bleed, but there are precautions you should take; for instance, avoid exerting any pressure on your brain, including tasks as simple as blowing your nose too hard or exerting yourself while passing waste. Also avoid riding roller coasters, sky diving, riding in a hot air balloon, and scuba diving. Weight lifting and high-contact sports are out of the question (I have no desire to participate in sports anyhow); and certainly, avoid blows to the head. Try also to minimize your level of stress."

I don't feel worried about riding roller coasters (never have been on one), sky diving, hot air balloons, scuba diving and the like, but blowing my nose and going to the bathroom? Am I to be anxious about getting a cold? How hard it was going to be to avoid getting sick during cold and flu season; and being told to avoid stress, in itself feels stressful and impossible. I feel a little betrayed by God and by my own body. I can't take comfort in guesswork and theories! How could they not know how to help me? This is crazy! I'm only sixteen.

It was a crazy week and my life was going to look very different, but in some respects a change was a good thing.

My doctors and Dad searched surgical options, wrote to and spoke with other doctors across the nation. No one had a definitive answer; gamma knife surgeons said, "The benefit ratio of surgical intervention is not warranted," and another surgeon said, "I would probably recommend that your daughter be allowed to recover from the hemorrhage and see where we stand." And in some of Dad's research on hemangiomas, he highlighted "Hemangiomas are most often only of cosmetic significance; however, if present in the brain, hemorrhage can be a *lethal* consequence." This was definitely more serious than we'd anticipated. My mass couldn't be treated or removed. I felt helpless, but not hopeless.

I had a strange feeling that the LORD had given me this privilege to grow in faith and trust Him with a condition only *He* knew all about, and only *He* could fix. I relaxed knowing God was in control and knew what to do even if my doctors didn't. And yet, from that day forward I continued to daily regress. Each day I lost more movement in my hand, arm, leg, foot, and even in my face.

Soon it would be Christmas break, and I'd already been away from school for several days. At first, I enjoyed the opportunity to relax, take a break from school and from practicing my violin. I took a guilty pleasure in missing violin lessons. But after visiting with Dr. Shah, I realized I may be on Christmas break indefinitely. I was lonely and hated the fact I'd be away from photography and friends a while longer; but I had Dad, Mama, Angie, my other sister Ellen and my best friend Adam to keep me company. Adam especially made the circumstance more bearable.

As soon as I had known, I called Adam to tell him the results of my MRI and my visit with Dr. Shah to explain to him what I'd be dealing with, as if I really knew myself. I had little to no doubt that Adam would be by my side through this trial. Adam to me has always been a sweet man and a loyal friend. Adam's and my relationship started in first and second grade. I fractured my right wrist the summer prior to first grade. I met Adam (a second grader) the first day of school and my first impression of him was that he was cute, rat tail and all! Our teacher Bonnie introduced us, "This is Adam; he broke his arm in a soccer injury last year, so he certainly knows what you're going through. He'll be helping you in class until your wrist heals." Adam encouraged me and helped me write with my left hand in place of my right and encouraged me as I learned to do other tasks with my left hand that I would have normally done with my right. When I needed two hands to do a task, he took over. We became fast friends; best friends. Instead of playing on the playground during recess, we walked around the perimeter of the playground over and over again until the bell rang. We did that every day, each recess. I don't know what in the world we talked about; we were kind of weird. Other kids made fun of us and teased us that we were boyfriend and girlfriend and sang that taunting song that will go down in history as one of the most annoying songs ever, "Adam and Megan, sittin' in a tree, K-I-S-S-I-N-G. First comes love, then comes marriage, then comes the baby in the baby carriage." We honestly didn't care. I think we both kind of liked the idea of being together in that way. Adam in fact took me on my first "date" when we were in third and fourth grade. We were best friends through the remainder of grade school until he moved to a different school in fifth grade. I missed him so much and no other friend could replace him.

Although we lost contact between grade school and high school, in 2000, five years later, we'd reconnected at our grade school reunion. He was tall, dark and handsome. He had a smile that could make you blush and a great head of hair, like me. He was much like I'd remembered him, minus the rattail. We wrote to one another, talked on the phone, he sent me a beautiful bouquet of flowers on my sixteenth birthday and shortly after, asked me to be his girlfriend. It was so sweet how he doted on me and wooed me. I referred to Adam as my godsend. He came back into my life at just the right time, and I knew it wasn't by accident. God had sent him to help me during this difficult time. Just as he had done ten years prior, Adam coached me and encouraged me to use my left hand. I needed to reteach my hand all the things it had done before, especially when working together with my right hand. They were such simple things that I took for granted and I could no longer do: use the toilet, bathe myself, fix my hair, pull on jeans, button a shirt, clasp a bra, tie my shoes, and above all, play violin. Violin consumed a lot of my time and effort. Although I didn't particularly enjoy it, I allowed my violin to become my identity. I felt a little lost without this skill and wondered where I should direct my time and attention instead. Being stripped of my violin gave me the opportunity to use that time once allotted to practicing, to focus on Christ and discover who I am in Christ (something I would have liked to do long before my bleed).

I was raised in church and had attended Church of the Savior with my family since infancy. Even so I only knew *of* Christ, and His story in the Bible, but I didn't know Him as my Savior and friend until the seventh grade. I went to a Franklin Graham crusade with some of the youth from our church. Franklin Graham introduced Christ in a way that I seemed to have never heard before. I was miserable in middle school and in seventh grade only had one friend whom the entire seventh grade class thought was obnoxious, including myself. She was a pathological liar and had no other friends, so I really did try to be one. At school I felt like a lost soul. I was lonely and clearly needed something to give. When Franklin Graham said that Christ could be my best friend, I immediately felt the desire to know Christ in this way. I came forward and gave my life to Christ. I felt the indwelling of the Holy Spirit for the first time in my life and I couldn't sit still. It took everything within me to keep from screaming my joy out loud as Franklin prayed over us. Never had I felt such love for all people and experienced the peace that the Bible talks about that surpasses all understanding. It was a supernatural moment that I will treasure forever.

When we left the crusade, I wasn't sure how my life would change after that. I expected my life to look different after the crusade experience. My awareness of Christ had been changed, but the world around me looked and felt the same. I needed something to change, but didn't know how to implement the change, so I began to pray.

The diary that I kept with entries starting from 1993 simply kept records and secrets of my daily life until late 1999, when there was a turning point in my writing. I directed my entries to God in the form of prayers. Prayers full of fear, anger, anticipation for a better future, and I was seeking the LORD's will. This particular entry I believe is important and marked the beginning of something deeper with the LORD:

10-20-2000

Dear God,

My dad recently bought for me the book, "Jesus Freaks." It has many stories about martyrs (people who died for Jesus). I've been really impressed so far with the stories I've read. Most of them are terribly gruesome. All these people in the stories never denied Jesus. They were threatened with their lives but they stood strong for Jesus. I'm sure if Jesus helped me, I could stand too. I would definitely be very afraid though. Usually the people in the stories were thrown into prison and beaten (enduring a slow death). I really admire these people and wish I could be like them. I've read many stories, some even made me cry, and I don't cry! These stories inspire me to read my Bible and pray. Hopefully now I can keep a lasting, strong relationship with You LORD. More later.

Love,

Meg

Little did I know when I wrote this in late October that God would bring a heavy trial in early December in which I would need to stand strong for Him and never deny Him no matter what was thrown my way. My faith was put to the test. The bleed came as a shock, but I seemed to be stable in my faith and even was growing closer to the LORD, but physically I wasn't getting any better. I still hadn't been to school and still was resting a lot at home. One afternoon Dr. Kim and her husband Rick, who are also very dear church friends, paid me a visit at home. They arrived around lunch time and were visiting with my parents while I made macaroni on the stove. Kim asked me, "How have you been feeling, Megan?" "Fine," I said confidently. I turned back to the pot of macaroni and suddenly realized that my left thumb was touching the hot pot. I pulled my thumb away. I stared at my thumb shocked; I had hardly felt it burn. I didn't realize I was burning my thumb until I turned around and saw it. Although I kept insisting I was fine, later that day, my walking worsened, and I was told to go to the hospital that evening. Adam was visiting and left with a warm embrace and a promise that he would visit every day I was there. I held back tears until Adam shut our front door and backed out of our driveway. My lip quivered as I watched him drive away and I stumbled upstairs to my room. I sat on my bed patiently, and sobbing as Dad packed. Angie, ten years old, sat next to me on the bed staring at me in disbelief. I'm not sure that Angie had ever seen me cry and certainly had never seen me so afraid. I'd never been to the hospital and didn't want to go. "Dad," I pleaded, "only people who are seriously sick go to the hospital; I'm not seriously sick." Dad didn't say anything, but it was apparent that he was frightened and frantic. We were rushed to the car, and I'm sure Dad sped to get us there. His anxiety made me feel more anxious and he scarcely said a word. I don't know why he hurried us so much; perhaps he thought if we didn't rush, I would get worse. It was really not an unfair or illogical assessment, because it was apparent that my mass was still bleeding and it needed to be stopped. When we got out of the car into the parking garage, Dad and my sisters seemed to sprint for the stairs. I was frustrated that I couldn't keep up. I tried to run after Dad, but my left leg gave out. I collapsed on a garbage can at the bottom of the stairs. Dad ran back and carried me, panting all the way to the ER. He put me on my feet and the first nurse we encountered asked me, "Can you walk to the elevator? We'll need to take you to the pediatric floor on the third floor." Another nurse noticed my eyelids fluttering and Dad trying to steady me on my feet, and before I could answer, she intervened and pushed a wheelchair up behind me. I was so relieved and readily welcomed the chair. I pressed my tired body into the chair, slumped down and dozed off. Dad kept saying, "Are you Ok?" and I heard a tremor in his voice as he said to the nurse, "Is she Ok? Will my daughter be Ok?" I tried to reassure Dad; I needed him to be Ok himself. "Yes Daddy, I'm Ok, just very tired." I could hardly keep my eyes open as they lifted me up into the bed and attached wires to me to get a constant reading of my pulse, oxygen, and blood pressure (my vitals). A very quiet male nurse also put an IV in my hand so they could administer decadron (a steroid to help stop the bleeding in my brain and decrease swelling). The bleed was making me feel weaker and weaker and although not entirely at peace, sleep came to me easily that night.

Once in the night, my nurse came in to change the patches that held the wires to my chest. Without any sort of warning, he turned on the very bright light above my bed and my eyes behind closed eyelids burned. "Ah, what's going on?" I momentarily forgot where I was until the nurse pulled open my gown and forcefully ripped the patches off my skin. He readjusted the wires and put new patches on, then left the room without a word. I cried bitterly as soon as he left the room, not only because he abruptly awoke me and made my chest feel sore, but because he exposed me. Since

I had developed breasts, no man had ever seen me naked. I was very private and wanted to reserve that right for my future husband. I realize it was his job and it meant nothing to him, but that's what bothered me! I hated the nurse for the way he treated me and exposed me. I was troubled and had a hard time going back to sleep. As I began to settle down, however, I thought of sweet Adam and how much he respected me and my privacy. I also prayed that God would restore peace and my self-dignity.

After what I felt was a traumatic evening, I woke up the next morning asking the staff when I could go home. It was close to Christmas and I did *not* want to be in the hospital for Christmas. Mama never left my side and stayed with me through the night and all day. I had several visitors, some of which I was surprised to see. It seemed that half the congregation of Church of the Savior came up to see me that day. All of my family from in town and some from out of town came in too. I was swimming in cards, stuffed animals, flowers, and most of all love. It was an overwhelming, but a wonderful feeling to know so many people cared about me and my family. Although the visits fatigued me, I was always sorry when my guests left. They went about their day while I lay helplessly in bed. I had many tests in the duration of my stay. I put on a brave front, but the tests were unnerving. The staff continually allowed me to bring my stuffed giraffe with me as a comfort during tortuous tests and labs. My second night in the hospital I experienced an awful night of pain. Mama stayed with me while I moaned and I watched *Toy Story 2* to distract me, but I was still such a nuisance to Mama. I kept nagging her, "Mama, when can I go home? I want to go home with you now."

I fortunately didn't have to stay long, I was able to leave the hospital the next morning. So, I was in the hospital for less than a full three days, but to a restless sixteen-year-old girl it felt much longer. I was thrilled to be home in plenty of time before Christmas. I was also comforted and assured that Adam held to his promise and visited me in the hospital.

Although home from the hospital, my leg was still incredibly weak and I felt terribly unstable as I attempted to put weight on it. My leg swung out violently as I tried to walk. My right leg wasn't much help either because I was so tired. Our house had three flights of stairs; it was nearly impossible to avoid them. My room on the upper level shared a floor with a bathroom, but I'd have to descend a flight of stairs to go to the kitchen or leave the house. And my room was not spacious enough to hold much more than my bed and dresser. So, my temporary living quarters at home was in our family room. I had a bathroom, a TV, space to set up a TV tray to eat, and a stereo. Mama and Dad also pulled out the bed from the couch, put fresh sheets on with plenty of blankets and my new collection of stuffed animals I carted home from the hospital. The family room of our house is the hub of our home. To my satisfaction, I wasn't locked away in my room, but instead was in the middle of the house and around my family. The only time I had to ascend the stairs was when I wanted to eat in the kitchen or needed to leave the house, neither of which happened very often. And the very best part of being in the family room was being within view of our Christmas decorations.

When my sisters were at school, Dad at work, and Mama practicing her instruments or getting other housework done, I rested in bed and stared at our Christmas tree at the foot of my bed covered in lights and Christmas ornaments, both bought and handmade, that each had meaning and a story. And the beautiful tree was iced with tinsel. With the aroma of the pine and the soft, warm glow of the tree, especially as Mama played Christmas music in the CD player, I felt the LORD's presence and again, peace that surpasses all understanding.

Christmas in previous years had been about the excitement of giving and receiving gifts, and fun traditions, but this Christmas was different in many ways. For the first time, I truly reflected on the meaning and celebration of Christmas. My bleed made me painfully aware of the value of life and of my relationship and need for Christ. I reflected on Jesus healing the sick various times in the gospels and how much more profound and personal these miracles felt to me. I then noticed that the scriptures are filled with examples of suffering, which I could now relate to. I wept that Christmas in gratitude and reverence to God, for subjecting Himself to suffering and also healing others who obviously were in need of physical healing.

Gifts were not at all important to me that year, and yet, my parents and extended family showered me with gifts. In previous years I would have prized such an outpouring of gifts. Although grateful, I felt humbled and a little embarrassed. Among my many gifts, I received a latch-hook rug from Mama and Dad. Mama bought it for me prior to my bleed and in addition to being a picture of a violin once completed, she felt bad that I probably wouldn't be able to do the project now with my hand crippled as it was. However, it proved to be helpful in my recovery. I did a few rows of my latch-hook rug every day and in doing so began to strengthen my left hand. It was impossible to do with one hand and demanded the use of both. I was pleased that I could do something fun and aid my left hand in recovery while doing it. Unfortunately, however, I would need more aid in my recovery than just my daily rows of latch-hook. I would have to start therapy, and soon.

2

I had my first physical therapy session just after Christmas. The only therapy services I'd heard anything about, prior to my bleed, were drug rehabilitation and counseling services. There was a rehabilitation center just across from my high school and thus very close to our home. Although I saw it every day, I paid no heed to it; I didn't have any reason to. The rehabilitation center didn't have drug rehabilitation, but I soon learned that they had inpatient and outpatient physical therapy, speech therapy and occupational therapy services. I had no need for speech therapy, but I attended both physical and occupational outpatient therapy. The concept of therapy was so foreign to me; I didn't know what to expect.

I was told I'd need a lot of physical therapy to regain strength and control of the left side of my body. My first therapy session with my physical therapist, Ante (Katochiku in Japanese), showed Mama and me just how weak my body had become. He asked me to walk across the gym floor for him, but I couldn't stand up. I could hardly keep my eyes open. After collapsing many times toward the floor, with my eyes closed and my legs dragging underneath me, Ante and Mama dragged me through the gym. Even with my closed eyelids, the lights seemed so bright that they hurt my eyes. I told myself to keep them shut tight, lest my eyes become damaged. And although there didn't seem to be many people there, every noise I heard seemed amplified in my head and made me dizzy and inexplicably fatigued. I was completely relieved when Ante took me to a quiet, dark area behind the gym. We were in an area with curtains pulled around us to create more privacy, and no one else was within earshot; good! I was able to open my eyes briefly and get a better look at my therapist, but my eyes still strained to stay open. Ante told me to close my eyes again. With a very heavy, tired sigh I closed them again and said, "Thank you." I felt bad not being able to keep them open for more than a few seconds, so I was grateful to get the permission to close them; now if only he and Mama would let me alone to rest. I needed to lay down and sleep.

But, to my dismay, Ante proceeded with a test. He asked me to hold out my left hand. He said he was going to put different objects in my hand, and with my eyes still closed, he wanted me to turn the objects over in my hand to determine what they were. He put four different objects in my hand.

"Here's the first," he said. "Move it around in your hand." He watched me roll it around in my left hand. "Now, what is it?" He said.

"A pin," I replied, a little puzzled.

"Okay, here's another, what is this?" Ante implored.

"A pin," I said.

I told him the third and the fourth objects were also pins.

Not only was I troubled the first time I got pricked with the pin, but by the third and fourth I was rather annoyed. I didn't think I'd signed up for acupuncture.

Ante asked me to open my eyes.

"Now, watch your hand as I place the objects in your hand again," he said.

The first object he placed in my hand was in fact a safety pin, but he pointed out that it was clasped and didn't stick me as I said it did before.

The second object was a dime. At this point I thought he was pulling my leg. However, I watched as I rolled it in my hand and I could see now that it was a dime, but it still felt like a pin sticking me. The third object was a button and the fourth a cotton ball; they all still felt like pins and needles!

I felt myself get panicky and I was just a little more alert. Other than frighten me, I wanted to know what the point of the exercise was. Ante apologized for upsetting me, but explained that he needed to get a starting point to help him determine how much damage I had and what he would need to do to aid me in my recovery to get back to *me* as I was prior to December 11th. He caught my attention and I was interested, but I still pleaded with Ante and Mama,

"Please let me be, I just want to go home to sleep."

But, we continued the session against my wishes. Ante's eyes showed that he had compassion on me and was aware that he couldn't possibly understand what I was feeling because although he'd been a therapist for several years and seen similar behavior and deficits in other patients, he'd never experienced such a physical trauma himself.

Ante was so patient with me and a very good therapist to be my first. He was a thin Japanese man who, like me, was quiet and shy and very kind. It was apparent at my first therapy session I was at a bad place, with a long road of recovery and hard work ahead of me. I went to therapy three times a week for several months. I saw Ante for physical therapy. He spent 45 minutes to an hour with me each session, having me go through a regimen of exercises to strengthen my leg so I could safely walk again. Ante had me climb stairs, ride a stationary bike, lift weights with my legs, and do balance exercises; it felt drudging, but I was determined, and I had hoped to also relearn to swim, ride a bike and run.

Although the debilitation of my hand was the lesser of the two evils, I saw an occupational therapist just as often as I did a physical therapist when at the rehab center. The goal of occupational therapy is to regain use of the arm and hand to do daily necessary activities like maintain hygiene, dress, eat and drive independently. I regularly had Dana for occupational therapy. I thought therapy with Dana was fun and creative.

Ante was quiet, whereas Dana liked to talk. She asked me about school, about my Adam, my family, my interests, and dealing with my new situation. Dana provided both occupational and emotional therapy; I looked forward to our visits. In occupational therapy, Dana and I worked regularly on fine motor skills. I used tweezers to pick up pegs to put in a puzzle board; although right-hand dominant, I attempted to write and draw with my left hand; I pinched clothes pins with different levels of difficulty and reached to place them on a "tree"; and did many more exercises that simply felt like games. Dana even had a board that reminded me of a doll my grandma had. She handed me a board that had a lace to tie, buttons to button, a zipper to pull, and snaps to fasten, I laughed and said,

"My grandma has a doll that taught me these tasks as a child."

It's true that a lot of the things that came naturally to me before and that I'd learned to do as a child had become very difficult for me. It was terribly frustrating not to be able to tie my own shoe, a task I learned to do independently by kindergarten. It was humbling and infuriating to need to ask for help with such a simple task I'd learned and mastered at age six.

As I progressed through therapy and my leg and arm got stronger I continued to go to therapy, but didn't see Ante anymore. Whoever was available at the time of my visit was my therapist for the day. Mama and Ante, just before he stopped working with me, added pool therapy to my therapy schedule. I consistently worked with Sue in the pool and with Dana as my occupational therapist, but with a new physical therapist each session. I felt I spent half the session each time explaining my situation and what exercises I'd done with some other therapists in their facility. A few therapists didn't seem to have a clue what they were doing. I must have rolled my eyes a thousand times behind each therapist's back.

I knew I needed it, but I hated going to therapy. While Adam and my friends were sitting in class, I was exercising in my cute sweats next to men and women well into their 70s and older who had suffered from similar debilitating injuries. A teenager like myself didn't belong alongside old folks in therapy. I got tired of being gawked at and pitied by the old folks at therapy. I tried to be polite and smile, but avoided talking to them. Mama talked to the nosy ones for me and often shared more than I would have liked her to. I got tired of hearing, "Oh you poor thing," or "You're so young." Yes, I was attacked with this debilitation at a tragically young age and I clearly should not be here; thanks for reminding me how unfair this is.

Although I felt alone in my mess, Mama shared the burden of my disability with me. She says, and understandably, it was a very difficult season for her. In addition to my sudden physical trauma, while I'd been in the hospital, one of Mama's symphony friends was shot and later died in the same hospital. She was completely grief-stricken and sorrow surrounded her. More than anything, she hated seeing her daughter suffer when there seemed to be nothing she could do to make it better. Praying for a miracle didn't feel like enough. It was all costly, but Mama would do whatever the doctors recommended to rid me of my horrible mass. Mama made herself available. She used any "extra" energy she had beyond her music and house work to selflessly serve me.

Unfortunately, my sisters were often deprived of Mama's attention because I took so much of it. Much of Mama's day was planned around my care. She cared for me during the day while Dad was at work and my sisters at school. Mama brushed my hair, helped me dress, tied my shoes, and she drove me to any and all medical-related appointments. She tried to also be a friend to me, but I resisted her effort to provide companionship. I wanted to be in school and with Adam. I loved Mama, but I was angry about what was happening to me. My anger was misplaced, but I wanted to blame somebody, hate somebody for this mess. I couldn't hate God; I didn't hate God. I felt angry that Mama "let this happen" to me. And how could she not have known? Although aware of the injustice of my emotions, I silently festered and harbored bitterness toward Mama. She prodded me to talk about it, always analyzing me and trying to guess what was going on in my head. I didn't want to cry, process or talk about what I was feeling and going through. I just wanted to get better. I often held back tears and any expression of grief because I didn't want her to try to console me. Everything she said bothered me and I felt tired of being with just her all the time. We listened endlessly to oldies on tapes that Dad had so graciously made for "us" to listen to in the van. My personal favorite was "One Is the Loneliest Number." Just being with Mama all the time and not with friends in school was cause for loneliness.

The things Mama and I did during the day, including therapy, were not normal for me, and I was growing tired of therapy and running errands. Although I didn't have the body of a sixteen-year-old girl anymore, I certainly had the attitude of one. I didn't like being alone with Mama so much and hated what my daily routine had become.

However, when my sisters came home from school and Dad came home from work, our family seemed more normal again. Everyone was home together in the evening as they always were, and nothing was different about that. I needed to spend time with my family and forget about the pressing need of physical therapy and not being able to be a normal teenager for the time being. I looked forward to evenings when we were all together, as it should be. We each had time together doing different things. Dad and I had quality time over a mutual interest: puzzles.

In addition to my many gifts for Christmas, Dad and I received a new 3D puzzle. We'd been working on a few leading up to Christmas, and Mama bought us another to build. It was our hardest puzzle by far, yet also the most interesting. It was a village with little shops, a cobblestone street, cottages, and complete with a watermill (which was possibly the hardest part to construct 3D). Dad and I worked on puzzles the nights that Adam was unable to visit. Although we didn't talk about much else, Dad and I bonded over puzzles; and much like the latch-hook rug, it aided in my recovery. The puzzle helped stimulate brain activity, sharpening mathematical and spatial skills. I bonded with Dad by constructing puzzles together, and I bonded with my sisters in play.

Although sixteen and a young lady, I would have done anything just to connect with my sisters in such a desperate time. I needed them. I had left Barbies alone for two years or more but desired to play with my sisters as often as I could, even if it meant playing with dolls again. Playing was a good escape and I was not ashamed to be a little girl with my sisters again. We spread Barbies out across the basement, making houses out of cardboard boxes, apartments from shelves, and incorporating anything we could to make our play more enjoyable and creative. I generally wasn't embarrassed playing dolls with my little sisters, but the person I did *not* want to find out was my boyfriend Adam. With Adam I was trying to grow up, but with my sisters I was a child, trying to be the big sister they knew and loved playing with. I suppose I wanted to show them that the change would not change me and my relationship with them. Ellen, Angie and I played until we heard the doorbell ring upon Adam's arrival. We'd scurry upstairs to a board game laying out on the family room floor, acting as though we'd been playing Christmas Monopoly for hours. I hoped he was none the wiser. I really enjoyed having uninterrupted time with my sisters, no school, no practicing, just play.

Play with my sisters provided an escape from my new way of life, but time together with Adam provided the ultimate escape. My heart skipped a beat and I momentarily had butterflies each time he rang my doorbell. "Yay, Adam's here!" Adam's companionship was a good distraction from the physical trauma my body was going through; he helped lift my spirits, and helped me forget how different and difficult my day-to-day life had become. He came over every night that his mother would allow him to and took me out of my corner of the world. Adam lived on the east side of Wichita whereas I lived on the west. He was more familiar and comfortable with the east, so he took me out there a lot. We only lived fifteen miles apart, but the east side might as well have been a whole new city; every place he took me was new. I was also far enough away from home that I didn't run into any classmates, which was a relief. Adam made it clear that wherever we went he enjoyed being with me, and my cane that tagged along for walking support never seemed to bother him, so it didn't bother me.

He took me out a lot to experience new restaurants and east-side venues, but when I needed to "cool it," we watched movies. I was on an Alfred Hitchcock craze, so we watched a lot of Alfred Hitchcock flicks at each other's houses. It was fun trying to hunt down ones neither of us had seen before; and we saw some very disturbing flicks. I would not recommend *Marnie* to anyone; creepy! Although my house had the better popcorn, we preferred to watch movies at Adam's house because we didn't have siblings and parents joining us. Adam was an only child and his parents often worked late, so on many occasions, it was just the two of us. Especially when we were alone together, neither of us could stop smiling. I loved the way he held me and winked at me. I craved Adam's company, especially while laboriously trying to get through my regular therapy sessions. I'd never experienced such a close bond with any one person as I had with Adam.

I knew Adam felt the same, but he seemed to desire more out of our relationship. I wanted to take things slow, but he wanted to be more affectionate, kiss me, and snuggle me. His intimate desire for me made me uncomfortable, but aroused interest too. I wanted to feel safe enough to make myself vulnerable with Adam. I'd never considered or given any thought to sex before dating Adam. Adam and I talked about it, and it was fun to talk, but the more attracted to the idea I became, the more anxious I got about being affectionate at all. I withdrew from Adam and felt strong convictions from the LORD, no doubt, concerning my thoughts and where my heart was leading me. I knew I had to think and pray about my emotions. I talked to Mama about sex. Her response surprised me and made me a little uneasy. I expected her to say, and almost *wanted* to hear her say, "It's bad, get those thoughts out of your head!" However, Mama took pause and looked very thoughtful before she spoke. She said, "You must know that you truly love who you give yourself to and should never be forced to do something you're not comfortable with, or that you know you will deeply regret. Sex is not to be given away freely. It's your decision to make, but I advise you to make that choice carefully. Your dad and I love and trust you and want you to know that you're worth waiting for." I wanted Mama to tell me what to do or not to do, but she said it was my choice. Her words of wisdom shook me and challenged my feelings for Adam. That conversation with Mama turned out to be very uncomfortable for me. I knew I was too young and not ready. She was right. I am worth waiting for, but on the other hand, I wanted to prove my love and commitment to Adam. I then understood and could identify with those girls in the very cheesy films we watched in sex education that said they felt pressured into having sex or felt a need to with intention of proving their love to their boyfriend. I used to make fun of those very cheesy, unrealistic films. Oops, I felt myself in the same sticky situation, but for real!

I wanted to talk to Adam about my mixed feelings, but I felt afraid to. I just continued to keep a safe distance. When the two of us were alone, I lay on one couch and he lay on the other. I needed to sort through my inner conflict quick, because I didn't want it to jeopardize our relationship. I wanted us to remain friends and continue to develop deeper feelings for one another. I just felt Adam was ahead of me and fell for me long before I fell for him. What's more, I still felt like a child. I slept with a stuffed giraffe, was playing dolls and Mama was dressing me, bathing me, driving me and tying my shoes. Good grief, I wasn't ready to make a grownup decision to have sex.

However, Adam seemed so grown up to me and mature. He was only a year older than myself, but I teased him that he reminded me of my dad and acted more like an adult rather than a teenager. He listened to Queen and big band groups, like Chicago.

His favorite show was *Mash* and he was reading a book on how to be a gentleman to a young lady, while we were dating. I relentlessly teased him one afternoon as we were on our way to his house and listening to oldies in his car. I said, "My word, you are so much like my dad!" When he parked the car in his driveway, he came around to my side of the car, grabbed me and kissed me. He said "There, now would your dad do that?!" I giggled and said, "Not on the lips!" Ha! Poor Adam, that really didn't sit well with him. Sometimes he made me uncomfortable with his young man-ness. I just wanted him to be a kid, like me. Wear holey jeans instead of slacks, slouch once in a while, don't always talk proper and use words I don't know; that's just annoying. I'm sure I seemed imma-ture and very childlike to him, but he was never unkind. He was always a gentleman and doted on me.

One icy night, instead of driving me home after his school's homecoming dance, I stayed overnight at Adam's house. Our parents were worried we may get into a car accident on the way home. I was a little giddy. "Thank you for ice. I get to stay the night at my boyfriend's house!" It was very exciting and I looked forward to all-night conversation. However, I couldn't help but wonder if Adam expected or had hoped for something a little different; and I was nervous. But, when he came in my room just before bed, fully dressed in his airplane pajamas, I smiled, stifled a laugh and realized Adam may *act* grown up and pretend to be grown up, but he was still a child too. Neither of us were ready for sex, and that was a relief. So, I was certain Adam didn't expect sex, but I was disappointed that he never made it down to my room to talk late into the night or to just snuggle. I laid awake waiting for him and didn't get much sleep.

Despite our differences, and different desires or expectations for our relationship, I sincerely loved Adam, and enjoyed being his girlfriend. We were childhood friends and then high school sweet-hearts, what a perfect love story. So, I was upset and confused when headed home from his house that I felt the Holy Spirit say it was time for me to end our boyfriend/girlfriend relationship. Deep down, I knew why; it was because emotionally I was too dependent upon Adam, and I set unfair, unrealistic expectations of him that he could not humanly fulfill. I expected him to drop everything when I needed him and to come see me. Homework wasn't important, his friends weren't important, I had to have him by my side. Also, I knew the LORD was protecting me from doing something I would most definitely regret. Although I was pretty well decided to abstain from sex, the temptation to give way to the flesh was still there. I loved Adam, I thought it would be fun, and I trusted Adam to be respectful. I was comfortable with the idea of Adam being my first. I wanted to solely trust and rely on Christ, but I felt I also needed my sweet Adam. I referred to him as my godsend. I dismissed the inner voice and decided it was absolute nonsense; I could not have heard such a word from the LORD! "LORD, please don't ask me to distance myself from the only friend I have."

Although I kept my thoughts to myself, Adam felt I was hiding something from him. I kept insisting I wasn't, until he broke me and I shared some of my most intimate pages in my journal, most of which spoke of my ridiculous infatuation for him that I had difficulty expressing to him face to face. He enjoyed the praise he read about himself in my journal and delighted in the fact that I'd frequently written "I love Adam." His smile disappeared however when he read this:

02-16-2001

Dear LORD,

Today and yesterday I've been thinking a lot about my relationship with Adam and You. I have been pretty depressed that I haven't been able to see Adam yet. Thursday he was out with some friends and today he was grounded, but he isn't sure of what he did! I've really been wanting to see him. Whenever I'm depressed, he always cheers me up. He's a very good friend and boyfriend. I feel almost mad at his mom; it seems he was grounded for no reason. This was a week that I really needed to be with him. I was depressed Thursday, so I told him how I felt, and why I was so depressed. I remember telling him that it was all up to God now to heal me. The hemangiomas are very much still there. I told Adam that I strongly believe that only You can heal me now. His response really surprised me. He said that maybe I don't have enough faith in man. What a ridiculous thing to say. Then he said something that disturbed me; I was kind of offended! He said that not everything can come from above. But of course, I believe that You are in control of all things; nothing can happen without You. Adam clearly thinks differently than I do.

He further explains that man sometimes needs to fend for ourselves and depend on our own strength. But, hadn't he seen what I'd been through, how out of control of the situation I'd been?

I just think that our relationship could be stronger if we were of the same religion. I wish he were Christian, then maybe I could talk to him more openly about my faith without annoying him or making him feel uncomfortable. Adam has accused me of not telling him everything that's on my mind; of course I don't. There are some things that need to be kept between You and I and no one else. I can talk to you about anything at all and I don't feel uncomfortable (I bear my soul unto the LORD). You are also the only one whom can ever be there for me when I need You. Adam disagrees. He says that he will always be there for me. I argued with him and said it's not possible. He has a life of his own which involves school, work, homework, and other people in his life…

You LORD never need to leave me for sleep, nourishment,

school, You're there when no one else can be. I wish that Adam could fulfill a similar role, but I need to realize that he's human and cannot possibly be God…

Love,
Megan

Although our difference of opinion and perspective on God didn't bother me enough not to be together, once Adam knew how I honestly felt, it bothered him. He called less and soon after his spring break, Adam said he thought it best that we not date one another anymore. I was heartbroken and so angry. How could he do this to me? He seemed to enjoy being my knight in shining armor and seemed to make it clear that he loved me; didn't he love me? I was getting better and nearly ready to go back to school and that was in part because of him. It didn't make sense; I was finally getting better. Why would he leave? I still needed him and I desperately wanted him. Did he think he wasn't needed anymore? It just wasn't true! Ugh! I knew I shouldn't have shared my journal pages with him!

"But Adam, I really do love you!" Perhaps it was too little, too late to say so. I wish I could have said it more often to his face.

3

I regretted not being more open with Adam and withholding affection that I so desperately wanted and needed to give him. He was gone but even with a broken heart, I physically progressed so swiftly in the following weeks that I was back in school the next month. I was so excited to walk through the high school doors again and go to each of my classes as a normal student. My closest friends knew ahead of time that I was coming, so they weren't terribly surprised to see me. No one else, however, seemed to have noticed my extended absence and thus didn't acknowledge my return. A fellow student in my history class thought I was a new student and flirted with me. My name had been removed from all of my classes' roll call sheets, and when standardized tests were handed out in math class, I wasn't given one. Did the school think I had transferred or died without telling anyone? I had a homebound teacher while away from school, but I had missed so much class work, that I in fact felt like a new student and I would have to play catch up. Most of my teachers were good about getting work and instructions home to me, but my biology teacher was not. On many occasions I didn't have the means to do the lab assignments at home or simply didn't understand them (even with the aid of my homebound teachers and my parents), so upon my return, my biology teacher told me I had a "D" in her class. We went through her grade book together and she pointed out assignments that I hadn't turned in, most of which I insisted she either never gave me or I couldn't possibly do at home. And without a word, just a smirk, she then handed me a stack of homework that she'd apparently forgotten to send home to me. How is this happening to me? My lab partners in biology didn't even acknowledge my presence until the bell rang for dismissal. Finally, one said rather rudely, "And where have you been the last few weeks?" I sat dumbfounded for a moment, then muttered, "I was really sick," but he hadn't heard me because he was already on his way out the door. Seriously, where have I been the last few *weeks*? I've been gone three months! I was angry as he turned and walked out of class; that was the last straw. I wanted to cry and scream, "You jackass. This whole school sucks!" Since I didn't have a need to go to orchestra anymore, biology was the last class of the day. It was a horrible way to end the school day. I don't know if I was expecting a welcoming committee or special recognition, but I was heartbroken that no one shared the excitement I had upon my return to school.

I hadn't been in school for three months, was disconnected from my school friends and somehow felt more invisible than I was before. Didn't anyone want to hear about what had happened to me? I longed to share the news of my supernatural experiences and spiritual growth with someone, *anyone*, but no one cared. Since I had been gone so long, my best friend Tina befriended another classmate and they spent more time together than she and I did for the remainder of the year. I no longer had orchestra, Adam or Tina. I had lost what little sense of belonging and the friendships I felt I'd had.

In addition, I didn't realize until I didn't have it anymore, how much I relied on my musical ability to express emotion. I couldn't even begin to play my violin again. Even after many occupational therapy exercises, I had lost my fingering hand to play. I had to find a new avenue in which to express myself. I wrote many average poems about my broken heart and lost soul. I also loved art, especially photography, so I was determined to excel in photography. Photography, however, didn't come as easily to me as music did. I really wanted photography to feel natural, more effortless. I took lots of pictures and often stayed after school and wouldn't head home until my teacher was ready to go home herself. Even so, I didn't feel as though I was very good at photography, at least not compared to how good I was on the violin. I had been blessed with the gift of beautiful tone while playing my violin. It was something that I felt came naturally, and couldn't be taught. But, much like beautiful tone can't be taught to a musician, it seems a photographic eye can't be taught to a photographer. And I clearly had not been gifted a photographic eye. I was just determined to find something I was good at and that would make me notable, to feel significant. Desperate, I even tried playing the violin again. But having to start back at square one, teaching my fingers to play "Twinkle, Twinkle, Little Star" was humiliating and frustrating. I didn't enjoy playing enough to try to build the skill back up again.

I prayed and prayed and prayed for God's direction and assurance, but slipped into a deep depression. I continued to read and pray, but soon lost heart in that too. I could feel myself slipping away from Jesus. He seemed distant and absent for the first time since my bleed. I held on to the hope of rekindling a relationship with Adam. But, even after my many attempts to repair our friendship and my desperate pleas for his companionship, Adam stood firm in his decision. I had to accept that Adam wasn't going to change his mind about me or about God. I spent too much time alone and with my head down the remainder of my sophomore year of high school. I spent many nights spread out on my bedroom floor, grieving the loss of a dear friend and godsend and finally began to process and grieve the change in my body. I laid in the dark, and watched many candles burn to the ground while listening to somber music. Whether it was a weekend or weekday, I spent nights in my dark bedroom, door shut. I shut out my family and what friends I might have had, and I simply prayed, pleaded to God, for something to change.

I felt somewhat guilty for doing so, for I know the LORD is to be my strength and friend, but I felt the answer to my problems was for the LORD to provide another friend such as Adam to come into my life. I swore that the potential friendship would not keep me from depending on God. And that it would not distract me from seeking God, as it had with Adam.

In November of 2001, I received a mass email from a woman at my church. She said her son would be apart from the family for the holidays because, being a Marine, he was stationed in Okinawa, Japan at the time. She asked if members of the congregation would be so kind as to send him a holiday greeting from home. I had never met her son, but have loved to write and loved an excuse to, so I wrote him a letter. I've written to many people: friends, cousins, and my boyfriend, all of whom took many days, weeks, months, sometimes years to reply to my letters. I had been praying for someone to be able to keep up with my pace of writing. Within just a few days of sending my greeting to her son Cameron, I received a letter back. I was pleasantly surprised by his speedy response, and thus began our relationship as pen pals. I wrote to Cameron frequently and he to me. His letters were long, always interesting and thoughtful. I looked forward to hearing from him; it was always the highlight of my day and sometimes the only joy I felt regularly. Although a stranger thus far, in a short amount of time I felt I'd grown close to Cameron and as if he and I knew each other well. I kept to myself at school, but I poured out my heart to Cameron on paper. He had experienced some pain in his life and sympathized with mine. It was nice to have someone to share my feelings with. Because I'd never met him, I didn't fear his rejection or judgment. I didn't care. However, there came a time when I had wished he didn't live so far away and that we could meet face to face. And yet, I had vowed to God that I would not put an earthly relationship ahead of Him again, and Cameron's distance made it easier to keep that vow. Then my prayer became, LORD, when You feel I'm ready, and my relationship is steady with You, please provide me with a Christian friend who is close. I was so proud of this poem when I wrote it, now I'm a little embarrassed to share it.

A Pleading Prayer (poem)

God listen to my cry for help, wash away my pain.
Lift my burdens from my heart and make me free again.
I still feel the tremors and slight pain of throbbing in this
fragile brain of mine.
To ask to heal me completely could be too much to want,
or even too much to imagine.
So, I asked for a friend and You gave me many, but can
they ever fill my hole?
Through my eyes I see only one solution, and that is to be
friends with *him* once more.

Cameron is my marine friend who always manages to lift
my spirits and make me laugh.
But Cameron lives so far away and is headed down a
different path.
Matt Westfall is my distant cousin who has encouraging
words and is on my level of thinking,
But the distance between us keeps us apart. The last time I
saw him was just after Thanksgiving.
Tina is my school friend who shares my love of art and
always walks me to my class.
But, Tina and I only know each other's outside
appearances, and we simply leave it at that.
Kerri is my longest lasting friend; we went to grade school
and church together.
But, Kerri and I have gone our separate ways and we
hardly get a chance to speak to one another.

Ellen is my younger sister who is constantly available to
converse,
But Ellen is a Corman and I a Mitchell, two families that
are entirely too diverse.
So, I ask You now for a friend that lasts.
I ask You to wipe out my haunting past.
Since this hemangioma I have doesn't seem to be going
away,
I need an extra pair of legs that is willing to stay.
Who will be the friend to pick me up when I fall?
Who will be the friend when I'm upset that I'll call?
An understanding and faithful friend is the best gift You
could give me.
With a friend like *him* again, I'll be able to rest easy.

I believed I needed the accountability and spiritual challenge that a Christian brother or sister could supply as well as the closeness and affection I'd experienced with Adam. I joined Campus Life at school, but unfortunately, was not readily welcomed. Occasionally, being impatient with the LORD, I tried to force myself on people in Campus Life in hopes of finding the Christian friend I desired and felt I needed. And when that didn't work, I always repented and turned back to scripture. To ensure that I didn't become dependent on Cameron to fill my emotional need either, I read scripture and prayed over the scripture before I opened his letters or wrote him back; but doing so served a second purpose. Although not an agnostic as Adam was, Cameron was also not a Christian. We'd been raised in the same church, heard the same gospel, both been through some trials, but responded to the LORD's message differently. As often as I felt prodded to, I shared my faith with Cameron. I didn't share the new me, the changed me, with Adam often enough and regretted it. With Adam, I wasn't being true to myself or to the LORD. I was only having fun and wanted to enjoy it while it lasted. However, I felt comfortable sharing my faith in writing with Cameron or anyone who would take the time to read it. It was an incredible feeling and a good start to my spiritual growth and confidence in sharing about Christ. I owe thanks to my friendship with Cameron for renewing my passion to read scripture. I felt I had a purpose in doing so, not only to edify myself, but to learn from it. If I was challenged in my faith, I wanted to be prepared to respond confidently and with an educated answer.

I've read a comment I believe was made by Philip Yancey, an author I'm incredibly fond of, saying, "Reading the Bible at random, will yield random results." I have two or three journals full of "random" scripture that I felt the LORD led me to that prove otherwise. Being new to the Word and not knowing where to start, I prayed over my closed Bible every day, saying, "Jesus, turn me to the passage you'd like me to read today." Wherever I turned to, I felt the LORD speak to me every day through His Word; and I expected to hear from Him daily.

Just in writing, I felt closer to Cameron than I ever had to Adam. I felt the break-up with Adam and especially the recovery of the bleed changed my life forever and it forced me to grow. I made an unseeingly close bond with a Marine before I'd met him and didn't feel as anxious about developing new friendships anymore. I made an active decision to take more social risks and to push myself out of my comfort zone from then on. First, I decided to take a church trip.

I was surprised my parents allowed it, but the summer prior to my final year of high school, I went to Mexico. Our youth at my church joined up with the youth of Asbury United Methodist to go on a weeklong mission trip to Santa Ana, Sonora Mexico. It was the first trip I'd taken outside the country. I doubted my physical ability to keep up, but I felt secure and comforted that both Dad and my sister Ellen were going. I wore a brace for my left foot and ankle that my physical therapist had fashioned for me and I was put on the work team that required the least amount of physical strength. Although I had recovered from my bleed, the trip was a physically challenging experience. I slept very little each night and did a great more physical activity than I'd become accustomed to. I woke up so tired each morning. I was on the painting team, and as we painted each morning I could not keep my eyes open. I often painted with my eyes half open, but the LORD sustained me and the social benefit of the trip far outweighed the physical strain.

I absolutely did not fit in with my youth group at Church of the Savior, all boys with whom I had nothing in common. They talked about science and time travel and all sorts of bizarre topics or theories I thought were ridiculous and I had no interest in. I was quiet and often overlooked. The pain of being ignored in my church youth group was greater than the invisibility I felt at school. I needed their support and concern, but didn't receive it.

Needless to say, I was thrilled to go to Mexico with a large group of youth from a different church. I met other Christian men who were nothing like the goofy boys of my church youth. They were kind and interesting and many of their young men were on fire for Christ, and it showed. Ellen and I made fast friends of the Asbury youth and enjoyed being with a different crowd. Their worship was powerful, and their passion contagious. I didn't know a church youth could be so inviting and accepting. I decided when we got back home to the states that I would attempt to remain friends with these amazing people of God from Asbury church.

4

The Mexico trip and my new-found friendship with Cameron stirred up a new sense of confidence in me. I felt determined to continue growing and developing as an individual. At school, my reputation as a forgettable misfit seemed impossible to shake, but as my final year of high school approached, I had decided that I'd make the last year count. I was determined to go to all the school events and to be more vocal, so I would no longer be the Megan that no one knew.

I was off to a good start by attending the first few football games and the welcome back, "Aloha" dance. I joined a few clubs and had an event calendar to check off the events as I attended them. I prayed somehow that my plan for school involvement would produce happiness, recognition and significance. It was fun to attend the events, and I did feel more a part of the school, but it didn't exactly bring about the change that I was hoping for. I found myself standing in the bleachers, walking across the dance floor alone and still feeling invisible.

To fill my void of loneliness, I poured myself into my art and tried to distract myself from despairing. My faith had grown and I grew to have an appreciation and love for scripture, but something was still lacking. I missed God; He seemed silent. I longed for the tender, intimate moments and revelations from the LORD that I'd experienced through the suffering of my bleed in December of 2000. I was grateful to God for my pen-pal relationship with Cameron, but I still dearly missed Adam. I missed God and I missed having a friend to talk to, but I didn't know how to change that, so I prayed and waited. By mid-October, God answered my prayer with His unexpected, but perfect plan. First, God blessed me with a friend.

In addition to photography, I enrolled into a second year of pottery. My love was genuinely in photography, but I wanted to work with my hands too. Photography wasn't an easy art for me and pottery was even more difficult, but I enjoyed trying.

At the start of the year I didn't know anyone well in my pottery class and I didn't necessarily care to, but that soon changed. For a project, Mrs. Brown broke us into pairs and I got paired with Nate. I only knew *of* Nate and really didn't know much about him except that he played sports. Football maybe? I was a straight "A" student and had anticipated I'd do the "group" project alone. However, he surprised me when he actually showed interest in the project and we worked together. After the project, Mrs. Brown assigned Nate and me seats next to one another. I felt pressed to get to know Nate and share my testimony of faith with him. I spoke to him about Christ and brought a paper I'd written and read at church. He openly shared with me that he too believed in Jesus as God's son and accepted Him as his savior. I was a little perplexed; why was God asking me to witness my faith to Nate if he already believed? Although Nate already knew God, he still seemed interested in hearing what I said about Him and what I believed to be true about God and His Kingdom myself. Nate was the first Christian friend I'd had since Kerri in grade school. Nate was indeed the Christian friend God placed in my life that I'd been praying for. I had been looking for such a friend and didn't find one on my own. Once I stopped looking, God placed Nate in my life. Nate was the friend that I'd hoped Adam could have been in more ways than one. Not only was Adam not a Christian, but he was so different from me. He said his friends made fun of me and called me naïve. Adam rarely made me feel stupid, but he was quite smart and studied things I couldn't comprehend. He was only seventeen, but tried to be and act so much older. He was so neat and proper. Even when he wore casual clothes he was so neat and proper. He was gentlemanly and awkwardly romantic. Adam was still sweet and I loved him, but I must admit it was refreshing to have a friend like Nate. Nate wore tattered jeans, T-shirts, a worn ball cap and waited entirely too long before he got a haircut. He listened to country music and drove an old beat-up truck. He was just a kid, like me.

In addition to that, Nate loved Jesus too. We talked to one another as we molded and shaped our clay. Nate was much better than I at forming pieces on the wheel. I felt like I had to work a lot harder than he did to manipulate the clay as it spun round on the wheel. Trying to center that darn lump of clay was the hardest part of creating a decent work of art. So, talking to Nate was a welcome distraction and I didn't get quite so frustrated when pottery was really difficult for me.

The sophomore seated across the table from us joined in on our conversations many times and we listened to her stories. We talked about our families, friends, faith, churches, spiritual influences, our teachers, assignments, and our future. We never ran out of things to talk about and we talked every other day in pottery. It was something I looked forward to.

One afternoon in class, Nate and I were sitting next to one another on a pair of the electric wheels. Facing the wall, our backs to the class, we were frantically trying to get a piece finished before the bell rang to end class. Nate and I were both struggling, but he had at least moved past centering and had begun to pull the clay to form a vase. I still struggled to center that very hard gray lump of clay. No matter how much water I added to soften the clay, the clay felt like a rock and wasn't moving. Instead of throwing the clay back and getting a more malleable lump, I stubbornly fought back. I put a lot of force into the clay using my hands, arms and all of my upper body strength to attempt to center the equally stubborn lump. While pushing and pulling in vain of success, I suddenly felt lightheaded. I got the sensation in my head just as I have before when I've fainted. I dropped my hands, let the wheel spin and stared at the wall. I turned slightly toward Nate and told him something happened; and then my head hurt and I didn't feel well. Just as I had turned toward him, he accidentally smashed his pot and cursed. He didn't hear what I'd said, or simply paid no heed to it. As the class came to a close, we cleaned up, got back to our tables and started to pack up our things. I sat down slowly and told Nate I was dizzy. I suppose he thought I was just trying to get attention, and maybe I was being too dramatic because he dismissed my concern, but something told me that something was amiss.

A fellow classmate of Nate's and mine had recently been confined to a wheelchair because of some flare-up in his rheumatoid arthritis. He seemed to be doing well overall, but needed the chair to give his legs and back a rest. After the incident on the wheel, I told Nate that, like Stephen, I soon would be in a wheelchair. I can only imagine how foolishly dramatic and stupid this sounded to Nate. Nate got mad at me and said, "Why would you say that?" A little surprised at my response as well, I said, "I just know." Nate rolled his eyes and said nothing more. As I said it to him I knew it was absurd; I just felt a little dizzy and paranoid. Why would I possibly think I'd soon be in a wheelchair like Stephen?

However, it was soon made clear that the LORD had given me a premonition and had prepared me for the news that soon became a reality. I had in fact been broken again and had another brain bleed, most likely at that moment in pottery when I was trying to center that damn lump of clay, and I had nothing to show for it. Staying home from school to recover was suggested by Dr. Shah, but Mama and I didn't even take it into consideration. I was not going to subject myself to the same emotional turmoil I'd felt two years prior. Staying home was not an option.

So, we decided to try a wheelchair at school. I had an aide available to me if I needed her to help push my wheelchair around the school, carry my books and help guide me through assignments in class. But, I never took the school up on their offer for an aide. Instead of being ignored or made fun of, old friends and new friends of all kinds embraced me and helped me through my disability. I had friends in each class who were more than willing to help me with anything and everything. As hard as it was to have another bleed, I enjoyed the attention. I felt loved by my classmates, which was another answer to prayer.

Contrary to what research says about consecutive bleeds being more severe than the first, this particular bleed was far milder than my first. I sat during most of my classes, but was able to stand as needed in the darkroom and I had very little trouble focusing in class and keeping up with the assignments.

I had a feeling this bleed would take no time at all to recover from; but, I had another bleed two months later in December. I was in English class; we were all silently reading the books we'd chosen to write book reports on. I was reading Ayn Rand's *Fountainhead*. Although a very engaging book, and I usually couldn't pull myself away from it, I must have read the same couple of pages a dozen times because I anxiously awaited Cameron's arrival.

I had met Cameron for the first time the week prior. After writing and reading several letters, I finally met him one year after we had begun to write. He came home from Okinawa, Japan to visit family and friends before he left to be stationed in Yuma, AZ. We were leaving church when Mama asked me if I'd like to go see him. Of course I would! I considered changing my clothes and getting "dolled up," but eventually decided it would be more appropriate to go as I was. I had a photo of Cameron that he'd previously sent me in a letter, and although I'd sent him a few of my senior portraits, when we finally met face to face, Cameron seemed pleasantly surprised by my appearance. I was both flattered and embarrassed. I was nervous sitting next to him on the couch. He was giving me his full attention as he talked to me. He was genuinely interested in me. And I thought he was more attractive in person than in his photograph. He was so handsome and I was immediately attracted to him. It was difficult to hide my nervousness for, as we sat next to one another on the couch, he saw my left hand shaking and my tight nerves rolling my fingers into a fist. Cameron grabbed my hand and flattened it, held it between his. My body and my nerves relaxed. I have no recollection of what we talked about; I just liked that he so naturally and comfortably held my hand. I was simply elated to meet Cameron.

Our initial visit was short and around many other people. Today he was coming to see *just me*. He said he'd come see me at school and take me to lunch. I was excited to get to spend more time with him, especially if it meant getting away from school for a while. The time could not pass fast enough; I sat in my wheelchair very restless and uncomfortable. I finally slumped down out of my wheelchair and sat on the floor. I laid my book on the floor in front of me, legs crossed and my head in my hands, looking down at my book (not an unusual position for me to read, as I often sat this way on my bed at home). But, suddenly I felt a rush to my head as I had in pottery class in October. It alarmed me and I thought perhaps I should draw attention to it, but when the time was right. I wanted to enjoy some time with Cameron first.

Cameron arrived in town in time to take me to lunch. I was thrilled to get away from school and to be with him. He struggled to get my wheelchair into the trunk of his 1979 Firebird, a car he took pride in restoring. I was incredibly embarrassed and apologized profusely for the inconvenience of my chair: "Sorry, I wish I didn't need it." I don't remember where we ate lunch together that day; I just remember again feeling elated to see Cameron once again. I was stiff and nervous as I had been the week prior when we initially met, and I could scarcely eat.

When Cameron took me back to school, I coaxed him into coming with me to my pottery class. It was obvious that Nate didn't like the attention that my attractive friend Cameron was getting. But, I felt really comfortable with Cameron in my element and enjoyed showing him off.

When the time came, I had to tell Cameron and my parents that I felt I'd had yet another bleed. We scheduled an MRI for the following morning, and Cameron volunteered to go with me. I'd never been to an MRI alone and didn't want to. He arrived a little late and seemed extremely tired. His eyelids were heavy and I'd wondered if he'd had much sleep. Cameron sat in the exam room with me. As with all MRIs, I had to sit very still and couldn't talk to him. However, I saw there was a small square mirror above the helmet that held my head in place. It served the purpose of being able to see the technician, but I kept my gaze on Cameron and gave him a slight grin as often as I could. At one point during the exam I thought I saw him shed tears. His heartache and compassion for me melted my heart; how could I not love this guy? MRIs tend to fatigue me and result in a headache afterward, but I pushed through so I could spend some quality time with Cameron.

Our previous visit together had been brief, but this visit we spent a great deal more time together. Shortly after the MRI, we drove to the county park, and I made him climb trees and get dirty, so I could take photos of him—not only for class, but for myself to keep. I tried to walk all over the park myself, but on the way back to his car my ankle turned and my leg dragged. Too weak to walk, I had to have Cameron carry me back to the car. I apologized to Cameron, but must admit that I liked being carried by a strapping young marine. I wish my friends could have been around to see that.

Once we got to my home, I popped the film canister out of my camera and handed it to Cameron. I needed him to help me properly get the film in my light-tight canister to develop the images while he was still there. Film must be rolled in an entirely dark place; if light filters in, the film is ruined. The only appropriately dark place in our house was in our storm shelter, which was our closet under the basement stairs. Although it was our storm shelter and should have been empty, we kept our old play kitchen, stuffed animals and doll beds (toys we'd outgrown) in there. It was terribly humorous to watch Cameron position himself on one of our old doll beds (there was nowhere else to sit or stand in the closet). Before I shut the door, I said,

"Are you sure you can do this?"

With a smirk, he said,

"I've assembled many guns in the dark in under a minute, I'm pretty sure I can do this for you." I laughed, and left him to it. I gave him instructions through the door, but before I finished, he came out and handed me the canister.

"I told you I could take care of it," he grinned. "Ok smartass," I replied. "Thanks."

When the film was secured in the canister, I poured the developer through the top, shook it and Cameron and I talked as we waited for the developer to do its magic. Once the film was developed, I was pleased to see the negatives turned out some decent images despite my struggle to keep my left eyelid closed as I used my right eye to look in the view finder. I promised to send Cameron some photos once I got into my darkroom at school and had an opportunity to print some. We spent the rest of the day together, and continued to over the next few days. He and I went to a few movies together during his visit. We went to a movie the night he'd planned to leave, and we sat in his car after the movie in the parking lot as I cried. Cameron had the car furnace blowing full blast. I was bundled up in my vintage leather jacket from my auntie Mona and was soon sweating. He was confused as to why I would possibly be sad. Although I was surprised he had agreed to, we had just watched *My Big Fat Greek Wedding* together. We had laughed and enjoyed our time together.

Cameron leaned in, "What's wrong?"

I said, "I asked for this, you know."

"Asked for what?" Cameron was utterly confused.

"I asked God for another bleed!" I responded.

"Why in the world would you do that?"

"I don't know, I suppose because I've been so miserable and felt when I'd had my bleed two years ago, my faith grew, I found a wonderful friend in Adam, and lately I've been feeling so lost. I felt like I'd been waiting for something different and missing out on happiness and joy I couldn't seem to attain, so I prayed for a change even if that meant another bleed."

All Cameron could say was,

"I'm sorry Meg; I want to make this go away."

Then, Cameron kept quiet and as best he could over the car seats, awkwardly held me until I stopped crying. He dropped me off at a church New Year's Eve party before he left. I embraced him and asked if there was anything I could possibly do or say that would keep him from leaving me.

He sighed and said, "No."

I squeezed him a little tighter and said, "I love you, Cam." Without hesitation, he said, "I love you too."

I let go of Cameron, he left to go to Yuma and it really hurt to see him go. I felt I needed him to help me recover, walk alongside me to comfort me and distract me as Adam had. However, it was made clear that the LORD needed me to continue to rely solely on Him and I was angry at Him for it.

I vented and cried as I shared my frustration with Nate. Although hard to hear, Nate shared a passage with me from 1 Samuel that he thought would help, which was surprising: Nate had never before pointed me to scripture when I had talked about my trials and heartache. We had talked about God, our walk of faith, the creation of the world, but never specific scripture. Still being fairly new to the Bible, I hadn't yet read 1 Samuel 8 for myself.

Nate shared that God sometimes lets us do things outside of His will. It's sometimes the only way He can show us that His way is in fact better than our own. In this particular passage, the Israelites demand that Samuel ask their LORD for a king to rule over them. Samuel is astonished at their request but, even so, prays to God. God simply replies to Samuel that it is not Samuel they've rejected as their leader, but God himself. Before giving the Israelites the king they had asked for, Samuel warned them that their king would make servants and slaves out of each and every one of them! Yet, the Israelites still seemed to think that a new king would solve their problems. I believe denial plays a big part in this passage as well as an inability to see the big picture and know that the LORD was truly best for them.

I have frequently acted as the Israelites did specifically in 1 Samuel 8. When I feel down, I plead to the LORD for a friend to pull me out of the pit of depression. Although I know a friend could never suffice, I persist until the LORD blesses me with one. I've been fortunate to know and love Adam, Cameron, Nate and others. But, I've been heartbroken by each of them because when putting humans in God's place, they always fall short and will disappoint.

I have to keep reminding myself of this passage, being mindful that God's way is always best. "'For I know the plans I have for you,' declares the LORD, 'plans to prosper you and not to harm you, plans to give you hope and a future. Then you will call upon me and come and pray to me, and I will listen to you. You will seek me and find me when you seek me with all your heart. I will be found by you,' declares the LORD, 'and will bring you back from captivity'" (Jeremiah 29:11-14).

I don't want the LORD to let me be to my own devices and give me anything that is outside His will, so I must yield to His will and trust He knows what is best for me and what will encourage my growth with Him.

Cameron and I still wrote to one another and talked on the phone while he was working in Yuma. He said he wished he could be closer to me and help me through my rough time, but said he was glad Nate was being such a good friend to me. It wasn't long after Cameron's return to Yuma that he was sent further away to Kuwait in February 2003. It had been two years since the September 11th terrorist attack on the United States, but the war still raged on in the Middle East. I feared for his life and prayed constantly. I held one of his photos that I took of him with me all day and often wore a sweatshirt he gave me, to always be mindful of him and pray for his safety physically, mentally and emotionally. He wrote to me as often as he could and I to him. A few times we were able to talk on the phone. My letters and conversations so uplifted him that he asked me to write to one of his fellow Marines as well.

In the meantime, I was recovering at home from my October and December bleeds. Still attending school in a wheelchair, I went to my classes and it seemed much harder to concentrate on the lessons and homework. I was more mentally tired than physically tired.

In fact, at the start of the second semester, I did some physical therapy at school. Nate was a proctor for the nurse for seventh hour, he was on the swim team at school and worked as a lifeguard in the summer. The school nurse, Mama and I collaborated and thought that I could use the pool at school during seventh hour for pool therapy and Nate could supervise. From past experience I'd already known what exercises to do. Nate and I had become close friends, so he agreed to help. On the dates we couldn't use the pool, we took walks in my neighborhood for my physical therapy. Even at the end of the day I was still able to muster enough energy to either swim at our school's pool or take walks with Nate every other day.

Nate's and my friendship grew stronger because, in addition to pottery, he did my therapy with me too. I appreciated Nate's friendship and he was someone I could easily talk to about my faith and fears more openly with no one else around. And he freely talked with me as well. Therapy didn't feel like work; it was valuable time spent with a friend. By senior year, social groups or cliques seemed to dissipate and I had friends of all groups. I was finally noticed and I didn't care if it was because of my chair; I loved it. It also gave me an opportunity to share my faith.

Although I had two bleeds so very close together, they still were far less debilitating than my bleed at age sixteen. With the aid of regular walks and pool therapy, preceding my senior bleeds, I felt stronger faster. By March of 2003, both Stephen and I were out of our wheelchairs and roaming the high school halls again.

As the year came to a close, I was asked by the yearbook team if I'd write an inspirational piece to put in the yearbook about my rough year and how in spite of it I'd overcome my trials, and with joy. And as we parted, some unexpected classmates commended me on my strength and good attitude through adversity. I took the opportunity to credit my strength and joy to Christ, even in the midst of difficulty. In April I had gone to my prom, danced and stayed up late, I graduated in May in the top 10% of my class despite my extended absence and catch up required of my sophomore year and the mental handicap I occasionally battled my senior year. I had to do one more thing before I left the high school grounds indefinitely; I mustered up the courage to pray aloud for a classmate.

I had prayed for him all year long and worried about his future and his soul. Because of the trials I'd been through, many of my fears of rejection and social judgment melted away. I had a new confidence in my relationship with Christ; I prayed aloud over this man and didn't fear his rejection. I wanted him to know that someone truly cared about him, not just me, but the living God. I've known very few people in my walk of faith, whether they're Christian or not, that reject someone's offer to pray for them; I was glad he allowed me to. I pray he has since found Jesus too.

5

I had spent the first three years of my high school career watching the clocks in class and checking the dates off my calendar as they passed, hoping just to survive. I was sick of the popularity contests, mundane classes, and many of my classmates. However, in my fourth and final year of high school, with God's help, I'd finally begun to *enjoy* high school and made invaluable friendships with several of my classmates. Social cliques seemed to have finally dissipated, and I was actually sad to leave friends and familiarity behind.

I had a hard summer following the end of high school. I felt I had a purpose in high school, a feasible way to minister to people daily. I didn't know how to continue to serve Christ through the summer without people. Although Nate said we'd remain friends after we left high school, we only saw each other a few times before he left for college, and we grew apart. Cameron was still overseas at war and I heard from him much less that summer. I missed Cameron and his letters and I missed Nate and our daily, lengthy conversations. I found myself feeling very lonely. But my days of moping needed to come to an end at long last.

I needed to be in fellowship with my brothers and sisters in Christ. Although still very much a part of COTS (Church of the

Savior), I started attending Asbury's church services and young adult group. I still wrote to Cameron and his friend Dan, even when I didn't hear from them. I continued to read and pray over scripture as I wrote. After graduating high school, it felt only natural to go to college. With the influence of some preexisting friends from Asbury who went on the Mexico trip, I decided to attend Friends University, in my home town, for college. Mama and Dad felt more comfortable with me staying in Wichita for college, given my recent physical traumas. Although for some reason it seemed to me unlikely, the truth was I could at some point have another bleed and I needed to be close to family.

I was still shy even at my new Asbury church group, but I quickly developed friendships with fellow classmates in college. It was the perfect place to start fresh; no one knew me and I could make a different name for myself. People were going to know who I was, and I wanted to have some fun. I made friends with two other young ladies in my writing class the first day of school. It felt uncomfortable and unnatural at first, but I was very chatty and friendly. It would be my new norm. I was so tired of being lonely. I was immensely grateful to have a fresh start. However, no one in my college group had walked with me through any of my physical trials. Looking at me, no one would have ever known that I'd been through something so physically challenging. I missed that particular comradery, understanding and support.

By college I had regained nearly everything I'd physically lost. I was typing again with both the right and left hand, fixing my own hair, bathing, tying my shoes, walking to each of my classes, taking a full load of classes and working part- time at the Friends library. I had a handicap tag for parking to save some steps to get to my classes, and occasionally had a foot slap or a foot drop as I walked when I was heavily fatigued, but otherwise I felt back to *me*.

I generally enjoyed college much more than I did high school. The men were nicer, and I felt like royalty each time a young man ran ahead of me to open the door for me. At first it made me uncomfortable, but it didn't take long before I started to expect it.

My classes were more interesting and challenging, and most importantly, I had true friends. Friends is a small Christian college, so I didn't feel lost; I rather felt that I fit in, and I was at home there. I was more vocal and people knew who I was. It seems fairly standard that teenagers tend to rebel against their parents and explore things they probably shouldn't; but by the time I was of age to drive, I'd had a bleed, knowledge of my masses, and their potential to bleed again. I had the temptation and access to partake in drugs should I choose, just so I could occasionally escape the emotional pain my bleeds inflicted upon me. However, I knew the risks I'd be taking by experimenting with drugs or alcohol, and that it would be a very probable death sentence for me; and that would be a foolish risk to take. I had also become a Christian, which naturally brought a desire to please the LORD and honor my parents. I had a deeper love and respect for both Dad and Mama after they'd selflessly nursed me back to health *three* times. There was no way I was going to actively cause more physical damage to my body or emotional grief for my parents. So, through high school, I was not the obstinate unbearable teenager that every parent fears.

However, I took full advantage of a healthy body and felt I'd earned the right to be a little "naughty" in college. The group of girls I hung out with were solid girls and they couldn't believe that I was ever pegged as quiet and shy prior to meeting me. I made them laugh, enjoyed being the center of attention and often embarrassed them with my "friendliness" toward strangers and other classmates (attractive men) and my habit of skinny dipping. I was very proud of my healed body and wanted to fully enjoy it. I was deemed a flirt among friends. I'd spent too many years being quiet, invisible and shy and was never going to be again. I liked who I was in college and with my friends. I was happier, healthier and had fun! My girls and I spent a lot of time together on and off campus. Although each of us was very different, our commonalities drew us together. Besides all of us being Christian women, we all lived off campus. We missed out on a lot of campus life events and we weren't a part of the on-campus community, but we created our own community. We spent many late nights at Starbucks, one another's houses and at various parks; we often talked until we were all ridiculously hysterical from fatigue.

And yet, I missed having a close guy friend. I'd had a close guy friend for each year of school. I was attracted to and wanted to date, or at least befriend, some of the incredible Christian gentlemen on campus; but I felt awkward or a little disingenuous doing so since I felt so attached to Cameron. However, I still didn't know to what degree he cared for me.

Although we had not physically been in each other's space much yet, I treasured and valued our long-distance correspondence. I had invested a lot of my heart, trust and loyalty to Cameron. While he was away in Kuwait, I worried about him. I tried to keep him informed, in writing, of the events in my life he'd missed out on. I wrote to him about my final months of high school, graduating high school, my lonely summer proceeding high school, starting school at Friends and developing what I knew would be long-lasting friendships.

As long as Cameron was overseas I prayed for him and thought of him. My last letter from Cameron was dated June eighth, 2003. He told me not to worry, that no news is likely good news, but I worried all the more. I anxiously awaited his notice of his return; he had been away too long. And yet, I was surprised when he did announce he would be homeward bound in late September. Cameron returned to the States in September of 2003, after having been at war nearly eight months. When he showed up at my front door I was shaking, my stomach in knots, and I threw my arms around him, "Welcome home, soldier."

Cameron wouldn't be in my space for long, maybe only two or three days, so for the time that he was home, my head was not at school. I didn't know when I'd get to see him again, so I made every effort to be around him. I suppose I expected him to act and relate to me as he had when we last met face to face, but his demeanor was changed. His friend Dan, who I had also been writing, traveled with him to Wichita before returning to Arizona together. Dan was friendly, happy, and laughed a lot. Why was Cameron so different? He came back fragmented, troubled, distant. I didn't know how to respond and frankly I was a little afraid. This wasn't the Cameron I'd spent time with before. I had longed to hear the stories he had alluded to in his letters and that he told me he wished to share with me when we were in each other's space again. Although I made every attempt to be near him, he very seldom spoke to me or even looked at me. Before I knew it, Cameron was gone again. I wished I could have talked to Cameron alone, but he didn't seem at all interested. I didn't get the time with him I'd hoped for to tell him how deeply I truly cared for him. I loved him.

Sadly, because of the disappointing and awkward "visit," I felt it best to give Cameron some space to get readjusted to civilian life. I waited a month or so before I wrote and mailed to him a very heartfelt letter. I said in writing what I wish I could have said to him in person. I still have a copy in a journal I've kept. I anxiously awaited his response, and when his response was simply "Thank you;" my heart broke a little, but I certainly wasn't going to force the issue. Although I was flirtatious at school, I had no intentions of pursuing anyone, especially not Cameron. I wanted to be desired and fought for, not the other way around. He kept pushing me away. There was very little depth to our conversations over the phone and they were few and far between. And he no longer wrote to me. As he put it, he "had stuff to work through." I wanted to wait for him, but he made it clear that he didn't want me to. I didn't like it and was so disappointed, but I respected his space, left him alone and I prayed for his soul every day. It heavily grieved me to do so, but I let go of the hope that something further would manifest with Cameron. I had to move on emotionally and "romantically" somehow without jeopardizing and losing his deeply valued friendship. I didn't like the thought of opening my heart to someone else; I felt I needed to take some time to heal. I knew in my heart that Cameron wasn't exactly right for me.

He didn't love the LORD as I did and led a different life, but foolish as it may have been, I had never loved and cared for another person more deeply. I had hoped that God would more perfectly align our paths.

I had hope for marriage and spending the rest of my life with a man I dearly loved, but I felt so foolish, angry, embittered and hardened. I had a guard up emotionally and I didn't talk to anyone about Cameron, not even to my close girlfriends, but I was transparent and honest with the LORD. In the privacy of my room and on Sunday mornings at Asbury, I prayed, worshiped, and asked the LORD to console me and guide me. "Is there anyone for me? What do You desire for me to do and who do You want me to be? LORD, I had *my* plan, but I want *Your* plan."

I needed fellowship with other Christians and thirsted for the Word. I faithfully attended church and the young adult college group affiliated with my church. The group I attended met in different members' homes. Nicole, who had started attending group around the period that I also began to attend, decided to host a group at her home. I primarily went to the group to learn. I didn't feel as knowledgeable or as well versed as many others in the group, so I listened and certainly gleaned a lot from our leader. Although young, our group leader (Joe) had a lot of biblical wisdom and I loved hearing him teach. I was drawn to his wisdom and felt uplifted by the group. As I attended regularly to both home group and church at Asbury, my faith continued to grow.

I really respected Joe and valued his opinion and insight on the Bible. One evening, two guys in my small group and I were discussing marriage. One of them had said he desired to find someone to marry, but doubted that anyone would want him. I told them I personally didn't have a desire to get married. I wanted to pursue my dreams, do and go where I please, be independent. One of them declared with heated passion, that the institute of marriage was one of the most sacred bonds on earth: a gift and privilege from God. Joe happened to come by and I asked him what he personally thought of marriage. He said he too once believed that he would be better off alone and could expand his ministry better without a family to commit to.

"However," he said, "I've recently had a change of heart." He had decided he desired a family to share his life with.

Joe's response surprised me, but I knew in my heart I felt the same way. I was suppressing my feelings. I *did* desire a husband and a family, but I couldn't bear to admit it. In our small group, we shared prayer requests. Although I thought it terribly petty, considering that I knew what true suffering was and the consequence of such, I asked my two brothers in Christ to uphold me in prayer as I felt anxious about school work. In light of my anxiety, Marc gladly offered to help me with a college paper I had been struggling with. I had sort of had my eye on another young man in our group and hoped to eventually befriend him, but Marc was upfront and assertive; I accepted his help. In some respects, he reminded me of Adam; he was very intelligent. But unlike Adam, he lacked humility. He was puffed with pride. I remained cautious and guarded, but he began to more frequently come around my house to help me with other homework, he came to dinner, invited me to meet his friends and we regularly saw one another at church and home group. He continued to be assertive, confident and made a point to talk to me and invite me in. Do I dare let him in? He was attractive, and a brother in Christ. He had been the first Christian to express any interest in me, but his occasional display of arrogance was very unattractive. I couldn't put my finger on it, but Marc confused me; I couldn't perceive what he was thinking or feeling at any given moment. We were together a lot, but I couldn't decide if I liked him or even if he liked me. I wanted to just let our friendship run its course, to see what may develop.

In the meantime, our group was growing and started to feel crowded in Nicole's home. If I was late, and I usually was, I sat furthest from Joe on the floor by the door. Although already squished together in her back room, in late November or early December, Nicole started inviting more people to join us for Bible study, including her brother Mike. Mike had very recently become a Christian and needed a group to nurture him in the faith.

At first introduction, I didn't pay Mike much attention because I wasn't taken to him and was preoccupied with other things and people. On the other hand, unlike Marc and many others, Mike made his affections for me very clear. Although I wasn't attracted to him, I was flattered that he was so interested in me. I had shared a prayer request to the group that I was struggling to gain weight. I weighed only ninety pounds at the time and was experiencing dizziness and lightheadedness, among other health burdens. My doctor advised that I strive to break 100 pounds to be healthier. I also asked the group to remember me and pray for me through the month of December, because December in particular had been a hard month in previous years, having had a bleed both in December of 2000 and 2002. The group laid hands on me that night and Mike put his hand over my head. At the Christmas party the following week, Mike caught me by surprise as I sauntered in and he said I ought to eat the "three-pound cookies" that someone brought and I'd hit my 100-pound goal that night. I was touched that he'd remembered me and my prayer need. Toward the end of the party, only Mike, Nicole, and a few other close friends of Nicole's, remained. We all visited together in the kitchen and Mike cornered me as he talked to me about who knows what. I was amused at his attempt to impress me.

Shortly before Christmas, Marc and I were taking a brisk walk around the outside of the shopping mall. Although I didn't feel I was "ready," Marc seemed to push me into a relationship with him, but I didn't know what he was thinking; so, I had to ask,

"Marc, what do you call this exactly, what are we doing, are we dating? Or were you hoping we would?"

Marc never made eye contact with me and responded very smugly, "I believe that the LORD is telling me I shouldn't date anyone right now."

He puffed with pride and continued to smile with clearly no

sign of remorse for leading me to believe otherwise. I didn't feel hurt; I was burning hot with anger. He had wasted my time, and I realized after that response, I didn't even want his friendship anymore. I felt my face flush and I wanted to punch him square in the mouth, but couldn't find the courage to do so. I wanted to walk away, but when he offered to give me a ride home I accepted because it was so cold and icy and certainly would have been too far to walk. Totally oblivious to my anger, he turned up the radio and belted out the words to some annoying pop song all the way back to my parents' house.

When he dropped me off at my house a wide smile spread across his smug face and he said,

"Goodbye, and Merry Christmas."

Humph, Merry Christmas indeed. Just to get my rage out, I wrote a letter to Marc that I would never deliver. I then decided that I wasn't going to sulk and be depressed; I was going out. I called Nicole's best friend, Catie, to ask if she'd like to go to a movie, I didn't care which one, I just had to get out of the house. She said she was out shopping, so I asked for Nicole's number. I called Nicole and, rather confused because she heard Catie giving me her phone number, she said,

"I'm out shopping with Catie," but her voice picked up speed and raised in pitch as she said, "But you should call my brother Mike."

"Uh, ok" I hesitated; but I wrote Mike's number down.

When I hung up with Nicole, I stared at the piece of paper that I'd written Mike's number on. I told Mama and Ellen the situation.

Then I laughed as I said, "You know, I know one thing for sure, Mike Wohler likes me." Joe had taken a special interest in Mike and made a point to make him feel welcome in the group, and at church. I respected Joe and wanted to know what it was about Mike that appealed to Joe. And what it was about me that appealed to Mike.

I pondered this a moment, and from the bottom of the stairs, as I sat with the receiver in my hand, Mama and Ellen chanted, "Call him, call him, call him."

I must be crazy, I thought, but I never back down from a challenge; so, I called. Mike answered his phone sounding groggy and confused, as if I'd woken him from a late nap. I said, "Uh, this is Megan Mitchell from group. Is this a bad time?" Mike perked up and said, "Oh hey, what's up?" We had more awkward conversation, but he casually agreed to go to a movie with me. I felt somewhat successful. I freshened up my make-up, reapplied my Bamboo Pink lipstick and all the way to the theater I laughed to myself and thought, this is so unlike me. I arrived at the theater before he did and bought our tickets. My normal instinct while waiting for a date would have been to feel nervous, maybe even intimidated, but with Mike I felt at ease. I knew I didn't need to work to impress him in any fashion. He already liked me. I waited for him in the lobby and I immediately spotted him as he walked in. There was no way I could have missed him. He had a bright red oversized button up shirt on with red sneakers and baggy pants (which I have since learned was a carefully devised outfit which he deemed suitable for our "date"). He also had a huge goofy grin on his face. Wow!

"Oh man, this was a mistake," I thought.

I nervously waved and he came over to greet me.

"What's up?"

When he was so friendly and relaxed, I relaxed too.

He was so late arriving that we had to sit up front and as we sat down he said, "So, who else is coming, Joe, Josh, Catie?"

"Nope, just us," I said bashfully. Now I'm feeling a little embarrassed. I think to myself, no dude, you're sort of my rebound date.

During the movie, Mike wore his phone on his pants by his hip. His phone was on silent, but went off several times during the show. And as it did, his phone flashed wildly. I was terribly annoyed and it was hard to concentrate on the movie. Although I thought it was generally an awkward evening with Mike, I enjoyed his company. As we exited the theater, Mike very smoothly worked his way into a second date. He said, "You bought my ticket tonight, so I think it only fair that I take you to a movie and buy your ticket."

I laughed, and said, "Ok."

Because I was on Christmas break, I had my days to do with what I wanted. I slept in and then went to the YMCA to work out. Several times Mike would call me while I was at the Y. Although I put on the façade that I was put off by his persistence, I appreciated that Mike pursued me; he was always upfront and never beat around the bush. Mike and I spent a great deal of time together during my Christmas break. We played lots of games of double solitaire, pool, watched movies and got to know one another.

Mike was fun, different, and continued to make it clear that he adored me. It was refreshing to be with someone in close proximity that I could spend lots of quality time with. It was only in January that Mike asked if I'd date him and officially become his girlfriend. I laughed and said, "I kind of thought we were already doing that." Mike helped me get out of my pit of depression; he taught me how to have fun again and taught me a love for food. With his finances and influence, I steadily began to gain weight. I looked forward to our time together, as if a new adventure awaited us upon each encounter. Although we seemed polar opposites, my affections for him grew. One evening we were watching a movie together on his couch. I laid down lengthwise with him behind me. He wrapped his arm around me, I pulled it around me a little tighter and without thinking I said, "I love you." As soon as the words spilled out of my mouth, I opened my eyes wide. Uh, did I just say "I love you?!" I didn't love Mike romantically, I just really liked Mike. He was fun to be around and I felt really comfortable around him, but I didn't *love* Mike. I thought, "Yikes, maybe he didn't hear me." I held my breath and my body was rigid as I awaited his response. He said, "Oh wow, really? Are you sure?" I wanted to say "Oops, no sorry. I didn't mean it."

Instead, I turned toward him slightly and said, "Yeah…." Mike's response then was, "Aw, thank you." That was so embarrassing; I wanted to take it back. *He* was supposed to say "I love you" first and *I* wouldn't have said it back until I meant it. At that moment, I wanted to sink into the floor and disappear. I wasn't going to do that again! LORD, if I could take it back I would. I was going to guard my mouth a little more carefully. I think Mike had known that I didn't mean it; that it had just slipped out, but perhaps I was on my way to loving Mike.

I knew early on that Mike was unemployed, had previously been an electrician, and was receiving unemployment. It's why we were able to spend lots of time together. I had nearly forgotten that he took a trip to western Kansas between our first and second date, to see his uncle just before Christmas. Soon after Mike and I began to officially date, Mike's uncle hired him for a job in sales that would move him three and a half hours from home and me. Although I really liked Mike, I was not interested in managing a long-distance relationship. We had hardly begun to date, so I assumed a clean break would be best. After all, one of the most valuable pieces of our relationship together was that we were geographically close to one another. I had every intention of saying "Goodbye and good luck." Our time together was fun, but I would move on.

However, Mike really liked me. He wasn't willing to accept a "goodbye"; he wanted to make it work and continue to date me. I hated the idea, but agreed I'd give the long-distance relationship a two-month trial. I helped Mike move into his new apartment in Garden City, Kansas; a place where he knew only his uncle, aunt and two cousins. Mike came home to Wichita and myself every weekend and we talked on the phone each night before going to bed. Mike was making a valiant effort to keep our relationship alive. I decided that perhaps Mike was worth the work of a long-distance relationship. Two months stretched into many more. He sacrificed so much money and time to see me and still date me. Although it was challenging to truly get to know one another living far apart, Mike residing in Garden City and I in Wichita during the week made it much easier for me to focus on school and for Mike to focus on work. Also, we spent time with the LORD individually. We were allotted the opportunity to grow in our faith apart, which I believed was important for Mike. As a new Christian he needed to adopt his own beliefs and grow in the LORD apart from me. However, when we came together on the weekends we forgot about work and school; we dated, and we went to church with one another at *our* church. And we felt united in our passion to impact the Kingdom together. I didn't want to be too hasty and rush into anything, but after being together exclusively for five months, we'd already begun to talk about forever.

06/28/2004

Dear LORD Jesus,

For some reason I feel moved to write my prayer tonight. At this point, I'm simply trying to stay awake. To start my praises, I want to express my gratitude for Mike, a man you have given me, I believe, to spend the rest of my life with! Sometimes I prayed with despair, but usually I prayed hard in faith. I had even reached the point in which I thought I was destined to be alone forever, but to serve You. As soon as I had fully accepted that task for my life, You graced me with an answer to prayer.
I thank You for being so faithful, and giving me the best friend I've prayed my heart out for. My poems and journals are proof that I was so hungry for a companion to love and to love me in return. Every time I think of Mike, talk to Mike, and most importantly, see Mike, I am eternally grateful and filled with joy. For truly, he is the greatest gift You've given me outside of Your very love. Please God, always be our rock and our guide from now into eternity.

After having read the book *A Life God Rewards*, about the different rewards God gives us in heaven, all I can hope for is that I serve Your Kingdom to my fullest potential. And that I may serve You next to my best friend Mike through my life on earth and through eternity in heaven.

Now, two very important people I need to lift to You. LORD God, I pray that Mike and I have the words and wisdom, whether it be in prayer or face to face, to help our two closest friends find and walk with You. I pray with faith, patience, and hope in You that Your ultimate will for them is to come to You. I just pray that You help Mike and I to remain close friends to these lost souls. And I ask that You bless them with the awareness of Your presence and steadfast love. As I like to repeatedly say, "Open their eyes and proceed to their hearts!"

Help us to be good examples of Your love and mercy. Help us to be leaders of lost friends as well as followers in the body of the church. Thank You for everything You have done, do, and will do for *us*!

Lovingly,
Meg McKay Mitchell

I had fallen in love with Mike and prayed he'd be the one that would stick around. I relied on him and trusted and believed that he would never leave me. It was a different and wonderful feeling to feel so secure in his love.

08/02/2004

Dear Jesus,

As is frequent occasion for me, I feel the need to write out my prayer tonight. I again thank You for Mike. As we grow closer together, I see him also growing closer to You and hungry for more of You. What a blessing it is to be in Your presence and enveloped in Your love. My ongoing prayer for Mike is that You provide him with the wisdom and courage to walk out his faith in his daily life no matter who surrounds him. I pray you give him a desire to spiritually lead me and share his heart with me. I ask that as we pursue You that we may continue to grow and that we may also grow with one another. Help us and guide us so that we may never fall into temptation. Give Mike the strength and courage to gently lead me in our relationship as You have intended. And in turn, I ask You to help me fulfill the part you created me for in this relationship. As Mike prays, I pray that Your voice be heard so he will undoubtedly experience Your involvement and presence in his everyday life.

Last of all, I pray that Your will be done between Mike and I. If we are meant or not meant to be together, I beg of You to give us courage, patience, and understanding to do things right according to You. Please Jesus, be our focus and our center in all circumstances: happy or sad.

Lovingly,
Megan McKay Mitchell

I wanted to do things right by God and not find myself in a situation similar to my emotionally dependent relationship on Adam or even Cameron.

It sometimes frightened me how quickly I fell for Mike. Perhaps I was too hasty and should have been more cautious, but somehow being with Mike just felt right. I was so happy with him.

God seemed to bring us clarity as Mike and I began talking about marriage, which led to discussion about children. Considering my heath condition, I shared with him that I wasn't sure that I could in fact safely have children. I had nearly always had in mind the intention of adopting rather than having children of my own; but as I fell in love with Mike, I desired to have children with him. My heart ached thinking that I might not get the satisfaction of bearing Mike's children. I apologized to him and cried with him. Although he knew about all the potential dangers of my physical condition and the possibility that my body might not be able to bear children, Mike wasn't discouraged from proposing marriage to me on Christmas Eve of 2004. Mike's proposal was not elaborate, but was rather spontaneous, simple and sweet. We snuggled on the couch in my parents' living room, enjoying the quiet in the house and the stillness of the night. As we gazed out the window, he held my hands and pulled my attention away from the window and gently turned my head toward him. I fixed my eyes and ears on him; he had my full attention. He said, "I don't have a ring yet, but I can't wait any longer to ask you, and this seems as good a time as any. Megan, I love you, and I want to keep on loving you for the rest of my life; will you be my wife?" I squeezed his hands, kissed both of his bristly cheeks, and said, "Of course." Mike and I were thrilled to announce our engagement to friends and family, but rather than get married right away, I was "persuaded" by my parents to finish college first.

Mike and I had only begun to date shortly after my first semester of college and we were engaged after I'd completed only three semesters. With only three semesters under my belt and many more ahead, Mike and I were potentially in for an extended engagement period.

Mike hated being apart from me; it felt especially difficult for us both after we were engaged to be married. Mike had work to keep him busy and preoccupied, but he initially was very lonely in Garden City and seriously missed me. We asked that the LORD would open doors for Mike to find a church and even to bless him with a friend like Joe. Mike found a church, by "accident," in Garden City that he grew to love. He helped with the youth on Wednesday nights and he did in fact find a friend that reminded us a lot of Joe. Our faith was strengthened and we were encouraged by the LORD's answers to our prayers for Mike. The LORD's blessings that He bestowed upon Mike in Garden City proved to us that the LORD deeply cared for Mike and his position in Garden. I felt happy for Mike and relaxed knowing that he was well cared for.

Meanwhile, I continued work to attain a degree in Psychology at Friends. I had the ambition to become an art therapist or a marriage and family counselor. I also had an interest in religion and Spanish and pursued them as minors. I really enjoyed learning about the human psyche and filling my mind full of biblical knowledge. My most intriguing classes were my religion classes. I favored a professor in the religion department. He was hard, but very knowledgeable, and I felt I got my money's worth from his classes. Additionally, I enjoyed my Spanish classes because it was fun to know and speak another language. My best friend Becca and I could use our knowledge of Spanish to talk in "code." With my major, two minors and a lot of interest in several different classes, I had a full load each semester.

In my four years at Friends, there were several opportunities to travel with classes or groups of fellow classmates out of state or even out of the country. Although not a requirement to complete my Spanish minor, my Spanish professor and best friend Becca persuaded me to agree to go to Cancun, Mexico to study abroad for the entire month of June in 2005. I was strong, but knew my body still had some limitations. For my safety, my professor suggested that Becca and I stay in a home together. All of us were in our third year of Spanish and knew enough to understand and communicate our needs. We stayed in Cancun, but we didn't stay where many Cancun vacationers would. We were immersed in the Mexican culture and stayed at different families' homes in the heart of Cancun. Becca and I stayed with a single woman who worked during the day and partied out at night. Becca and I were still living with our parents back in the states and had never shopped for groceries or cooked before. Although we were both novices, I was glad we had each other. It was an opportunity for Becca and me to grow closer and learn together. Our Spanish professor told us we had to speak to one another in Spanish in the home as our other classmates would; but that didn't last long. We played games together until we were too tired to think or when we realized we still needed to do our homework for the night. We experienced a lot of new things together as friends and as a class. Every day was packed with activity. We had studied the Mayan ruins and culture back home in class and had the privilege of visiting several of the sites. We also each had the opportunity to teach English to our own individual classes at a very low-income school, we visited a Mayan theme park, ate great authentic Mexican food, shopped, and of course had classes at the collegio (a high school in Cancun) each afternoon. In addition to our full days, Becca and I walked a LOT. I felt strong when we left home in Wichita, but still felt slightly worried about my ability to physically keep up in Mexico. I spoke with my professor in the second week of our stay and told her I felt I was pushing myself too hard. She suggested I take breaks once in a while, which meant I'd miss out on some fun activities. I hated missing part of the events that my classmates were experiencing, but I knew I needed the extra rest to keep myself from further physical trouble; I wanted to be able to perform my best in the classes at the collegio.

I was embarrassed and angry that many of my friends were embittered toward me for not "having to do" everything that was required of them. I cried as Becca shared with me how our classmates spoke of me when I wasn't around (with disrespect and a lack of understanding). They were questioning my integrity, which infuriated me. I didn't want to be pitied, but I also didn't appreciate being subjected to criticism and judgment; I was so hurt. I suppose I assumed they understood my weakness to some degree and would extend some grace, maybe even some compassion.

However, I appeared healthy at home and they didn't know the extent of my scary history, fragility of my brain and the dangers of a potential bleed. The cause of the bleeds I'd had before was still a mystery and I felt I couldn't take chances. I had to try to forgive my unforgiving friends and dismiss what they might think of me. I hated the idea of living in fear and being perceived as fearful, but I had to continue to listen to my body even if it meant losing the respect of friends; it wouldn't be worth the risk.

Even with fairly regular rest, my left foot drug and slapped on the ground as I walked to class each afternoon. Becca always knew I was coming as she heard my foot fall. Being in Cancun exposed what physical weakness I still had and that I didn't know still remained. I have beautiful photos, stories and some memories I treasure, but I wondered if I was a burden to Becca and a nuisance to my classmates in Mexico. I wondered if it was really very wise that I travelled to Cancun.

In spring of 2006, against my better judgment, I took a second college trip to Chicago to fulfill a psychology credit requirement; it seemed a better alternative to the longer boring class available to take on campus. I thought it would be much less taxing than the Cancun trip because the Chicago trip would be less than a week long. We met as a class weekly to discuss what we'd be doing in Chicago and what was expected of us as a class. Recalling Mexico, the more my professor explained about Chicago, the more anxious I got. It sounded like it was going to be more physically demanding than I'd originally thought. I wasn't comfortable or familiar with anyone in my class. And I certainly didn't want the possibility of being a burden to my teacher or classmates, as I felt I was in Cancun. One morning after class, I approached my professor and told him I'd still like to go on the Chicago trip, but would feel better about going if my fiancé could too.

My professor didn't feel comfortable with this, but after some convincing he decided to allow Mike to come along. Although a much shorter trip than the trip to Cancun, like Cancun, the Chicago trip was actually very physically trying. I had my own room while in Cancun, but while in Chicago I shared a room with eight other ladies. I'm such a light sleeper and don't sleep well away from home anyway. Every little noise kept me awake or would wake me up. I got very little sleep while in Chicago. We visited a lot of very interesting places, but with very little sleep, I started out each day heavily fatigued. We often took subways and other transportation, but we also walked *all over* Chicago. I was not prepared for the amount of walking we did. I wore out my shoes and injured my knee. Mike and I made a side trip to get a knee brace and for the latter half of the trip he carried me. I was so glad Mike went with me; he was so sweet and never acted burdened or discouraged, and I loved him even more for that. But, I was discouraged that even with Mike's help, I struggled to keep up with the group.

I didn't enjoy needing to still rely on people to help me. Would I ever be normal again; could I eventually be strong and independent? Perhaps not.

6

A t the close of the 2006 school year, I decided that I would like to live in Garden City in my own apartment for the summer. I had visited Mike several times and stayed in his apartment during spring break, fall break and many extended weekends, but I wanted to get better acquainted with the people and town and even my fiancé Mike before Garden City became my home. Mike and I planned to be married the following summer, after I graduated college.

With the exception of my month-long stay in Cancun, I'd not lived away from my parents before. Garden City would soon be my home, and much of Mike's and my relationship had been long-distance. I wanted to be in his space a little more, and date more regularly before we "tied the knot." I had my own apartment, cooked for myself, bought groceries, cleaned, had a part-time job that paid for my rent, utilities, food and gas, and I took a biology course at the community college. I missed my girlfriends (it would have been our last full summer together), but I had a great summer with Mike and felt so independent and grown up with my own space. I got to know the people of Mike's church better, and I believed the transition I'd make the following summer once

Mike and I were married, would be a little easier since I'd spent several months there already.

However, after a fun summer with my fiancé and our daily face-to-face contact, it was tough to come back home and finish school. I had two semesters left. I could not wait to start my life with Mike, and it was beginning to get harder to wait. My heart yearned for Mike and marriage, I could hardly stand it. I longed to be Mike's wife and start that new chapter of my life.

I felt anxious and lonesome for Mike when I came back to Wichita. He came home less and the time between visits felt unbearably long. But, I wanted the LORD to use that time to teach me and help me grow stronger in my faith. The day I'd become a wife, I'd no longer be one, but part of two. I needed the LORD to prepare me for marriage, and to help me be patient. Joe's sermons each week at Asbury of my final year in college brought me to my knees; I felt he was speaking right to me. I bore my soul unto the LORD and felt deeply moved in His presence. I experienced immense spiritual growth and gained the preparation I needed for a change. I didn't realize that the LORD was actually preparing me for a mighty storm. The memory is terribly bitter-sweet; tears still cloud my vision as I recall the monsoon.

Mike and I had been engaged for over two years. Our wedding date was set for post-graduation, 7/7/07 (a perfect day). I took my long breaks between classes to work out and tone up. I couldn't wait to show off my beautiful body to my husband for the first time. It was mid-March, I had just completed and aced midterms and our big day was drawing near. Soon I would graduate with my psych degree and be married. I felt more than ready to start my next chapter with Mike in Garden City, but in that month of March I had the unexpected yet inevitable occurrence of a *fifth* brain bleed!

This bleed was more intense than any of the previous I'd experienced in high school. The body I had worked so hard to perfect was broken once again. The deterioration came quickly; years of hard work to recover were in vain, meant nothing. In a matter of days, my body was broken all over again. My left-leg and left-hand motions were gone, my vision was impaired, and I was overwhelmingly fatigued. I tried to continue to go to classes, like I had done as a senior in high school. I was determined to finish the semester strong; but I didn't even have the focus and stamina to make it through one fifty-minute intro class. Mama brought me in my wheelchair and left for the music building to pick up her music while I was in class; but, within minutes, I got incredibly dizzy, lightheaded, and my head throbbed. I sent an urgent text to Mama just ten minutes into the class, "I can't do it Mom, my head hurts so bad and I can't hardly focus, please come get me!" Trying to concentrate on anything was exhausting, even in such an easy intro class, and trying to sit upright in a chair was torturous. My body begged to lie down. I dropped my head in my hands as I anxiously waited for Mama to rescue me. I was frustrated and scared; this was serious.

I scared Mike too. I encouraged him to wait to drive back to Wichita until after I'd met with my neurologist and we knew more about my condition and course of action; but Mike insisted he be with me. Before he excused himself from work at the radio station in Garden, his coworkers formed a circle and joined him in prayer. By the time we went to consult with my neurologist, Mike was right by my side. Being the fifth bleed from the same mass in seven years, my neurologist was insistent that we again consult with the renowned surgeon in Phoenix, Arizona. Enough was enough! My heart raced, and for the first time in seven years, I cried in front of my doctors and I kept shaking my head. I was a few months away from graduating college and getting married. This couldn't be happening to me right now; not now! I couldn't have brain surgery; there had to be another way! I wanted to continue school, stay on track to be married and move, and I denied what was happening to me, right before us. I kept asking my doctor, "What about school? I'm almost done with school!" My doctor was trying to explain to us why he thought surgery would be the best option, but I wasn't listening. I kept asking, "What about school?" Finally, my very quiet, patient doctor turned to me and said firmly, "That's a moot question at this point!" Then I understood what Dr. Shah was telling me; that my perfect plans for my near future were being rewritten. I was silent the rest of the visit and didn't hear anything else beyond the doctor's firm statement that school was out of question. I was in a state of shock and feared for my life.

When we came back home from the doctor, we were ALL in a somber state and, being emotionally and physically drained, I could hardly keep my eyes open. Mike sat next to me on my bed and I very seriously said to him, "I wouldn't blame you if you left me. This road I'm about to take is not going to be easy." I wasn't sure if Mike was spiritually ready for the battle at hand, but Mike said, "No; I'm in this. Whether you like it or not, I love you, and I'm not going anywhere!" He was very adamant that his place was with me, and there was no use fighting him. Although neither of us really knew what lay ahead for me, Mike was willing to take this scary intense journey with me. I smiled, squeezed his hand, let my heavy eyelids close and soon fell asleep.

As days passed, I continued to battle insurmountable fatigue from the bleeding, and my condition was worsening. I spent most of my day resting in bed, praying for the LORD's mercy, and desperately trying to journal. The surgeon in Phoenix, Dr. Spetzler, said he was willing to do the surgery to remove my hemangioma, but I had to decide for myself if I wanted to take the risk. He said there was a small chance of permanent paralysis, even smaller chance of death, but also the strong possibility of being rid, and no longer burdened, of my nasty mass. I didn't know how to respond or what to expect, but the truth is, I was terrified. It was not a decision I was comfortable making. I didn't want to have to decide my fate. Mama recounts an afternoon when she passed by my door and heard me tossing back and forth in my bed, and moaning. I didn't want to go through with it; I wanted a way out and I begged the LORD to take my life. Over and over I said, "LORD, please just let me die. I don't want to do this! I don't want to have surgery, but I also don't want to risk more bleeds by opting *not* to do the surgery! Please LORD, I want to be with You and not face this. I'm so scared. I'd rather take a thousand finals than go through with this. Please, please take me."

I was terribly impatient and was not willing to endure more hardship, physically or otherwise. I waited for God's answer to my plea. I was afraid God might not answer at all, but He did. His response was clear. The Spirit stirred within me and the LORD said, "No, you're not coming home yet." I sobbed harder in complete agony. "Have mercy on me, and let me die." Then the LORD simply responded, "You are to be a wife and mother first." Suddenly I stopped crying, I felt caught off guard. "Huh, really? I'll be a mom?" I wiped my tears on my already tear-stained, wet pillowcase and responded, "Ok, then You need to help me through this." God gave me the answer I needed to go forth. I cautiously, but faithfully decided to go through with the surgery. God gave me a promise that I would survive and I trusted that He would be with me, but I undoubtedly knew it was going to be hard.

Once I received God's promise, I had to journal it. I could barely sit up and see, but I had to write this down as a reminder and encourager.

Dear LORD Jesus,

I struggle to sit up and focus, my hand is unsteady, and I can hardly see the words I write in front of me, even with these nifty cheaters that Mike got me, but I must write. LORD, I now know that death is NOT in my near future, and I'm sorry that I'm a little reluctant to receive and accept life. I am trying to trust You and allow You to perform a miracle in my life. I know You have a plan for me to marry Mike, to become "a wife and a mother first." Thank You for that word God. LORD, I feel that Satan has already been defeated because we still are turning to You for peace in the midst of this storm. I continue to love

You no matter what I'm put through. Satan can't have me; I'm Yours. I thank You that Mike loves You and still deeply loves me genuinely through thick and thin. You've done a great work in both of us already. LORD, we are both scared of what will become of our future, especially with brain surgery inevitably around the corner. LORD, I ask as I've asked numerous times in my life, that You please hold my head, cradle my weak, tired body and to continue to nurture Mike and I's relationship. You are my rock LORD. Forget all my requests to be with me to get through finals at school, this is so much bigger than any of that! I need to feel You hold me at night and lift me during the day. Mike had to let go for a while to go to work. I miss him. Jesus, always be with us, never let go of us. Be with Mama, Dad, Ellen, Angie, Mike and anyone else who is suffering LORD.

-Meg

Upon receiving the word the LORD gave me, my decision was clear; I would yield to God's will and go forward with the surgery. So, I told my parents that a decision had been made, and now I just had to wait for a surgery date to be set. Once I had declared my decision, I was ready. Let's go and get this over with. But it wasn't as simple as all that. I was still slowly bleeding; I vividly remember the day when my left hand could no longer help pull up my pants after using the restroom. I felt helpless, but my condition wasn't classified as "urgent," so I had to wait. In waiting, I painfully remember the many lonely nights I spent in my room, in bed. I was sad especially when Mike was *in* town, because I couldn't be with him as I was before. I was too weak and frail to go out with him. Mike is a very boisterous man, and excitable. Even when he was quiet, I could hardly stand to be in his company without feeling overwhelmed and tired. So, Mike spent time with my sisters instead. Mike, my sisters and my sister's boyfriend all went to see *Blades of Glory* together in theaters while I lay at home in bed. They also went to a Jeremy Camp concert together. Jeremy Camp was my favorite Christian artist at the time. I was extremely disappointed to not be able to go with them. Mike said he would use his "art of persuasion" to talk Jeremy Camp into coming to my house to see me. Mike knew how hard it was for me to miss out on that experience because I was such a big fan. He sent to my phone several thirty-second clips of the concert, so I could feel as though I had experienced the concert live with him. It was so sweet, but each new video I received provoked me to sob louder. I hated not being able to be there with them. When they finally returned home, I half expected Jeremy Camp to be following them, but Mike said he didn't even get to talk to him. Instead, he bought me a T-shirt and sweatshirt hoping to cheer me up. It did cheer me up a little. I know they felt bad that I couldn't go and they were trying to somehow include me and love on me.

I often felt left out, but I did feel deeply loved. I felt loved all over again by many people. As we had been before, people from all our social circles surrounded us in love and prayer. I remember nights my girlfriends came to pray with me and we dyed Easter eggs, and a large group from COTS crowded our family room and spent an evening praying over me and my family. Some stayed to further pray and comfort Mama and Dad after I'd gone up to my bed to recover from the excessive crying and emotional stimulation. Although it was exhausting to have visitors during that time and try to socialize, I truly cherish memories of the masses of people who had surrounded us in our home with love and prayer.

Finally, in late March a surgery date was set, and we headed for Phoenix, Arizona for my brain surgery. Mama, Dad, Mike, Ellen, Angie and Mike's parents Tim and Therese, were all coming along for the ride. Mama, Mike and I all boarded a commercial flight. Everyone else took to the road. I hated to fly and couldn't imagine it would go well (I was convinced my first bleed had occurred when I flew for the first time in 1999 and ever after I got sick on every flight), but it was the fastest available option, and I had Mike, Mama and my wheelchair to assist me. Once we'd arrived in Phoenix, we made our way to the hospital to meet Dr. Spetzler for the first time. We all squeezed into his exam room. When Dr. Spetzler knocked on the door, Dad squeezed himself behind the door as he opened it to let Spetzler in. Dr. Spetzler peered behind the door, smiled and said, "Thank you." I anticipated he'd be a little annoyed with such a full room that he could hardly *squeeze* through, but he very warmly extended his hand to each family member and asked them their name and relation to me. Last of all, he shook my hand with both his and with a warm smile, he said, "Quite a family you have here." Rather than annoyed, he seemed touched that I had such a strong group of support. After introductions and an analysis of my physical condition, he proceeded to tell us about the surgery. My body was tense and nervous as I tried to listen to Spetzler throw out medical terms and procedures I didn't understand. I couldn't concentrate because I was still so tired. It took all my strength just to sit upright on his exam table and to keep my eyes open. I couldn't make much sense of what he said. But my researched dad was there, and I trusted he had a much better understanding than I did. Here is what I heard and did understand. Dr. Spetzler and his team of fellows would make an incision, drill through my skull and make a path through my brain tissue to get to and remove my hemangioma once and for all. That's all I needed to know. When he was finished explaining the procedure, I nodded nervously, smiled and said, "Ok." He returned the smile and asked if any of us had any questions. Dad asked a number of questions and I may have too, none of which I now recall. However, there is one question I *do* remember: Mike's one and only question.

Mike asked, "Yeah, are there any disc golf courses around here?" My surgeon said, "Pardon?" I was immediately embarrassed and angry. I muttered to him, "You *can't* be serious." He answered me aloud and said, "Well yeah." Mike was my *fiancé*; didn't he have any *other* pertinent relevant questions to ask about his fiancée's *brain* surgery?! To our surprise, however, Dr. Spetzler was truly intrigued and asked Mike to explain what disc golf was. Once Dr. Spetzler had a better understanding of what disc golf was, right there in the exam room, Dr. Spetzler got his phone out of his pocket and called his son to ask him if he knew where any disc golf courses were! In his German accent he said to his son, "You know, Frisbee." When Dr. Spetzler got off his phone, he got a piece of paper and drew a map for Mike of a place his son thought might have a disc golf course. I was horribly embarrassed that Mike asked my *brain surgeon* about disc golf during my consultation, but Mama said, "It did show us that Dr. Spetzler is human and has a family. He isn't a cold surgeon, you aren't just another patient and we aren't just another family to him. Although Mike's question was absurd, Dr. Spetzler's response was comforting and shows us his character." As we left the exam room, Mama faced Dr. Spetzler and said, "I hope you're having a good day tomorrow." I had the same feeling, but after meeting with my kind, warm brain surgeon, I was absolutely certain that God had placed me in good and steady hands. We had been told that Dr. Spetzler was the best surgeon to be doing my terribly invasive and risky surgery. He was the best in his field and had travelled around the world teaching fellow surgeons how to do the surgery he'd be performing on me. He was highly revered by his fellows and beloved by his patients. He was and is nothing short of the very best. The next time I'd see Dr. Spetzler would be in the morning, for my surgery.

Once in our hotel, we talked of dinner plans. I was not allowed to eat anything after 8 p.m. and was not allowed to drink beyond midnight. So, my last meal would be a hearty meal. We had steak my future father-in-law (Tim) and Mike, cooked on the hotel grill. Mike wasn't accustomed to using a charcoal grill and put so much charcoal on the grill that he nearly set the hotel ablaze. I was thankful I wasn't outside to witness the near catastrophe, I only heard about it. Thankfully Tim had come to the rescue and took over. A near crisis was averted, and the steaks were very tasty. We talked and we laughed as if tomorrow (surgery day) were just any other day. After Mike and his parents vacated to their own room, my family prepared for bed. As a family, we prayed together and a few tears were shed. Then, I snuggled in next to my sister on the queen bed to relax and go to sleep. Because I was still so fatigued from the bleeding, even any anxiety I had surrounding surgery couldn't have kept me awake. I didn't have any trouble sleeping. As I slept, my parents sat together watching me for a few moments and Dad said, "She looks so young." My parents thought I was *too* young to have to go through something so perilous and even life-threatening.

I groggily woke up early the next morning. It was Friday, March 23rd. It was finally the morning of my surgery. We walked across the street (myself in a wheelchair) from the hotel to the hospital. I was promptly admitted, led to a hospital bed, and my family crowded around me in my pre-op room. I got my hospital gown and bracelet and they stuck me to set up an IV site. A nurse rolled a saline drip in to connect to my IV. "I brought you breakfast," she laughed. I didn't think it funny. "Unless you're serious about breakfast, don't mention it; I am so hungry," I said. I was unbelievably hungry, thirsty, nervous and anxious. Although I knew the outcome, that I would survive brain surgery to become a wife and mother, I didn't know what state I'd be in afterward. What would the recovery look like? Dr. Spetzler only said that I would quite likely experience approximately six weeks of pain. He forewarned us the surgery risks included, but were not limited to: death, coma, paralysis, blindness, infection, hematoma (more brain bleeding), or anything else they could think of. I trusted Dr. Spetzler, and more importantly I trusted God no matter what the outcome might be. Even so, I couldn't control my nerves while lying in waiting. My left leg shook nervously on the bed, and my empty stomach was in knots, but I was still talking and laughing with my family to pass the time and try to take my mind off the "what ifs." I could not, and would not allow fear to overtake me. "God give me peace, God give me peace."

The last thing I consciously remember is the anesthesiologist coming in to give me my healthy dose of anesthesia. Just before they took me in, however, I responded physically to something Mike had said to me many times before. "Show me what ya got little lady, show me what ya got." I jiggled on the bed in response, and the nurses laughed as they pushed me through the operating room doors. By the time they had situated me in the operating room, I was in a complete state of unconsciousness. I have no recollection of the sight, smell or feel of the operating room, only that I was in a place of peace I can't quite describe. I had slipped into unconsciousness trusting and believing that God had equipped, and was using, Dr. Spetzler to preserve my life and completely remove my right-sided hemangioma.

My family stood and watched as I disappeared into the OR. After several moments of staring silently at the closed doors, a nurse came by and said to them, "You can go wait in the waiting room." They said, "Yeah, we know." Dr. Spetzler had told my family that the surgery would take approximately eight hours. The surgery was risky and intense. My family needed to not let themselves worry, but eight hours was a long time to wait and wonder what was happening to me. They eventually pulled themselves away from the OR doors and made their way to the waiting room to settle in. Mama listened to opera music, Ellen and Angie listened to music and prayed, Dad visited with an old friend who lived in Phoenix, Mike played his computer game and his parents started a movie. In the meantime, I was being positioned for the lumbar drain to be put in my back and then for my suboccipital craniotomy for supracerebellar transtentorial approach for micro-surgical resection of cavernous malformation with Tisseel duraplasty (I copy this directly from my surgical records and there are red squiggle lines under most of the words I just typed.) The suboccipital craniotomy was, simply said, an incision through the back of my skull. Dr. Spetzler cut through the three layers of my dura (Ouch!), at which point my brain was exposed. Once Dr. Spetzler could access my brain, he used what neurosurgeons refer to as wand guidance. Dr. Spetzler would be moving the wand from the back of my head to the center of my brain. To me, it seemed like a long way to go. The very small wand was used under a microscope and also transmitted a live feed to a computer screen to see my brain as Dr. Spetzler navigated very carefully to my lesion. As he approached the lesion, he saw there was blood surrounding the lesion from the bleeds I'd had. "Gentle suction" was used to remove the blood and finally, FINALLY "microsurgical instruments were used to remove the cavernous malformation." He took out the nasty, dreadful hemangioma in pieces. Once he believed he'd removed all of the lesion, he moved his way back out of my head, stitched up my dura, and secured my skull back together with three titanium plates and six screws. One of Dr. Spetzler's fellows stitched my scalp back together. It was my first time to have stitches and I got them both inside and outside my head; go big or go home. Surgery was finished. I imagine Dr. Spetzler and his team breathing a sigh of relief and shaking hands or even giving each other high fives; once their gloves are removed, of course. It was a difficult, scary invasive surgery that other surgeons deemed impossible, but Dr. Spetzler made possible the impossible. It appeared to be a successful brain surgery. I was still alive.

My family had anticipated a long wait, but the surgery took half the time anticipated. After four hours, my family was informed that surgery was over, successful, and they could see me soon.

I was told that Dad was shocked and shaken, and Angie couldn't stop crying; the nurse asked her to leave so she wouldn't upset me. They said I was momentarily conscious, but I don't at all remember the first time they saw me. I woke up more consciously aware by night. I was in the NICU (neuro intensive care unit), and everything was dark around me. My family wasn't there, and as far as I knew, I hadn't seen them yet. I was confused. Where am I? What happened? I wanted to scream, but I had a breathing tube in. I wanted to reach for my nurse call button, but my only good arm was tied down to the bed rail. They said I'd tried to pull out my breathing tube (a very common reaction in patients post-surgery.) It was then that fear truly gripped me. How can I communicate and get answers? I just wanted someone to tell me surgery was a success; that I was going to be OK. Where was everyone?

All I could think to do was kick my bed wildly to get attention. My bed shook as my legs hit the bed, violently; I was successfully making a lot of noise. I was hot and cold at the same time, in an immense amount of pain and so scared, but how could I possibly communicate that without being able to talk or motion with my hand? Instead of some much-needed comfort and some answers, my nurse came in a few times in the night to sedate me, and once I heard her say, "I'm not supposed to do this, but you need to calm down." The sedation of course helped me relax to fall back asleep, but my spirit felt uneasy and anxious, even as I slept. It was a rough night.

When my family came to visit me in the morning, I was still in a state of panic and very frustrated. I was frantic and scared in the dark of the night, but in the morning my room was so bright that it hurt my eyes and my brain. My breathing tube was still in and I was more aware of my pain. I couldn't focus my attention on any of my family and communicate with them. They had untied my right arm from the bed, but I couldn't sit up or focus long enough to write anything down to be able to "talk" to them. I just stared at them wanting to ask them so many questions. Mike's parents had been in to see me, Mike and Angie had been in to see me, and then Mama and Ellen came in. Mama came close to my bed and sat down beside me. She looked as though she had been crying, or had gotten very little sleep; maybe both. She gently caressed my hand, she seemed to be reading my mind, as she said, "Surgery went well, you're doing good." A few tears slid down my cheek. I gently squeezed Mama's hand, as if to say, thanks Mama. As groups of my family came and went, I became increasingly curious as to where Dad was. I'd seen everyone else. Where was my dad? I hadn't seen him, no one had even mentioned him. The only sign language I'd ever taught myself, was the alphabet. So as best I could, doped up on pain medicine, I used my right hand to spell out to Mama and Ellen, D-A-D. Ellen and Mama watched, really confused at first. Then Ellen said, "Are you trying to spell something?" I nodded impatiently as I continued to sign D-A-D.

They said, "Bad? Yeah, we know it's bad." I shook my head and tried again, D-A-D. "Bad Meg? We don't understand, what are you trying to say?" They kept thinking I was spelling "bad" instead of "dad," so I rolled my eyes, shut them and gave up. I couldn't concentrate much longer without increasing my insurmountable pain and fatigue. Mama said, "Sorry Meg, we don't know what you're trying to say." I'd just worry about Dad until they could get my breathing tube out and I could ask them. I heard Mama and Ellen talk quietly as I gave in to fatigue and dozed off again.

I was awoken what seemed just minutes later to remove my breathing tube. That was such a weird feeling and uncomfortable. When they got it all the way out, the first thing I wanted to say was, "Where's Dad?" Before I attempted to speak however, they asked me to swallow some ice chips. I successfully swallowed ice chips as quickly as I could, and let them soothe my very sore throat. I had scarcely swallowed the ice chips when I said hoarsely, "Where's Dad?" They didn't want to tell me right away because they didn't want to upset me, but Mama finally told me what had happened to Dad. She said Dad fainted when they had all visited me after surgery. He came out of my ICU room after having seen me for the first time, the color drained from his face, and he hit the floor. "Oh, my poor daddy." I immediately had compassion on my daddy and was even more desperate to see him and hug him; certainly, he'd feel better once he saw me more awake and without my breathing tube. After he had fainted, they took him to the cardiac tower and did an EKG just to be sure he hadn't had a heart attack. So, the next morning when my family had first come to see me, Dad was resting. Once I'd known Dad was OK, the breathing tube was out and I could talk to my family a little, for the first time since surgery, I felt more relaxed in my spirit; I didn't feel frantic and so scared anymore. And my first shift nurse also helped put me at ease.

The nurse who'd tended to me in the night ended her shift early in the morning, and a nurse named Dave took her place. Dave was an older English gentleman with a delightful English accent. I was so thankful for Dave. He had all the qualities I feel a nurse, especially an ICU nurse, should have. He was kind, gentle, caring and friendly. He always greeted me with a smile each time he came into my room and treated me and my family with the utmost respect. Late morning or early afternoon, Dave coaxed me into trying to eat a cup of Jell-O. I had not eaten anything since our steak dinner the night prior to surgery and I was dumping lots of pain medicine, among other medications, into an empty stomach. I was propped up and reluctantly, feeling overwhelmingly dizzy and nauseous, let Dave feed me a few spoonsful of cherry Jell-O. The first spoonful tasted good and felt cool on my throat; a successful first bite. I slowly allowed a second spoonful to slide down my throat and into my belly, but very soon after, I threw up. Dave, knowing I was terribly nauseous, had a puke reservoir close by, but he didn't grab it quick enough and most of the puke landed on me. I said, "I'm so sorry." He said, "Nonsense, it's OK. Thank you for trying. You know, it's about time we get you cleaned up anyway." He warmly smiled, warmed my cold left hand in his hands as we waited for another nurse to bring in some warm washcloths to wipe me down. Dave gently wiped my legs and arms and cleaned the puke off my face, neck and hair. He handed me a washcloth to wipe my chest, and he gently brushed my teeth. Although I was in so much pain and regularly emotionally shaken, Dave's joy and kindness was infectious and I couldn't help but smile too. I thought he was wonderful. My family was quite fond of him too, and enjoyed talking with him. I was thankful Dave took an interest in my family and took good care of them too.

Although the trip to Phoenix was trying on my family, I was

immensely happy to have them there; *all* of them. I had very few occasions in which I felt alone. I wasn't much for company, but someone was always with me; they came in shifts. Even through the night I was not alone. Mike insisted on sleeping in my room every night. When Mama and Ellen came in the morning, Mike would go back to the extended- stay hotel to get some better-quality sleep during the day. Mike, Mama and Dad seemed to be doing relatively well with my condition and were patient with the process. My sisters had a harder time adjusting to, or accepting, that I was so incapacitated. Ellen felt hurt and sad that I wasn't able to talk to her much and that I glared every time I looked her direction. Ellen would say, "Smile, aren't you happy to see me?" I'd give her a slight smile and often close my eyes and rest. El, frustrated, would say "You're going to sleep again? We just got here!" Mama and I couldn't convince her that it was nothing personal, I was just very sleepy and in a lot of pain. Each time Ang came to see me, she was very quiet and sad. I don't think she quite knew what to say or do. After all, Ang was still in high school (only sixteen) when I had surgery. And it pained me that *they* were in pain.

With visitors, the days were tiring, but the nights were quite possibly the hardest part of my hospital stay. The pain seemed to be more intense and I was tired but restless from being in bed all day. I was immensely thankful to have my future husband with me for those difficult nights. The first night (the night of surgery), I was alone and very frightened. But, my second night in the NICU was especially traumatic for *everyone* on the floor. I had my eyes closed, but I was not yet asleep, and Mike was sitting by my bed quietly talking to me. My nurse came into my room to check on me, but suddenly she got a call and without a word to either Mike or me, she bolted out of my room. Mike and I in fact heard *all* nursing staff running on the floor; we heard sobbing and felt increasingly anxious. My evening nurse poked her head back in, saw our anxious expressions, sighed and explained the situation. A young girl had been life-watched into the hospital because she was having a massive bleed. Much like my circumstance, she had a mass in her brain that she never knew she had. She was out with friends when it suddenly began to bleed and it was an aggressive, merciless bleed. My nurse told Mike to turn on the TV to distract me. She didn't want me to become upset. However, TV did not provide any sort of distraction; in fact, it made me dizzy and intensified my pain. Not only was I worried about the girl very close to my quarters, I was also in a lot of pain. I was suddenly wide awake. The entire NICU staff and doctors were trying to save the young girl's life, so I had to put any need or demands I had on hold. My nurse came in to us to give us updates once in a while; the young girl's condition worsened hour to hour, or rather minute to minute. There was no time to even get her into an emergency surgery; she was too fragile. My nurse, Paula, knew that Mike and I were people of faith and said "Maybe you should pray; if there *is* a God, only He can save her now." The girl wailed and screamed in the next room all night long. I cried long and hard for her too. I prayed that if her life should end that night, that she had known Christ as her LORD and savior and would ascend to heaven where pain and fear do not exist "He will wipe away every tear from their eyes, and there will be no more death or sorrow or crying or pain. All these things are gone forever" (Revelation 21:4). Early in the morning her struggle ended, and she died. We heard her wail all night long; in the morning we heard her mom and sister wailing. It had happened so suddenly and painfully. How could they have known and prevented that from happening? My heart was heavy for her family. Aside from the mother and sister's cries, the floor was eerily quiet and very somber all morning long.

After an emotionally and physically painful, trying night, I had hoped I'd again have Dave as my day nurse. He would be a familiar, kind face to comfort and care for me. However, I had a new male nurse. I was friendly and tried not to show that I was disappointed, but I was. He wasn't as gentle and kind as Dave, and although Mama and I thought it much too soon, he wanted me to try sitting up in a chair. I resisted because I was still in such a fog being doped on meds, very groggy, and still nauseous. Even so, he lifted me into a chair next to my bed. Immediately I felt disoriented, my ears plugged up, I felt my body swaying (I couldn't remain balanced). I desperately wanted, *needed* to lay down! He insisted that I try to sit up for at least five minutes; and then he left! Soon after he left I begged Mama to help me lay back down. I felt as though I could fall out of the chair; I couldn't grab focus of anything to get my bearings! I tried to close my eyes, but that made it worse; I felt dizzy and nauseated. Mama ran into the hall as I whined and cried, and she said, "Someone please help." Another nurse came to my rescue, and by the time my male nurse had returned, I had been under the care of a different nurse. Dad said he later saw Dave scold the nurse who'd left me unattended. Mama and I were so mad that we hoped the nurse had been fired. I felt discouraged and knew that I was a long way from being able to go home if I couldn't even sit up for a few minutes. The other NICU nurses I had were more attentive to me and pleasant. But my favorite NICU nurses were undoubtedly Dave and Paula.

Paula (my regular night nurse) couldn't have been more different from my day nurse, Dave. So, the difference was truly night and day. Paula was the nurse who had repeatedly given me a sedative my first night in the NICU, although she was unauthorized to do so, and who had come in to my room the next night, broke confidentiality and shared frequent updates on the girl next to me. Paula operated on her own set of rules and Mike and I somehow loved her for it. I knew she cared about me and had my best interests at heart, so I trusted Paula with my well-being. However, I must admit, there were times she scared me. I favored the left side of my head to lay on because the incision was on my right and very painful. While coming in to change my IV fluids, she told me a story about a patient who also had favored one side of his head and walked out of the hospital with his ear to his left shoulder. The point was that I needed to equally lay on my right and left side so my neck wouldn't get stiff. Although it hurt to lay also on my right side, she scared me enough to do it. On another occasion she told me that if my spinal fluid drain wasn't moved or adjusted every time I moved, that pieces of my brain would be sucked into the drain too. Not nice to toy with someone who's already loopy on pain pills. After that, I was afraid to even breathe! When I adjusted myself in my bed, I frantically said to my family members, "Hurry, adjust my drain!" Although she frightened me, Paula truly took good care of Mike and me both. She personally and promptly took care of my needs; we loved her. It seemed we'd made a good impression upon her too. She'd seen evidence of our faith and knew when she came into my room that we'd pray for the young girl and her family who had been life-watched into the building. On day three, I was no longer on oxygen, my catheter was removed (ready to take trips to the bathroom), and although I hadn't "eaten" anything beyond chocolate milk, I was well enough to leave the NICU. As we left, Paula told us that she had been in NICU nursing for more than twenty-five years, and in all those years there weren't many patients she'd remembered, but that she would never forget us. I smiled and said, "And I'll never forget you." I embraced Paula and said, "Thank you."

As they wheeled me to the elevator, I felt almost giddy. I got to leave the NICU! Mama pushed button six and we elevated to the sixth floor. They wheeled me to a spacious room and I gasped, "A window!" Being on a more "normal" floor, out of the NICU in a less urgent state was really nice. I again had a room to myself, and a small window. I watched the sunrise and sunset each day. Although I longed to be outside in the sun instead of in the sterile hospital room, it did my soul good to see the sun through that window.

Thankfully, my vision had cleared after surgery and I could clearly read things near and far away as I had before my bleed. However, other than the sunlight, there wasn't much else to look at in my room. Sitting up for a prolonged period of time was still difficult, so I couldn't yet read a book or write in my journal, but I had signs on my walls. Directly above my sink at the end of my bed, was a sign that read "Wash your hands/ Lavarse sus manos."

Also, I had a pain chart with faces on it on the wall next to my bed. I thought the chart wasn't terribly helpful in properly communicating my level of pain to my nurses. Pain is subjective. Everyone rates it differently. The nurses always asked when I requested pain meds, "On a scale from 1-10, how would you rate your pain?" The face representing number one on the chart had a broad smile, and number ten had a face with tears streaming down its cheeks. I hated that stupid sign. If we're saying my brain pain the night of surgery is gauged at a ten, then everything and anything else in comparison would not exceed a five; unless the scale is expanded, at which point I'd say *that* pain was a 20. How's that for intense? Through the duration of my stay in Phoenix, I compared my pain to the night of surgery when I can truly say it was a solid ten. It was the most excruciating pain I'd ever experienced or can imagine. Although I've had many debilitating migraines since then, it is nothing compared to the pain I experienced post-surgery.

I quickly discovered in the hospital that when I was more modest with my pain number, and said anything less than a six, their response was, "How about taking just one then?" "No, no, I want two; I'm still in a lot of pain. Forget I said six, it's a ten. The entire time I'm here, it's a TEN!" Brain surgery hurts! When I was moved to floor six, I no longer got the good, strong pain meds. They started giving me pain killers in pill form instead of through an IV. The pills weren't nearly as effective. But, in order to get well, I needed to wean off the heavy stuff that made me so drowsy; and I was in a hurry to get well and go back home. NICU's top priority for my care was to manage my pain and to keep me alive. But, the priority of floor six was to get me well enough to go home. I needed to eat, poop, and sit up as I would on a plane; all of which were difficult tasks. Ellen was especially determined to get me to eat. In the ICU, all I could stomach and sit up long enough to "eat" was Carnation Breakfast Essentials (a chocolate powder with protein and vitamins mixed with 2% milk). I sat up just enough to get two drinks and then laid back down to rest.

Through the duration of an hour or more, I only drank half of a cup. My lack of appetite and nausea hadn't changed from the ICU to the sixth floor, but the staff on the sixth floor pushed me to eat more. They brought meals up from the cafeteria. I don't recall if they brought up a tray for each meal, but if they did, I most certainly know that I did not eat at each meal. I tried to eat once or twice a day with Ellen's "encouragement." I often felt like slapping her. "Just two more bites, come on," she'd say, "Don't you want to go home?" I tried to fight against her, but she wasn't easily defeated. Each time they lifted the lid off my plate of food, I gagged and grimaced. My family claimed that the food in the cafeteria was actually quite good. Well, I don't know what they did to it between the cafeteria and my room, but I thought everything was awful. Occasionally I'd get a hankering for a particular restaurant food. My family was thrilled that I was even willing to entertain the thought of eating something else, but I couldn't eat any outside food.

By my fourth day post-surgery, I began to notice I was starting to feel better; perhaps it was the few bites of food here and there or that I was getting better stretches of sleep at night because the nurses didn't have to bother me as much on floor six. But I was well enough that I was beginning to feel restless. Reading books was still impossible for me to do; but I had Mama and Dad take turns reading the Bible to me. I could only concentrate long enough to listen to and comprehend one short Psalm or chapter, but I appreciated more stimulation beyond the two signs I had to stare at in my room. I was sitting up at longer stretches and was talking to my family more (although sometimes half asleep). I asked to take walks in the hallway, and when a young nurse offered to give me a shower, I readily accepted. I was so eager to get clean. After several days of laying around in bed, just wearing hospital gowns and going days without cleansing my body, I felt gross. I was excited to get cleaned up, but also terribly anxious about aggravating my incision. I told the young nurse that I was terribly nervous and asked her to please not get my incision wet. She was very gentle and successfully washed my hair and body without disturbing my incision. She also washed away some of the crusty blood that had dried into my hair. Ick! I felt a little embarrassed and uncomfortable that she, a complete stranger, saw me stark naked. Mama and my two sisters were the only people who'd ever seen me naked. She was roughly my age, was shy and appeared uncomfortable with the shower situation too. We were both very quiet. She was thorough, but quick and very respectful. I don't think she ever told me her name, and I didn't see her again. I was glad of that. It was uncomfortable, but I did appreciate her. I felt refreshed and rejuvenated after getting washed. It felt wonderful to be clean. Thank you, young nurse, whoever you are and whatever your name is! Sorry you had to see my malnourished body, naked.

And then, time to poop. Mike has tried to convince me to omit this next section, but I can't possibly omit a good and humorous story. I was well on my way to getting well, but still needed to pass waste. In addition to having taken a mass amount of pain killers, I had eaten very little since surgery and moved very little. I was going to need some "encouragement" to be able to poo. First, my nurse gave me milk of magnesia and had me take a lengthy walk around the hospital; when that didn't work, I reluctantly agreed to have a suppository. When that didn't result in anything either, she gave me a second suppository. My nurse was very beautiful and charming, sweet too. I thought she looked an awful lot like the actress, Amanda Peet in the movie *Something's Gotta Give*. I looked like crap, felt like crap and now my beautiful nurse was shoving suppositories up my butt to help me crap. Would Mike ever find me attractive again? Showered by a stranger, two suppositories in the butt, no dignity intact at this point! I was humiliated, but mostly embarrassed that Mike had to see me like that. Mike had actually seen every inch of me naked for the first time, not on our wedding night, but when I'd accidentally flash him in my hospital gown. It was not exactly how I'd imagined revealing my body to Mike for the first time, but Mike and I just laughed about it, and I laugh about it still.

After giving me the second suppository, my beautiful nurse said to give the suppository ten minutes to begin to work. Mike and I were sitting across from each other playing chess while waiting for the suppository to take effect. I had my legs hanging over the bed, waiting for the urge to poo. Suddenly, I felt the milk of magnesia, the walk, the two suppositories, all catching up with me and working all at once. Mike pushed my call button, but I couldn't wait for help. I stood up, and as quickly as my left leg would allow me to go, I made my way to the bathroom. Mike jumped up, grabbed my arm to support me, and I let out the most horrendous stench of gas. It was so bad that even Mike gagged! Mike fled the room and a nurse joined me in the bathroom. Once the nasty deed was done, nurse beautiful helped me back to my bed. Bowel movement: check! My poor, poor fiancé. I was eating bits of food here and there, I was sitting up at longer stretches, and I was finally able to poo. Time to go home?

Dr. Spetzler came to see me each day at the hospital to monitor my progress. By Thursday (day six in the hospital), he said he was pleased with my progress and he asked me if I was ready to go home. I answered with a resounding, "Yes!" He said I could choose to stay in Phoenix as an inpatient in their adjoining hospital for rehabilitation, but I said respectfully, "No, I want to go home." He smiled and said, "Ok then." Several phone calls were made to arrange transportation for me to get home. My doctor and family agreed that I wasn't well enough to sit through a commercial flight, so they secured an air ambulance for me to get home. In an air ambulance, I could lay down.

Before leaving my room, Dr. Spetzler congratulated me on already being well enough to go home and said he hoped I would have no need to see him again. But he said they would now have a clear pathway through my brain if ever I would have the need for surgery again. Uh, come again? The color drained from my face and had I not already been laying down, I believe I might have fainted. I had nothing to say in response, I was stunned. Dr. Spetzler didn't seem to notice. He simply smiled, shook my hand, turned away and left. The moment he left the room, I went into a state of panic. "Surgery again?!" I cried. "Why would he say that?" He just said surgery was successful. In my mind, it was finished and it was finally over. God used Dr. Spetzler to heal me, right? I'm done! But soon after he mentioned the probability of a second surgery the Spirit stirred within me and said the first surgery would not be my last. I was absolutely stricken with fear. "No God, I refuse to accept that. Get back from me, Satan!" I *need* this suffering to be over. I asked for the chaplain to come pray with me and for Mama to read scripture aloud; neither comforted me. I was so restless and scared. My nurse finally informed me that the doctors typically give us the worst-case scenario; it doesn't necessarily mean that I will in fact have another surgery. With that, I was able to settle down (a little), but Dr. Spetzler's words shook me and forced me to realize that this brain surgery was my first, but might not be my last. After all, I did still have another hemangioma in my head. Suddenly I felt a greater urgency to get out of that hospital and go home! I desperately prayed I would never have need to come back.

Thursday evening Mike was helping me eat dinner (filling in for Ellen). He too tried to force me to eat. My nurse really wanted me to eat one decent meal before I left the hospital the next morning. I took a bite of green beans and that wasn't too bad. Then Mike encouraged me to take a bite of mac n cheese. I reluctantly ate one noodle, scrunched up my nose, shook my head and said, "Yuck!" Mike said, "Oh it can't be that bad; take another bite." "You!" I shouted. Mike shrugged, took a big bite of mac n cheese, started to chew it, made a horrible disgusted face and spit it out. Needless to say, he didn't make me eat any more food after that. I thought to myself, "I should have had Ellen do that a long time ago." I kept trying to tell them the food was practically inedible. I drank my milk for dinner, had a good night of sleep and Friday morning, they prepped me for my flight home.

I told my morning nurse that I was terribly anxious about the flight. I whined, "I always feel so sick when I fly." She said she'd give me an anti-nausea pill long before my scheduled take off and something to help me relax that she assured me would also put me to sleep. My sister Angie had ridden home with Tim and Therese earlier in the week and Ellen had flown home shortly thereafter. Mama and Dad took to the road and began to drive home and Mike and I were flying home in the air ambulance. I so wished I could have had Mama, Dad *and* Mike in the plane with me, but there was only room for three: me, Mike and my air ambulance nurse. I hugged my very sweet nurse as we left the hospital and said, "Thank you beautiful Christine."

They drove me in an ambulance from the hospital to the airport. The streets were crowded, and I was disappointed they didn't run the siren and fly through traffic and stop lights. I laid on a stretcher in the back of the ambulance. I winced each time we hit a bump in the road. My head hurt, I was nervous and my stitches were terribly itchy. I couldn't scratch my incision, so I played with the hair around it as I tried to resist the urge to scratch. Some hair fell out in my hand as I played with it and the attendant said, "Didn't you already lose enough hair from having surgery?" I was kind of embarrassed and bashfully apologized for messing with my hair. I told him that I hadn't actually lost much hair. My surgeon only cut hair around where they needed to make the incision. I have so much hair anyway, that you can't tell any is gone. My cousin Rebecca had offered to buy me the best wig money could buy if Dr. Spetzler shaved my head. I won't need a wig for my wedding, cousin Rebecca! I sure do love and appreciate Dr. Spetzler for not shaving my head.

The ambulance dropped us off at the airport. To board the small one engine med plane, I had to stand up and climb the narrow, unsteady ladder and that was incredibly unnerving. The nurse aboard the air ambulance, strapped me to a very uncomfort-able "bed" (board). I was nervous and my anti-nausea pill didn't seem to be working. As we took off, my stomach dropped. I took my anti-nausea pill and relaxant long before take-off, that the nurse said would knock me out; however, I was miserable and wide awake the whole flight home. The turbulence all the way back home, was unbearable. I bounced off the bed numerous times, even when Mike tried to hold me onto it. He himself was also bouncing in his seat. It felt as though we were hitting massive potholes in the sky; it was awful! And for the first time since surgery, I was *really* hungry! The nurse aboard the plane had some peanut butter crackers. I uncomfortably ate a few crackers, but desperately needed more food. I kept asking her, "What time is it? Are we close to Wichita?" I was close to tears as my body jostled around and bumped up off the bed and slammed back down.

Once we were finally close to Wichita, I breathed a sigh of relief, but storms surrounded the city and we couldn't land the plane at the Wichita airport. Mike directed the pilot to the carrier in Hutchinson, Kansas (just an hour's drive from Wichita). We landed and waited in Hutchinson for the storms to clear. Mike and the pilot de-boarded the plane and used the delay as an opportunity to use the bathroom. I was growing increasingly impatient. "Can't you just let me out here and someone can take me home in a car?" They briefly discussed and considered having an ambulance drive me into Wichita, but as they were discussing, the storms were clearing and to my chagrin, we took to the sky again. My stomach churned again, and was now audibly rumbling with hunger. When we finally arrived in Wichita I was sore, dizzy and for the first time since surgery, famished. I craved a burger. Mike called his dad upon my request of a burger from NuWay (a Wichita locally owned restaurant, with loose meat sandwiches). From the airport, I was shuttled and admitted to a rehabilitation hospital.

7

The rehabilitation hospital I was admitted to was the same I'd been to seven years prior for outpatient therapy when I'd had my first bleed, and when the hemangioma mess all started. I'd had a decent, yet sometimes frustrating therapy experience as an outpatient in 2000; but in 2007 I came to the rehabilitation hospital as an inpatient and had a very different experience.

I was so happy to be back in Wichita. Although I preferred to be at home with my family, I knew I first had to get a little stronger through therapy before I could safely maneuver around my house. The ambulance EMTs pushed me through the doors of the hospital and up to my room. I had a spacious room and a large window that looked out on a courtyard. Thank You, Jesus, for a big window. There were two beds to accommodate two patients, but they graciously gave me my own room. I was getting settled in when Mike brought over the NuWay burger his dad had picked up for me upon my request. I scraped off the onions and savored each bite of crumbled meat, mustard, and cheese on a toasted hamburger bun. It was the best thing I'd tasted in over a week. As I was eating my burger, my first nurse brought in a dinner tray for me. She awkwardly said, "Oh, I see you already have dinner, do you want me to take this out of here?" I didn't want to appear ungrateful, but I said, "Yes, please and thank you." She then said, "Would you like to take a shower tonight?" I probably could have used a shower, but I wanted to eat and visit with my family before they went home. Again, I politely said, "No thank you." The nurse appeared upset with me, but quietly left me to eat my burger and visit with my family.

I had arrived at the hospital on a Friday evening and my nurse, Saturday morning, told me I had a few days to get acclimated to the hospital before I started therapy first thing Monday morning. Mike stayed and slept in the second bed, next to mine on Friday, Saturday and Sunday night. We watched TV in the evening and we explored the hospital together during the day. Even though my appetite had returned and I was eating well at each meal, I was still feeling unusually hungry more frequently. So, Mike picked up an 8 oz. "Love It" size bowl of Cold Stone Creamery's mint mint chocolate chocolate chip ice cream to satisfy my night time cravings. It was a delectable concoction, with mint ice cream, chocolate chips, brownie bites, chocolate fudge, all inside of a waffle bowl; ensue mouthwatering. It was full of calories and oh so delicious!

I got increasingly excited as Monday morning approached. I genuinely looked forward to starting therapy; I was absolutely determined to get better. But I was also sad because first thing Monday morning, Mike would have to leave town, to go back to Garden City. Mike wouldn't be with me any longer. No more night time snack or overnight company. He packed the last of his things early Monday, kissed me, said goodbye, and he was gone. He drove back to Garden City to get back to work. He had already missed more than a week of work. Of course, I understood his need to leave, but I knew I was going to miss him terribly. He had been such a help and comfort to me thus far.

The start of Monday morning turned out to be a rude awakening. Only one week out of a massive brain surgery and I felt the rehab staff expected me to do much more than I was capable of, or should have been asked to do. I was still in pain, dizzy and very tired, but was still expected to take responsibility for much of my own care.

Each patient had been given a wheelchair of their own. When Mike had been with me over the weekend, he pushed me around the hospital in my chair, but the staff told me, first thing Monday morning I would need to maneuver *myself* around in the chair. I lifted my crippled left arm and said, "I can't use my left hand to help, I'll just be spinning in circles." Then the nurse said, "Actually you'll be using your feet to pull you along." "Well, I have a crippled leg too" I said. She said, "Everyone uses their legs to pull themselves; it's part of your therapy and will help your leg get stronger. You'll wheel yourself to meals and therapy sessions all day every day." I looked at her perplexed and said, "You're kidding." But I then looked down the hallway and saw all the other patients sadly sitting in their wheelchairs pulling themselves along with their gripped socked feet. Everyone was looking toward the floor, not a one smiling. It was a sad sight to see. It was a community mostly of elderly people and I was by far the youngest in the bunch. Many of the rehab hospital's other residents were also there because of neurological damage either from tumor, stroke, or some other sort of brain injury. Some of that group had also had brain surgery. I squirmed when I saw these patients with half-shaved heads and gnarly scars that looked quite gruesome and almost like a hacksaw had been used to cut through their skull; yikes! I was again very grateful that I had my hair, and that an incredibly skilled, much better surgeon (clearly!) had done my surgery. Thank You, LORD, that I did not have my surgery in Wichita. The journey to Phoenix was well worth the trip. I hated to join this community of sad, damaged patients; but I had no choice. So even as frustrated as I was, I obeyed, and did as the nurse asked. I squatted to sit in the chair as she pushed it up behind me and she watched me shoot forward to plant my feet on the floor. I hesitated and looked up at her, as she said, "Go on then." Seated in the wheelchair, I shuffled my feet and started making my way down the hall toward the dining room. She seemed gratified and said, "That's it, you got it." I thought, Ok, great I've "got it," but I feel humiliated and demeaned. I thought to myself, "I hate you people for what you've done to these other hurting patients, and to myself. How are we supposed to get well in this cold and sad environment?" We needed some compassion and help from the staff, but too often we were all on our own. The nurse walked into another patient's room as I pulled myself along with many others, toward the dining hall for breakfast. Although my feet worked well at pulling me forward, I had a difficult time steering with one hand. I ran into the wall and a few other patients, who then glared at me. I wondered, how long have these other sad patients been here? I felt a deep sorrow for them. Most of them were truly in bad shape, but still were expected to get themselves to breakfast. No one spoke to me, or to each other. I had never felt more alone and abandoned, but I perked up when I saw Dad standing in the dining hall waiting for me. He was a person who loved me, had concern for me and wasn't oppressed by this horrible place. I cried a little when I saw him. He said, "What's wrong?" "Nothing Daddy, I'm just so happy to see you," I lied. I wanted to scream, "I was wrong; we came home too soon, I want to go back to Phoenix!" I slowly ate my breakfast before my first therapy session (because I wasn't in a hurry for Dad to leave). When I had finished, and my tray was cleared, Dad grabbed the handles of my wheelchair to push me to the gym, but I said, "No Dad; I have to do it myself." "Really?" Dad said. He was a little confused as he watched me struggle to pull myself across and down the hall to the gym. Other patients around us were doing the same and I saw Dad look around and he thought-fully said, "Huh." Once we arrived at the therapy schedule posted in the gym, Dad helped me write down my therapy schedule for the day since I was responsible for getting myself to each session. He met and shook hands with my first therapist of the day, bent down and kissed my forehead and said, "I'll come by again tomorrow before work." I sadly smiled and said, "Bye Dad." But inside I was yelping, "Daddy, don't leave me here with these people."

I met with a young girl just older than myself for occupational therapy. Even though I was already very tired, I was excited to see her. I wanted to get my hand fully operational again. My hand was in terrible shape, so I was especially eager and willing to work really hard. I'd done it all before and gained all mobility back. I was confident I could do it again. We started at the table, and she put games and tools before me that I'd all seen and done many times before. I eagerly lifted my debilitated arm to the table and she tried to hand me a clothes pin. I tried with all my might to grab it, but my hand remained clenched in a fist. I bashfully said, "I can't open my hand." She took my hand in hers and pried my fingers out so they could grasp the pin. She asked me to squeeze the clothes pin, but instead my fingers curled back up into a fist and I dropped the pin to the floor. She tried something else that should have been a little easier, but again my hand wouldn't respond. She had me try a few other activities, but we came up empty-handed. I couldn't even begin to do them. So instead, she instructed me to do some balance exercises. These were exercises I was supposed to be doing in physical therapy, not occupational therapy. I was disappointed she had given up on my arm and hand so soon. I left occupational therapy feeling really discouraged, and my therapist didn't feed me any word of encouragement. She acted indifferent, unattached. She was just doing her job, and I was just another patient to her. She had no interest in getting to know me. I missed Dana.

Fortunately, I had a much more successful session with my peppy and determined physical therapist. We spent the entire session on improving my balance. I walked through a ladder on the floor, climbed over short hurdles, and pretended to walk on a balance beam. My balance was better than I'd expected, but I wouldn't be allowed to go home until the therapists and staff thought I was stable enough to move around more on my own with minimal assistance. I wasn't there yet. After my first therapy sessions with my occupational therapist and physical therapist, I had a break before any more therapy and lunch. I was thoroughly exhausted, but I laboriously pulled myself back to my room. I pushed my nurse call button when I finally got back to my room. I impatiently waited for her to come put me back in bed. I desperately needed to lay down and take another round of pain meds. I needed to sleep, but because I was expected to make it to each of my therapy sessions and meals on my own, I felt too anxious to rest. I didn't know what to do to kill time. It was the first time I'd been alone since surgery. I didn't have any extra strength to either read or write. Everyone I knew was either at work or school, so even as I sent out texts, I knew I likely wouldn't get a response till late in the afternoon. So, although I didn't watch any TV while in Phoenix, it was all I could think to do while at the rehab hospital to kill time. I noticed it was what everyone else did all day too. I watched the clock as I remember doing in high school, how much longer until I need to get to the next "class"? TV was really the only thing I could manage on my own. The TV was directly above my bed, and I could adjust the volume and channels on the same remote as my call button to summon the nurse. Everything else I needed required assistance. My nurses had to bring me my water, my medications and even stuff from across the room because I was not allowed to get up. And each time I had to use the restroom, I had to call for help.

They appropriately put a fall risk bracelet on my wrist to alert all staff that I was not yet stable enough to walk without help. I was told I would always have to ask for help to get around my room and to the bathroom. A few times I did get up on my own, because I thought it was silly to push my button to ask the nurse to get something that was just barely beyond my reach. My nurse once caught me on my feet and put on my bed alarm for the remainder of her shift. Even when I shifted my weight to reach for something or sat up to adjust my blanket, the bed alarm sounded and it was ear piercing! After that incident, I never attempted to get up on my own. The Wichita rehab staff were much slower to respond to my call button than the St. Joseph Hospital staff in Phoenix was. Twice I nearly wet my bed waiting for a nurse to assist me to the bathroom. The first time it happened, when my nurse finally came in to take me, I said "Oh, finally; I almost wet the bed!" She said, "Better to wet your bed, than to fall down and hurt yourself." At that callous response, I wanted to give her a swift kick to the shin! After she'd helped me to the bathroom and back to bed, I glared at her as she turned her back and walked out, and then I cried. I missed people who cared about me.

During a break, late in the afternoon, I lay quietly in my bed; the TV was off, and I was praying. Dear LORD, I know I can do all things through You who gives me strength, so please LORD give me the strength required of me to get well enough to leave this awful place. As I prayed, I was suddenly overwhelmed with a horrible smell. I thought to myself, "I hope it's not the smell of dinner; yuck!" But the odor was so strong, it couldn't have travelled all the way from the kitchen. It took me several minutes to realize it wasn't anything outside the room or even outside my bed, it was *me*! I slowly lifted my right arm, took a quick whiff of my underarm, and gagged. I then ran my fingers through my hair and felt how wet it was with grease and oil. I pulled my hand away, and it was slick with oil; slimy! Ew, yuck! I was embarrassed. How long had I looked and smelt so horrible? Had I daily been putting on deodorant? I couldn't remember. I had only taken one shower in Phoenix. It had been four or five days since that shower, and I was desperately in need of another. Next chance I had, I asked my nurse if I could have a shower. She said, "You're not on the rotation tonight." I protested, "Look at me, my hair is an oily nasty mess, and I can hardly stand my own stench!" She again said, "Sorry hon, you're not on the rotation tonight, but you can have one tomorrow night." "What?" If I could have, I would have dropped to my knees and begged her to work me in to the rotation. As she began to head for the door, I yelled after her, "Please, can I have a washcloth?" She said, "I'll see if I can get one." But she never came back. The hospital staff was terribly impersonal, and terribly frustrating. They were so emotionally distant, uncaring and indifferent. I would have attempted to befriend some of the other patients, but I didn't have much of a desire to. All the other patients were as old as my grandparents, or older and all looked so sad. Many of them had a lot of mental brain damage as well as physical, and couldn't begin to carry on a conversation. How could I ever relate to them? I dearly missed my family, friends and the Phoenix staff who were so kind and helpful. I suppose I'd been spoiled. The Phoenix staff set the bar pretty high. Although not as knowledgeable, I did appreciate my Wichita rehab doctor. He was the only staff member that took the time to talk to me and ask me how I was doing each day. He was a very kind man, but I had the feeling I was the first he'd seen of my "kind." Cavernous malformations/hemangiomas are very rare and it's even rarer for them to bleed. I was very young to have had a brain bleed and then brain surgery. I don't think he quite knew how to help me exactly. I prayed for him, whether he knew Christ or not, that somehow God would guide him to help me, rather than harm me.

I specifically remember when he came in between therapy sessions on the afternoon of April third. He said a nurse would be coming in later to remove the staples from my incision. I was sitting up in bed with my brace boot on my left foot, holding it at a ninety-degree angle, my toes pointed to the ceiling. I also had a brace on my left hand holding my wrist flat, and fingers open, rather than balled in a fist. We were discussing my pain, and other symptoms. Although he had put me on a far less effective pain medication, I told him my pain was tolerable for the time being. But I told him I was concerned about some numbness and tingling I was experiencing on my left side, *everywhere!* Since surgery, I had been taking steroids (decadron) as I had in 2000. My rehab doctor had begun to wean me off the steroid, per Dr. Spetzler's instruction, but given my tingling and numbness, my rehab doctor increased my dose of steroids and extended the time period in which I'd take them.

Later that afternoon, a nurse came in to remove my staples. Some of them were stubborn and difficult to get out because either hair or dry blood held them firmly in place. I winced as she carefully pried out the stubborn ones. Once she'd pulled out the last one, we counted them. There were sixteen staples in all. I was surprised that they looked just like ordinary office staples. After having *finally* showered, with the assistance of my nurse, I showed off my staple free incision to my family and friends when they came to visit in the evening. My scalp was healing. By April third, I could handle longer stretches of visits. I often had company when I ate dinner and shortly thereafter. It was my favorite part of the day and the only thing that kept me sane in that hellhole of a place. I was always overjoyed to see Mama, Dad, my sisters, aunts, uncles and cousins. I also appreciated my college friends who came to see me. They kept me updated on things going on at school and sometimes it was hard to hear. I hated to miss out.

I was terribly tired April third after a long day of therapy, an important visit with my doctor, removing my staples and a shower. I had seen my sister Ellen and one of my cousins, and I was nearly ready for bed. I had trouble sitting up and keeping my eyes open, but still welcomed one last visitor. I hadn't seen this girlfriend of mine since before surgery. We had classes together, and I'd missed her. She sat down in a chair furthest from my bed; she was visibly agitated. I wondered if my physical state made her anxious and uncomfortable. She asked how I was doing, I gave her a slight smile and said, "Not great, but getting better." She then said, "Well, at least you don't have to take finals; I'm freaking out!" I raised my eyebrows, "Are you kidding?! I'd much rather be stressing about finals than lying here in this bed recovering from brain surgery! Would you like to trade places with me? I'll take your finals and mine too!" I responded. I wanted to shake my friend and say, "Get over yourself." And yet, she continued to whine about how she just knew they were going to be impossibly hard and a huge percentage of her grade and that she wanted to finish out her college career with great grades. I tried to console her, even though I would have preferred to tell her to get out! I finally, kindly told her I was very tired and needed to sleep. I told her I would pray for her and that her stress would be alleviated. I did mean that. I would pray that God give her *perspective* and help her to relax about something really quite trivial, and more importantly to consider the state of the person you're ranting to about something that seems of very little significance.

I was grieved that she was so insensitive to my circumstance and couldn't/wouldn't allow herself to empathize. She was so consumed with her own anxiety, that she couldn't even put it aside to be there for me. I breathed a huge sigh of relief when she left, and I asked the nurse for some more pain meds. The frustration I felt with my friend, was making my head hurt. Good grief; I'd be on cloud nine if I could instead study for finals! Even with the aid of drowsy pain meds, I became visibly agitated and couldn't settle down to sleep. I called Mama and Dad, and asked if they'd come see me. I knew my parents could help me relax and pray for me. Dad was in the middle of something when I called, but said he'd come in the morning again for breakfast, so Mama came alone. Mama brought with her some homemade strawberry ice cream for my bedtime snack. I was very hungry. I told her about my friend complaining about finals. We both rolled our eyes until our eyes were sore, then we laughed and shook our heads. Oh, how naïve and ridiculous people can be.

The morning of April fourth (day five in the rehab hospital), I woke up at four a.m., eager to have breakfast. It was still very dark and breakfast wouldn't be served for several hours yet. I couldn't fall back asleep because I was so restless, hungry, and struggling with some growing brain pain. To distract me, and to kill time, I turned on the TV directly above my bed. I watched *Saved by the Bell* and *Full House* reruns until breakfast time. The very second the clock struck seven, I pushed my nurse call button. Twenty minutes later, my nurse came to help me to the bathroom and to get me into my wheelchair. I scooted forward, planted my feet on the floor, and shuffled myself to the dining hall. I was getting quite good at moving myself about in my chair. I cried as I pulled up to an empty table. I was exhausted, hungry, and Dad was nowhere in sight. Dad had promised he'd come every morning for breakfast. I cried as I slowly ate my breakfast. Finally, Dad showed up with just ten minutes remaining in the breakfast hour. He came up behind me, saw my face full of tears, and said, "Meg, what's wrong?" "I didn't think you were coming, and my head hurts so bad!" I blubbered.

I think that moment is when Dad truly realized how miserable I was at the rehab hospital. He gently wiped my tears with his handkerchief. I didn't protest as he gripped the handles of my wheelchair and pushed me to my session of group therapy. I rested my pained head in my right hand as Dad pushed me into the gym. My cheeks and eyes burned from my tears. A big burly woman who was lining other patients up for group therapy abruptly shouted at Dad from across the gym when she spotted us. "Oh no, no, no what are you doing? You can't push her! She has to do it herself." Dad politely said, "She's in a lot of pain today."

She then addressed me and yelled again, "Everyone here is! Now wipe your face. You have work to do." Dad was reluctant to leave me, but did so when the woman (big bully) said, "Go on, she'll be fine." As she walked off, I muttered "Bitch" under my breath. I think she might have heard me, but didn't pay any attention to me. Through the session, I looked around at the other patients and realized I was beginning to mirror their faces and attitudes. My spirit deflated, I was expressionless and numb to my surroundings. I was hoping my stay would quickly come to an end, and I hoped that the other miserable patients could soon escape too.

My pain subsided as I tried to be more restful between other sessions and meals. I turned away visitors and didn't watch any TV before bed. That night, however, was a repeat of the night before. I was exhausted, but restless. I again woke up at 4 a.m., very hungry. Upon my request of food, my nurse brought me a package of crackers. I quickly ate the crackers and asked for more. She was clearly annoyed and insisted I wait until breakfast. I groaned and held my rumbling tummy. Pain pills weren't as effective as they had been for my head pain, but momentarily eating something helped ease the pain. As my pain and hunger grew, I watched some more TV reruns until breakfast. I was going through the motions of another day at the rehab hospital, and still numb to my surroundings. I had a short break between lunch and my first afternoon session, so I went back to my room and watched more TV. I was flipping through the channels and stopped when I caught a glimpse of a woman wearing a wedding dress on TV. I watched the show for a few minutes. She was trying on dresses, joyfully planning her wedding with her friends and family, bubbling with excitement. I burst into tears. I wanted to be excited and bubbly and finish planning my wedding too! July seventh was just three months away, and I still had things to do. Instead, I lay in this godforsaken hospital feeling so alone and depressed. I screamed and continued to cry as I sat and watched the show through my tears.

While still in my meltdown, a nurse walked in to inform me I was late for group therapy. I wiped my eyes, she turned off the TV, helped me into my wheelchair, bent down and sweetly said, "Why are you crying?" Between sobs, I told her I was getting married in three months and I wanted to be planning my wedding, not stuck in the rehab hospital. She said, "Oh, you poor thing. I'll help you to therapy, just this one time." I was extremely grateful for her kindness and compassion; other than my doctor, she was the first of the staff to show any expression of concern. I wanted to reach out and hug her.

Once in the gym for group therapy, I saw several patients sitting together, in a circle. The woman who'd brought me to the gym, and the therapist, moved a few patients in their wheelchairs to make room for me in the circle. I tried to stifle my tears as they moved me. For the group therapy, fellow patients were throwing a lightweight ball around to one another. They had paused the game on my account. Although the objective of the game seemed fairly obvious to me, the therapist explained the game as he placed the ball in my lap. He said, "Stay seated, and pass it around." I noticed that two very old women had fallen asleep and a few others couldn't understand what was going on and what they were supposed to do, so they sat and let the ball hit them or just fall to the floor as they left their hands in their lap. It was pretty sad, but a little humorous. I looked at the therapist, chuckled and said "I don't think this is going very well." The therapist shrugged his shoulders and laughed too. So instead, the therapist placed me across from another gentleman who was also fairly alert. He had us bounce the ball back and forth until the other patient tried to stand up and nearly fell over; game over. That was the first time I'd laughed and actually had a little fun at the hospital.

Later that afternoon, when my doctor came in, he told me I could finally leave to go home the next morning. I could eat breakfast, but wouldn't go to therapy. I could leave! It was Easter weekend and I was so excited to get to go home on Good Friday. Hallelujah! Praise the LORD!! I'm going home!

8

It was snowing that Friday morning that I was released from prison, I mean the rehabilitation hospital, and looked as though it had been for several hours. Snowflakes fell onto my head and lap, as the orderly pushed me out to the curb. She and Mama both carefully assisted me into Mama's car. I felt relieved when we pulled up to our house; my home, my safe place, my place of refuge. Mama helped me up to my room and into my bed. I thought to myself, "I'll do so much better, now that I'm home."

Just as she was all those years before, Mama was my caretaker during the day while Dad was at work and Angie and Ellen were at school. Angie was sixteen, and a sophomore in high school. Since I'd started college and had a more serious boyfriend, Angie and I lost touch with each other. I thought being home now with no other distractions, would provide opportunity for Angie and me to reconnect. Angie, however, was quiet when she came home from school, and her way of coping was to ignore and withdraw. She sat in front of the TV, did her homework in solitude and quietly helped me only when Mama or Dad asked her to. Like myself, Ellen attended Friends University. She was a freshman and lived on campus, so I didn't see her as much. She was wildly busy dating her boyfriend, studying, writing papers and wrapping up her first year of college. I was envious, and wished I could be there too; I had been doing so well at school.

Although I'd still been living at home during my college career, I had regained a lot of strength and independence since my high school bleeds. I was very excited and proud of all that I'd accomplished. The 2007 bleed and surgery broke me. I was heartbroken that I lost any independence I'd regained and that I needed to again rely on Mama for help.

However, I was immensely grateful for Mama's selfless love and sacrifice of herself. We cried together over my pain, and sometimes she just sat in my room to keep me company as she silently read to herself. She was a great comfort to me. I missed her and longed for her company when she was otherwise busy with cleaning, cooking, practicing her instruments or out working. I wanted her to always be with me. My love and appreciation for Mama grew, and Mama became my closest friend.

Especially when Mama was busy with other things, I didn't know what to do with myself. Prior to the 2007 bleed, I'd had a very full schedule. I was taking sixteen credit hours to finish my double minors and major, I was working part-time, exercising, planning my wedding and staying up late nearly every night doing homework, reading, journaling or talking endlessly on the phone to my fiancé. All of that came to a screeching halt when I had my 2007 bleed; ALL of it. What was I going to do now?

Friends knew I'd be restless, so they graciously brought me all sorts of things to fill my time. Some friends from my church life group, gifted me a journal before I'd gone to Phoenix for surgery. They each wrote an encouraging note to me. It was so thoughtful, and I was touched. I would have loved to journal through my pain and sorrow, but sitting up for a long period of time still made me dizzy and tired. I also still couldn't concentrate long enough to write or read. I didn't like the idea of wasting time in front of the TV; I'd rather do something productive, but I thought maybe it was the only thing I could do to pass the time. So, I tried to watch

TV. Mike had given me a small TV to put in my bedroom and I'd purchased a cheap, very basic, DVD player to go with it. The TV had no channels, just allowed me to watch movies. A college friend gifted me season one of *Full House*, my best friend, Becca, gave me her extensive collection of movies, and my aunt gave me a copy of the *Pride and Prejudice* TV mini-series on DVD. I was able to watch large amounts of television at the rehabilitation hospital to pass the time and fill the silence, but for whatever reason, my head couldn't tolerate more than ten to twenty minutes of watching television at home without feeling dizzy and my head in mind numbing pain. Mama, Angie and I watched *Pride and Prejudice* together, but it took us several weeks to get through the five-and-a-half-hour series, because I could only tolerate watching short segments at a time. TV was not enjoyable. So, I tried listening to books on CD; to me, that seemed more "productive" and satisfying than watching TV anyway. An employee at the library brought to me *The Chronicles of Narnia* books on CD. I fondly remember Dad reading *The Chronicles of Narnia* to me each night as a child. I eagerly anticipated listening to them read aloud on CD. I tried listening to them on both my stereo across the room and on my disc man with headphones, but that made my head spin too and I couldn't concentrate long enough to make sense of the story. I sadly asked Dad to please return the CDs to the Friends library. Yet another friend made me a mix of relaxing songs on CD to listen to; my head couldn't tolerate that either. I couldn't listen to music without feeling disoriented. To stay connected to school friends, I texted, but the screen on my phone burned my eyes, making it difficult to text very often. I only very briefly entertained the thought of trying to use the computer. I wanted to check my email, communicate with my mass group of friends and contacts, but using our computer would require me to descend three flights of stairs, to sit straight up and look at a screen just in front of my face, and read. If I couldn't handle television from across the room, music playing from my radio, or even looking at the small screen on my phone, I knew I was quite far from being able to tolerate using a computer. I felt incredibly bored, lonely and cutoff from society. I especially hated being unproductive.

When I was sixteen and had my initial massive bleed, I didn't return to school right away, but I was still able to go out with my boyfriend Adam, spend time with my family, do puzzles, play games, craft, journal, read my Bible, go to therapy, run errands with Mama, go to church, and connect with school friends on AIM (AOL instant messenger). I then had two bleeds when I was eighteen, but was still attending all my classes, doing pool therapy and had no social limitations. The bleeds I'd had as a teenager were tough and hard to deal with, but keeping busy and continuing to connect with people helped me work through the pain and sorrow of it all.

Unfortunately, post-surgery not only could I not keep busy, but I was also not able to stay connected with people. Trying to connect in *any* form, was exhausting and painful. It was horrible not being able to be with people. I missed seeing and talking to my friends; I *needed* them. It was especially difficult to not be able to talk to my fiancé. I sent the occasional short text to him, and I could tolerate talking to him on our home phone rather than on my cell phone, but still only for short periods of time. I was frustrated and truly missed talking to Mike. And he was frustrated too. We were accustomed to talking to each other for hours each day. It was maddening. I needed to connect with Mike after such a traumatic event in my life; we needed to discuss our upcoming wedding, talk about his life, simply communicate with each other. I had hoped the sensitivity to the frequency of electronics wouldn't last long and I could again connect. I was missing out.

I was also very sensitive to sounds and bright lights. Spring had sprung and it seemed every neighbor in the neighborhood was operating their leaf blower, mower or chainsaw! Even with my windows closed, the noise of the leaf blowers, mowers and chainsaws seemed deafening; I thought I was going to lose my mind! I buried my left ear into my pillow and clapped my right hand over my right ear, "Does everyone have to run their freaking leaf blowers? Use a darn broom!"

Dad and Mama often left my bedroom door open, so they could hear me and I could hear them, but all the sounds of the kitchen (which was on the level just below my bedroom) seemed incredibly amplified. The sound of them loading and unloading dishes in and out of the dishwasher sounded like they were crashing cymbals and clanging triangles. The words they shared with one another around the table and the ring of the kitchen telephone all echoed in my ears. Also, Dad liked to drink a cup of tea nearly every night, after dinner. He put water in the tea kettle to warm up on the stove and would walk away as it heated up. I screamed at him every time he'd leave the kitchen to do something else and let the tea kettle whistle for several minutes before getting back to the kitchen. "Dad, please; come make your tea!! Turn it off, turn it off!!" Worst of all was the cuckoo clock. Mama had bought Dad a cuckoo clock for his birthday that year. Every hour, the cuckoo bird came out to "cuckoo" the hour. Not only was the clock obnoxious, it reminded me of every hour I'd been lying in bed doing absolutely nothing; still wide awake, and still in pain. I didn't have any classes, homework, or a job to attend to. My only "chore" and responsibility was to get better, and my deadline was July 7th.

Mike's dad urged Mike and me to postpone the wedding to allow more time for me to heal, but Mike and I stubbornly refused. I knew Mike's dad had sound reasoning and part of me agreed with him, but Mike and I had already been long awaiting our wedding day, and we weren't about to let the perfect wedding date slip away. There would never again be a 7/7/07. Mama and I had the mutual goal of getting me well by 7/7/07. Mama knew I was absolutely miserable, but she was still tough with me and pushed me to get better. Mama would see to it that our goal was achieved. At Phoenix hospital, I was a patient; at the rehabilitation hospital, I was a patient. At home, Mama said I was NOT going to be a patient. She wanted me to do normal activities as often as we could.

My very first outing was to my salon. I was so consumed with pain, dizziness and fatigue, I didn't care what my hair looked like; but Mama insisted that I get a haircut. She said my hair was ratty and I had lots of split ends. "You need a trim and a good hair washing," Mama said. I think Mama thought it was also good for me to get out of the house to do something fun and "normal." "Ok Mama, whatever." I shielded my eyes from the sun on the ten-minute car ride to my salon. Hair dryers were noisily blowing and women were chattering about the latest celebrity gossip.

My eyes were half closed as Mama led me to Mandy's chair. I had been coming to see Mandy for my haircare needs for several years. She was quiet and shy, which I consider unusual for a hair-dresser, but she was very good at her craft. She was pleased to see me. I told her I only wanted a trim, nothing fancy. I wanted to keep my hair long and thick for the wedding. I knew it would feel good to get my hair professionally washed, but I was so anxious about my surgery scar on my head. Mandy promised to be gentle and keep product away from it as best she could. She was indeed very gentle and only briefly brushed her hand over my incision to wash the soap away from my surrounding hair.

Mandy, and all the other hair dressers in the salon, admired my clean and discreet scar. They were also amazed that I got to keep all my hair. Mama talked to them about my medical history, why I'd had brain surgery, and talked to them about my upcoming wedding. I was the talk of the salon.

After Mandy had helped me sit back up, combed and trimmed my hair, she turned the blow dryer on me. Oh LORD, that was awful! I cringed the entire time and felt like passing out. I couldn't tolerate the noise, especially so close to my ear, but I didn't want to walk out of the salon with wet hair, so I painfully waited for it to be over! I breathed a huge sigh of relief when she finally turned the hair dryer off, and put it away. "Thank God that's over." Mama apologized on the way home. She said she didn't consider how trying the noise might be on my brain. She apologetically smiled and said, "But you look pretty." I admired my hair in the passenger side mirror and thought to myself, "Yep, sometimes beauty is pain."

Mama then realized that maybe it was too soon to be out in public, but she believed I needed to at least be outside. Mama started taking me on wheelchair walks; it was uncomfortable, at first. The first time we got outside, the sun blinded my eyes; the sun had never seemed so bright, and all the noises of the outdoors seemed louder than usual: birds chirping, lawn mowers growling, leaf blowers screaming, the sound of the wind rustling against the trees, it was all so loud. I also felt every bump in the sidewalk as Mama pushed me in the wheelchair. I would wince and cry out, "That hurt!" Mama tried to be more conscientious of the bumps in the sidewalk and tried to avoid them. We hadn't realized before how uneven the sidewalk was around our house. Sometimes, even with sunscreen, I got a sunburn on our wheelchair walks. I must admit, however, that it felt good to be out in the fresh air; it smelled good, and the light breeze felt good against my skin. Mama took me out every day, and pushed me around the neighborhood.

Mama said it was also important for me to be clean and maintain good hygiene. Initially, when Mama helped me bathe, we did so in the upstairs bathtub, but washing my hair in the tub was awkward and ineffective. Mama thought, also, that I ought to be more independent with my bathing and to have more privacy. So, I started taking showers in our downstairs bathroom instead. Mama put a little plastic chair in the shower for me to sit on. I hunched over on the chair as she adjusted the shower head and temperature of the water. I didn't mind that the stream of the water pouring over my body was loud, it felt so good. Mama put shampoo and conditioner in my very long thick head of hair, lightly lathered it, closed the shower door and let me rinse it out. I washed my own body with a light creamy body wash. I cried each time I showered, but it was a cathartic cry. My filth was being washed down the drain, and just for a little while, my grief too. When Mama helped me out of the shower, she sat me back down on the plastic chair in the middle of the bathroom, and wrapped a robe around me. She gently patted me dry, gently combed my hair and helped me get dressed. I cried every time. I was immensely grateful for Mama and her selfless love. She never ever acted burdened when caring for me. Although my hair didn't need to be washed so frequently, Mama helped me shower every day, and I looked forward to it.

Additionally, even when I didn't feel up to going, Mama pushed me to go to therapy every week. I was back to being an outpatient at the rehabilitation hospital. I was reluctant to go, but being an outpatient was far better than being an inpatient. It was an improvement upon the therapy I'd received in 2000 as well. I consistently had the same therapists, and that was nice. I attended both occupational therapy and physical therapy twice a week. I was still having a lot of trouble getting my left hand and arm to cooperate; my hand was still not responding at all. But my OT didn't give up so easily. She was determined to help me any way she could. She stretched and massaged my arm and hand. She was more creative with my exercises. She always encouraged me to use my arm and hand any way I could and to keep pushing myself, but she also taught me some practical ways to adjust. She showed me lots of different ideas and tricks to be able to dress more inde-pendently, and we brainstormed together about different ways that I could learn to cook and clean. She was always positive and encouraging. I eagerly anticipated each of our visits, so I could learn something new from her.

My physical therapist was quieter and didn't push me too hard. I most often had occupational therapy just prior to physical ther-apy, and she knew how fatiguing OT was for me. My hand was in worse shape than my leg, and the more trying of the two. My PT seemed to understand that OT, at that time, was more important. I again had pool therapy as well. Sue was my pool therapist again, and I was thrilled. But, overall, pool therapy wasn't as enjoyable as

I'd remembered it. The water was uncomfortably warm, and when there was a crowd of patients and therapists, the echoing noises of their voices and splashing of the water were so loud and disorienting. I was relieved on the few occasions when it was just me and my therapist in the pool. I would have loved to talk to and befriend my therapists, as I had before, but doing my exercises took all my concentration. I couldn't also amiably chat. When my therapists noticed that I had to repeatedly stop doing my exercises so I could process their questions to answer and converse with them, they soon learned to be quiet. I so badly wanted to talk to them about my fiancé, my upcoming wedding, the surgery, my faith in Jesus; but it took too much out of me. Mama and Dad were paying for therapy so that I could have therapy, not so that I could make new friends. Sadly, I couldn't mentally manage both. I instead, occasionally listened to Mama converse and befriend the therapists. Every once in a while, I'd jump in and comment on whatever they were discussing. I was glad that Mama was with me to break the silence. I had to use all my energy to concentrate on the exercises the therapists gave me to do. It was very important to me that I gain a full recovery. I had a wedding to get to: *my wedding!*

Wheelchair walks were nice, showering was healing, therapy was helping, but my favorite time of day was meal time. Before, I'd always eaten to live, but while home recovering from surgery, I lived to eat. The doctor in the rehab hospital took me off of decent pain pills too early (in my opinion), and the medication I was then taking for pain proved to be ineffective. The only thing that truly made my head feel better, even if just for a little while, was food. When I ate, I also got to go downstairs. I sat with Mama for breakfast and lunch and ate dinner with the family. Eating at the table was one thing that made me feel "normal." I could be present, part of the family, it took very little effort, and it was enjoyable to eat. I looked forward to meal time, and I craved food. The rehab doctor had increased my steroid dose, and it spiked my appetite. While at the rehab hospital, shortly after the doctor had adjusted my dose, I asked for larger meals and snacks in between. I even had Dad bring me a Big Mac from McDonald's for a "snack," just hours before dinner; and I still ate a full dinner! Once home, Mama made me a full breakfast every morning (bacon, eggs and toast), a decent-sized lunch (I scarcely ate *any* lunch all through school), and I ate seconds, sometimes thirds, at dinner time. I got accustomed to having an afternoon and evening snack too. And, as time went on, my appetite and need for food grew.

When friends asked if they could come visit me, I often asked them to please bring me specific snacks I was craving (such as Twizzlers, chocolate chip pop tarts, cashews, etc.) I was disappointed when they came empty-handed. Once or twice, in the rehabilitation hospital, I woke up in the middle of the night a few times feeling very hungry, and could not get back to sleep. At home, I was still waking up at three or four in the morning, just ravenous for food. My brain screamed at me in pain if I didn't eat something. So, rather than lie awake for hours, waiting for breakfast, with growing brain pain, I very reluctantly and shamefully called Dad on his cell phone. He would groggily answer the phone, and I'd say, "Dad, I can't sleep because I'm really hungry." Each night he'd slice me an apple to eat with peanut butter (I often had to have protein with my meals and snacks to actually fill me up.) He'd sit on the edge of my bed with his shoulders slumped and his eyes closed, as I ate. I always thanked him, and he'd grunt in response. I'd cry softly as I'd hear him come back upstairs after putting the dirty dish in the sink and hear him sigh heavily as he got back in bed. I had become a food monster, a glutton, and I hated myself for it! But the nightly snack helped me get back to sleep and sustained me until breakfast. I called Dad night after night for several weeks.

My family was just baffled by my sudden increase and interest in food. I was just barely one hundred pounds prior to surgery, and while in Phoenix could barely stomach any food at all. Just two weeks after surgery, I couldn't seem to get enough to eat! It was truly bizarre. I gained twenty pounds in six weeks. I needed to gain the weight, but it was too fast. We now realize, at present, that the steroids weren't entirely at fault for my increased appetite and weight gain.

I had been dangerously underweight all through my teen years and well into young adulthood. I had a terrible time gaining weight. Sometimes I ate just because the clock told me it was time for breakfast or lunch or dinner; I wasn't actually very hungry. And even when I was very hungry, I'd eat no more than ten bites, and feel impossibly full. My family got used to it, but it frustrated my dates who bought and brought me out to dinner. I ate snacks in between meals, but still couldn't break one hundred pounds.

However, when Dr. Spetzler removed my hemangioma, he cleared away the part of the mass, and blood, that had been interfering with my hunger signals. I was finally, truly hungry and ate good-sized portions. Food tasted better and made me feel better. The steroids just made me more ravenous than I otherwise would have been. The need and "addiction" to food, was awkward and upsetting, and yet the steroids caused other upsetting and embarrassing problems too.

Additionally, when I woke up in the middle of the night hungry, my shirt was soaked. The first few times it happened, I thought I'd somehow spilled water on myself in my sleep. But I'd check my water cup and it was still full. I was embarrassed and frustrated when I realized I was having night sweats. My chest, back and forehead were perspiring in my sleep. So, when Dad came in to give me my nightly snack, he also used a wet washcloth to help me wipe the sweat off my chest, back and face; and he searched for a clean shirt for me to change in to. I was glad it was mostly dark and Dad was too sleepy to even notice my bare chest, but it was still embarrassing. I profusely apologized; he was so tired.

The steroids were also making me puffy and swollen. With the weight gain and water retention, my pant legs were too tight, I couldn't fit my swollen feet into any of my shoes, my eyes disappeared when I smiled, and because of the night sweats, I was covered in acne. I looked like a pimply chipmunk with nuts stuffed in my cheeks. I had never felt so ugly and awful. I ate too much food and was not getting much exercise; I felt so bloated and held my aching, distended belly each night as I undressed for my shower. I didn't feel as though I was getting better; I was getting worse, and I was getting increasingly angry and scared. I hated what the steroids were doing to me. They were making me more and more restless, impatient and hindering the healing process! I lay awake in my bed, late into the night and inwardly screamed, "God, remember when I said I needed you to help me? Well go ahead, help me! Please Jesus, have mercy and help me."

Mama was faithful with helping me shower and getting me outside every day. She wouldn't let me shut my door during the day, she had me sit up and interact with visitors, but even still Mama helplessly watched me as I spiraled into despair. I cried pitifully every time I showered, I silently rode in the wheelchair on each of our walks, I sat at the kitchen table when visitors came over, but stared off in space or put my head on the table as they talked to Mama. I kept my door open each day and night, but wore earplugs. Mama was trying, but what else could she do? It troubled Mama and Dad that I was suffering so much physically, but what was more troubling to my parents was my withdrawal and spiraling depression.

The church I grew up in, and that my family still attended, was a small church. The congregation had no more than eighty members and they had no pastor. It was a non-denominational church, and ran by its own set of "rules," but I'd never been in another church quite like it. You could walk through the doors, and immediately feel the presence of the Holy Spirit. I left Church of the Savior in high school, because I couldn't relate and connect to the other youth. I felt more welcome with the youth at Asbury, and enjoyed the church services there so much more.

The people at Church of the Savior however, still felt like family to me. Everyone knew me, cared for me, prayed for me, supported my family and loved all of us. Church of the Savior had recently started a program called "Stephen Ministries." Mama herself had become trained to be a Stephen Minister to another member of our congregation. Stephen Leaders in the church trained volunteer Stephen Ministers to be assigned to individuals in the church who were hurting (experiencing some sort of trauma) in their life. I was proud of Mama for stepping up and volunteering to be a Stephen Minister. Mama saw the value in the program, and requested that I be assigned a Stephen Minister from the church.

I was reluctant and anxious, because talking to people was still physically and mentally challenging for me. However, my Stephen Minister, Amy, still came to the house for a visit. She came, smiled warmly, and sat next to my bed. It was refreshing to have her there. She was so peaceful and quiet and patient. She asked me, "How are you doing?" I listed my physical ailments and symptoms and how my body felt: awfully awful. She patiently listened, nodded and then said, "But how are you doing with all of this?" She caught me off guard; no one had asked me that before. Perhaps that's what some of them meant when they asked me how I was doing, but I'd become accustomed to listing how I was physically through the process of healing, not how I was emotionally. I was at a loss for words, I didn't know how to answer. I responded, "I don't know. I haven't really let myself think about it." She just nodded, could see that I was tired, so she grabbed my hand and stroked my arm as she prayed for my physical healing and for my soul. She kissed my forehead before leaving my room, and I could hear her quietly visit with Mama for a while before she left.

I was glad that Amy had come to see me, and what she'd said made me think. I had been so preoccupied with my body that I hadn't given much thought or attention to my soul and my communion with God. My prayers consisted of, "God, please help me!" Otherwise, I was scared and mad. Amy encouraged me to write as I could. And with what strength I had, to pray prayers beyond my most frequent plea, "God help me!"

The following Sunday, Mama helped me get cleaned up and

dressed for church. I looked at her fearfully and said, "I don't think I can, Mama." She said, "We'll leave when you've had enough, but it will be good for you. You've missed too much church, we all need to go to church." I nearly cried, but agreed to go. I made Mama promise that we would indeed leave when I told her I needed to. She promised. It was a twenty-minute drive to our church. I slumped over in the back seat and rested my eyes. When we arrived at church, Dad situated me in my wheelchair. Dad pushed me into the building, and I realized I needed to go to the bathroom. I went to the bathroom, located directly to the right of the sanctuary. As I fumbled around in the bathroom, I heard the worship music start. Immediately, fear, bitterness and emotional pain broke free in me, as I heard the sweet singing of praise to the LORD. I sat back down on top of the toilet seat awhile and listened to my fellow brothers and sisters in Christ sing. I began to sob in the bathroom, and I felt the indwelling of the Holy Spirit, which gave me peace. Mama smiled when she saw me come out of the bathroom, she saw immediately my demeanor had changed, and she got teary- eyed. Mama and Dad situated me in my wheel-chair again, and they wheeled me into the sanctuary, finding chairs to each sit on either side of me. Every face that greeted mine and smiled seemed to glow and emanate Christ.

I only was able to make it halfway through the service before I felt my head would explode. Mama and Dad quickly got me back in the car and drove me home. I didn't want to necessarily admit it to Mama, but going to church was truly good for my soul. She was right; I did *need* it.

After attending church, I realized I had missed weeks of allowing myself to hurt and heal emotionally. I had ignored the opportunity to talk to my LORD and allow Him to comfort me as I lay in bed. When I began to let myself hurt and feel emotionally, I softened. I took my earplugs out, looked up more, and smiled more, even though I was hurting. Pain and restlessness remained, but I wasn't as angry anymore. I tried not to think about it too much, because it was painful to, but I began to think of my girlfriends and my fiancé, and all the time I'd missed being with them. My heart hurt so much.

On a dark Saturday night, I lay in bed with an awful headache. I let my mind wander, thinking about my fiancé and closest friends. What might they be doing tonight? I closed my eyes and imagined my college girlfriends at the Starbucks at Central and Rock (a place we frequented). I imagined them playing cards and could almost hear the coffee machines hiss, smell the coffee, and see the expressions on my friends' faces; all of them studying their cards and putting on their best "poker faces." Or maybe they're at Becca's house playing games, as we also often did. They're all squeezed around the game table, not doing a very good job of keeping the noise level down so as not to wake Becca's parents. I imagine them all with a soda at their side, and as the game comes to a close they're astonished at how late it is, but start another "quick" game anyhow.

I didn't know if the girls were together that night or if they were doing other things. They didn't keep me posted on their day-to-day activities, and I preferred it that way. It was too painful to imagine all the wonderful college experiences I was missing. I missed attending my classes too.

I was enrolled in a class called Paul's Letters taught by a very wise, knowledgeable instructor. His classes weren't easy, but classes like his were worth the extra time, work, and tuition. I missed his class most. My bleed and surgery occurred shortly after midterms; the exam was over Galatians and Ephesians, and I aced it. However, I missed his lectures on my favorite book: Philippians. The notes my friend gave me regularly from the classes I missed didn't seem to be doing the class justice. It did me so much good to attend church, I wanted to try to go to school, even if just to finish the one class, on Paul's letters.

Mama agreed it would be good for me to visit. She drove me to campus, we rode the incredibly slow elevator to the third floor, and Mama wheeled me into Dr. H's classroom. I surveyed the room and met eyes with several friends who were all genuinely concerned with my well-being, said they'd been faithfully praying for me, and they were glad to see me. There was one classmate in the class I was most eager to see. We had studied together, and he came into the library daily, drank our terrible coffee, and read. We frequently chatted when I wasn't busy with work. I turned around, spotted him in class and eagerly watched him, waiting for him to turn and acknowledge me. He never turned my direction and very clearly avoided looking at me. I thought he'd be pleased to see me, but he couldn't even bear to look at me. I was deeply hurt, confused and immensely disappointed in him. I had considered him a close friend.

I slowly turned back to the front of the class to face our professor. Mama sat next to me as we listened to Dr. H's lecture on chapter three of Colossians. I tried to focus and listen to him as he talked, but my head spun. I looked down at the worksheet he'd passed out, and I got dizzy trying to read the words on the page. It took too much effort and concentration. I couldn't do it, I couldn't finish my favorite class. Mama was enjoying the class and didn't want to leave, but I insisted. It was good to be on campus and see some familiar faces, but I knew I couldn't come back to finish. My brain required more healing. Even in a wheelchair, I wouldn't have the stamina to attend school again before the end of the year. Life continued as it would around me while mine seemed to stand still, and there was nothing I could do about it. I'd wished classes would stop and they'd wait for me to come back.

How long would it be before I really felt like myself again? It had been a long couple of months, and I couldn't bear to be in pain any longer! I was immensely grateful to God that I'd survived surgery and my attitude had improved, but as long as the pain remained, I couldn't get better. There was no escaping the pain. I was supposed to be weaning off the pain medicine, but Mama and Dad were so distraught they called our doctor friends who told us to take the medication as often as needed. We increased my dose and I began taking the pills more regularly, but they were not alleviating my pain; they were just making me nauseous and making it even more difficult to pass waste.

Managing my pain seemed impossible. Nothing they'd prescribed was working. I often longed for the care and the wisdom of the doctors in Phoenix. No one knew how to help me. I needed God's help to move past it, but He had seemed to be silent. I was at the end of my rope, hit my breaking point, had hit rock bottom; but it was then that God moved.

It was the night of May 6th, the rest of the house was sound asleep. I could hear Dad's heavy breathing down the hall; otherwise the house was quiet. I, on the other hand, laid wide awake in my bed, rolling back and forth, tears burning my cheeks and soaking my pillowcase. It was well past midnight and I had yet to fall asleep. My brain was so tired, and I desperately needed rest, but my brain pain was so intense, I could not relax.

My belly kept rumbling, and I knew it wouldn't quit until I got something to eat. I was tired of waking my dear dad up each night for food, so I took care of myself. I bumped down the stairs on my rump and crawled to the fridge to eat deviled eggs Mama had made. I felt furious as I ate each one, feeling out of control of my body. I didn't *want* to eat deviled eggs in the middle of the night! I crawled back up the stairs, changed my sweat-soaked shirt myself, and waited for the pain to subside; it did not. I pleaded to the LORD. "LORD, I long to go to sleep, but my head hurts so bad; this is level ten bad! The pain pills aren't working anymore Jesus; *You* be my pain pill Jesus! Please LORD, take away my pain. *You* be my pain pill! Please, please, please! Have mercy, Father, and take away my debilitating pain!" I whimpered and waited desperately for God to move. Unless my pain alleviated, I knew I wouldn't be getting any sleep.

I rocked back and forth on my bed, looked out my window and peered at the stars. Holding my head, and digging my nails into the bed, pulling them across the sheets, I muttered over and over, "Please, please, please, God." Then suddenly, my pain was gone! Just like that, my level ten brain pain was gone!! I abruptly stopped rocking, let go of my head and slowly laid down. I was completely amazed. I laid on my bed wide-eyed in wonder. I waited for the pain to return, but it didn't! My pain was really gone; there was no trace of it. In fact, I felt clear headed and at peace. A level ten brain pain dropped down to zero in a second!

I cried tears of joy and felt a renewed strength to quietly sing praise to the LORD who had answered my prayer and shown me great mercy. I needed that divine encounter to undoubtedly know that God was with me, cared about me and had not forgotten me. It's a night I will never forget.

That night, I had the best, non-drug-induced sleep I'd had since surgery. I woke up the next morning still pain-free. I laughed and sat on my bed, absolutely dazzled by God and His quick healing power. "Thank You, thank You, thank You, LORD!"

Finally, I had turned a corner. I wasn't constantly battling pain and was beginning to wean off of steroids. Slowly my appetite returned to normal, and I was sleeping through the night. When Mama and I took walks, we went further together for a while in the wheelchair, and I walked part of the time, on my own two feet. Every walk we took that spring we saw multiple rabbits. I just love rabbits; they bring me so much joy. On one walk around the neighborhood, we counted over a dozen rabbits. I just knew that those adorable rabbits were God's special gift to me each day that spring. I'd say to myself, "I love You too, God; thank You."

The months of March and April were brutally painful; but in the days and months following, I had college graduation, bridal showers and my wedding to look forward to.

9

I felt anxious and sad about not being able to complete my final semester of college. Would I be able to graduate, or would they require that I come back to redo my final semester? I didn't have all the credits required to graduate with my bachelors in psychology and my minors in Spanish and religion. I was getting married in July and moving to Garden City. Coming back to Friends to do another semester of classes was not an option! What could I do?

My teachers met together and discussed my predicament and the matter of my pending graduation. Mama and I eagerly awaited their answer. The dean finally called one morning, and informed Mama and I that he and my teachers put it to a vote, and they agreed to let me graduate that May. They would give me the grade I'd had when I left campus, and waive all other assignments, tests, and attendance. The consensus was I'd still graduate as planned, in May, and with honors. Mama and I grew teary-eyed when the dean gave us the wonderful news.

The day of graduation came, and Mike, my family (including my grandparents, some aunts, uncles, and cousins), Mike's family, and even some church friends, were all in attendance. Thankfully my graduation gown had lots of breathing room and covered my bulging belly. I took pictures with some of my fellow graduates, and then we proceeded to the floor of the arena to sit and wait.

To preserve my energy, I sat in a wheelchair as I awaited my turn to walk across the stage and receive my diploma. I sat on the end of the row next to my dear friend Joy. I was excited, nervous, and a little tired. I had a difficult time paying attention to any of the speeches, so I just closed my eyes and rested until it was time to go. Finally, when we were next in line to walk, Joy wheeled me up to the stage. The audience was clapping as each graduate ahead of me walked across the stage. I was trembling, nervous about climbing the few steps up to the stage. I was just certain I was going to trip, but one of the professors on stage came down to help me up the steps. The professor grabbed the crook of my arm, as I cautiously got out of my chair to ascend the steps. Before I'd even set foot on the stage, the crowd uproared in applause for ME! I took my first two awkward, shaky steps, and with the aid of my cane, I slowly walked across the stage while the crowd stood and applauded. Although I had to concentrate on my feet and stared at the floor, I was grinning from ear to ear. Each professor on stage warmly embraced me and said, "Congratulations, Megan." It was a very proud moment for me; and I was sincerely touched that many people in the audience enthusiastically celebrated the victory with me. Graduated college, with honors: check!

With graduation achieved, the upcoming wedding had our full attention.

A group of my college girlfriends threw me a bridal shower. It was the first time I'd been able to tolerate a social gathering in which I'd have to engage in conversation and be the center of attention for a while. The girls made special snacks, played a few games, and they each gave me an assortment of practical and senti-mental gifts. I was still very puffy and swollen from the steroids and was embarrassed to be seen, but the entire party was sweet and very low-key; which was just what I needed.

In the proceeding weeks and through June, I had four more bridal showers. My aunt threw a Mitchell/Corman family shower,

Mike's mom threw a Wohler/Lent family shower, Church of the Savior ladies threw a shower, and friends from Asbury church threw me a surprise bridal shower. Mike and I received nearly everything we'd registered for, and then some. I was feeling deeply loved, and definitely spoiled! We were having fun partying, but still at work planning the wedding.

We were tying up all loose ends, ironing out all the final details. I let Mama make a lot of the final, little decisions; after all, it was her money, and I was tired. I didn't have any strong opinions about candles, or boutonnieres, or the layout of the program. I just wanted to be well enough to attend. Mama and I prayed every day that God would give me the strength to get through my wedding day, and that I could also *enjoy* it. I continued to go to therapy, was still taking walks around the neighborhood with Mama, and was getting stronger every day. Unfortunately, I learned that I also needed to slim down.

I went to do the final fitting for my wedding dress. We'd ordered my dress a full year before the wedding, and it was gorgeous. We had ordered a size two for my itty bitty petite frame. But, after three months of steroids and heavy eating, I'd gained twenty pounds. I poured into my dress at my *final* fitting and they couldn't get the back fastened. Stupid steroids! I was immensely embarrassed and upset. The awkward weight gain was grotesque, and certainly inconvenient.

For the next several weeks, I did a SlimFast diet and ate so much less. Thankfully, I had been told I could stop taking steroids. The first time I slept through the night without the need of a snack, and woke up dry, was a huge victory for me. When the steroids were no longer disturbing my sleep or my appetite, I knew I could easily lose the acne and the weight.

Mike came home, one last time, just before the wedding to work out some details of the wedding together.

We met with our wedding planner at the church and talked about the ceremony and the order of events: where we'd get dressed, where and when we'd do pictures, etc. Although it didn't matter to me, Mike didn't like the idea of having to do pictures together before the wedding. He didn't want to see me prior to when I'd walk down the aisle. Mike had many strong opinions through the wedding planning process, and forcefully made them known. It wasn't always enjoyable to talk of wedding plans with Mike. For one, he wanted more than three groomsmen. I would have loved to have more of my friends in the wedding party too, but Mama told us providing for three bridesmaids was all they could manage and afford. I was a little disappointed, but completely understood. Mike, however, didn't let the matter go. He said he'd planned to pay for all his groomsmen. His dad insisted he include his brothers, but he wanted to also include his "family" of friends. So, Mike would have six or more groomsmen and I'd have only three bridesmaids? As far as I was concerned, that was selfish and ridiculous. "You are allotted three, Mike. Pick three." He was terribly frustrated he'd been told "no." He didn't like that at all! Mike was particular about the cake, the invitations, the pictures. He tried to stick up for me and fight for what I said I'd like, but I didn't want him to. Expense often prohibited us from having things and doing things as he would have wanted, and I often thought Mama's suggestions of compromise or substitutes weren't unreasonable, but Mike argued with Mama a lot. "It's our wedding," he would say. "We should have what we want at *our* wedding."

He argued with both Mama and our wedding planner, frequently. It was exhausting, and I'd never really seen this angry, obstinate side of Mike; it made me uncomfortable and embarrassed in front of Mama and our wedding planner. Why was he being so incredibly argumentative? I didn't consider any of it worth fighting over. Wasn't he just excited to be getting married to me? He was concerned about our party; I was growing concerned about our *marriage*!

Perhaps I was adding fuel to the fire by complaining behind Mama's back? I don't remember if I'd said anything contrary to Mama's actions and decisions, but any fraction of rage I may have displayed, either in text or in person, could not be trusted. I was under the influence of steroids and subject to the occasional "roid rage." Whether I contributed or not, Mike was consistently frustrated, and Mike's building anger finally came to a head, and he blew up at Mama. He accused her of completely controlling our wedding, and that she wasn't listening to him. I did not share his feelings at all. Mama was doing the best she could, and doing entirely too much. I don't know the exchange of words exactly, but I remember that his aggressive words were hurtful enough to make my very strong mama cry. I hated Mike for that! Here Mama had been working hard to nurse me back to health so I could be ready for the wedding, to marry *him*! If I'd been Mama, I would probably have said, "Fine, I won't plan or pay for the wedding; you're on your own!" Mike's anger deeply troubled me. I didn't know he had it in him. I thought maybe he felt bad that he couldn't have been the one to care for me and help me through my trauma; Mama and Dad were doing that for me. He couldn't be there to do a lot of the wedding planning; Mama was doing that too. But, shouldn't he have been immensely grateful to Mama and kissing her feet? Instead, he was yelling at her, accusing her of being controlling and making her cry.

As I overheard Mama cry, I began to cry too. "LORD, Mike's anger scares me, and is completely unfounded. How can he be so cruel? I hate him. Am I to choose between Mike and Mama? Mama has selflessly loved me and cared for me. If I ought to choose, I choose Mama. I'll stay home a while longer."

When Mama came up to my room, she had blown her nose and wiped her tears, and tried to disguise her distress. Although she was smiling at me, her face remained flushed and I could see she had felt beaten down, and wounded by Mike's words. I sobbed and said, "Mama, I can't marry Mike. He can't treat you like that. I feel forced to make a choice between you, and I choose you." Seeing my emotional turmoil and pain, Mama said, "No, Meg, I love Mike; we'll work it out. Settle down, don't worry about it. We'll work it out." Sure enough, Mike called, talked to Mama and

Dad, and apologized. However, Mike's angry outburst still scared me and gave me pause.

Early one morning, with the wedding less than two weeks away, I laid in my room, stared at the wall and prayed quietly to God. Then suddenly I thought I heard the LORD say, "Don't marry Mike; it's not My will." Oh crap, I thought, the wedding is only two weeks away! I debated within myself, "Yeah, Mike had an angry outburst, but we've been together so long, he's been there for me through a lot and fought for me. LORD, to make a drastic decision like that so close to the wedding? I don't know if I can do it! Steroids are still in my system; I could still be under the influence of drugs and not thinking clearly." Then I thought to myself, who knows if I really heard that from the LORD. I don't think the LORD would say that. A lot of people get cold feet just before the wedding, that's all it is: cold feet.

But I couldn't completely shake the uneasy feeling about it. The next time Mama would come into my room, I was going to talk to her about it and ask for her advice. Mama came into my room within the hour. She had a piece of paper she'd written notes on and had pictures in her hand. She showed me pictures of what the flower arrangements were going to look like that we'd discussed. We went over the program and some other details together. She seemed so excited about how beautiful the flowers were (Mama *loves* flowers). Mama said, "Ok, everything is coming together, not much left to do." She laughed as she said, "Too late to back out now!" When Mama said that, I knew she was right. I loved Mike, and he *really* loved me. What was I worried about? No way I had heard that from God. So, I didn't mention any of my previous qualms to Mama, and what I thought I maybe had heard from God, and everything continued to be carried out as planned.

My bridesmaids were my two sisters and one of my many cousins (Emily). We went to get the final pieces for their pale pink bridesmaids' dresses and their other "necessary" accessories. Meanwhile, Mike picked up and got the final fit for his tuxedo and picked up the other three for his groomsmen (his three brothers). The day before the wedding, my bridesmaids and I went to get our nails done. Ellen treated me to a pedicure and a manicure. I politely declined the offer for a manicure, but even after I showed the nail artist my clenched left fist, she assured me she could do it. She pried my hand open, laid my fingers flat, cleaned my nails, then started to sand them; she was tearing up my nails. I tried to tell her that I didn't want fake nails. Duh, because the long nails would dig into the palm of my left hand. The language barrier kept her from understanding. She kept saying, "But you the bride." I couldn't get her to stop. Finally, Ellen stepped in and put a stop to it. Ellen had to explain with gestures before the nail woman understood, that fake nails were a bad idea; but by that time she'd already sanded and destroyed all of my nails. She brushed off the nail dust and painted them with French tips, which is what we'd asked for in the first place, but the surface of my nail was rough and looked awful. No hand pictures for me.

The night before the wedding we held our dress rehearsal at the church, and Mike practiced putting my wedding ring on the ring finger of my left hand. It was not easy. As he gently opened my left hand, he said "What happened to your nails?" To which I replied, "Don't ask." Everything went smoothly in the dress rehearsal, he successfully got the ring on, and our anticipation and excitement for the wedding, was building. In less than twenty-four hours, Mike and I would be married.

Wedding day was a bit of a whirlwind. Mike and I had wanted to be married at seven, but the church would hold weddings only as late as two in the afternoon. We were disappointed but decided that I'd walk down the aisle at 2:07. The initial plan was to have a small wedding; we wanted family and close friends only. However, once I'd had brain surgery, Mama and Dad decided to expand the wedding invitation list to include many more.

They wanted all our supporters to share in our celebration. I stood at the end of the aisle and saw every pew full of our friends and family who had come to witness our joyous occasion and celebrate with us. A news team was present and covering our wedding too.

Daddy and I had carefully practiced walking down the aisle together at the rehearsal. He held my right arm tight in the crook of his left arm and was prepared to help me along if my left leg gave out. I wore very soft, thin slippers. My ankle would have rolled and sent me to the ground if I'd worn any size of a heel. My long, full head of hair was gorgeous. Mandy did a beautiful job of curling it; I was so pleased. I was able to lose enough weight on the SlimFast diet so that my dress fit. My Mary Kay director did a good job of concealing any acne I still had on my forehead and between my brows. I was still puffy from steroids, but I felt beautiful and happy.

I wasn't terribly thrilled that Mike had decided to wear a white tux instead of black or gray for our wedding, but he actually looked nice.

We successfully made it down the aisle, and Dad officially gave me away to my husband. Mike took my right arm and helped me up the steps to the stage. We couldn't decide who we wanted to officiate our wedding, our pastor from Wichita or the pastor from Garden City? So instead of choosing between the two, we had both; and it was perfect. Two of our dear friends sang Jeremy Camp's song "Wonderful Maker." Despite every trial I'd endured, I still declared my LORD a wonderful maker, and good. "What a wonderful maker, what a wonderful savior." We were making a declaration to our friends and family in the congregation that we loved and trusted our LORD with our present and future; God was still a wonderful God.

Mike and I smiled and laughed with one another as Joe and Kellen told stories about us, blessed us, prayed for us, and we exchanged vows. Mike winked at me when he said, "In sickness and in health." I chuckled and quietly responded with, "Check." When Joe said, "You may kiss…" Mike dipped me and planted a big sloppy kiss on me (we have a great picture of that). Then we turned to face the congregation as Joe announced us as Mr. and Mrs. Wohler.

The congregation stood, cheered and my aunt said there wasn't a dry eye in the crowd. Mike and I wiggled and danced down the aisle to my favorite worship song "Those who trust."

When I'd first heard that song at Breakthru church service, it had become my anthem, and I love it still; especially when my dear friend Chris sings it, and he did at our wedding. We did it. Mike and I had finally got married. With the ceremony then finished, it was time to party.

On the way to the location of our reception, Mike and I counted seven other cars who had "Just Married" written on the back window of their vehicle too. It was a popular wedding date. Once we'd arrived at the reception, we got out of the truck and the sun was blazing; it was one hundred degrees and rising. Yikes! Thankfully, all of the festivities would be held indoors.

We greeted our guests, we danced, we did the traditional cake cutting and shoving the first bite into each other's mouths, the traditional family toasts, the ever popular (and profitable) dollar dance, and the bouquet and garter toss. It was so much fun to party with all the people we know and love. We weren't just celebrating our marital union, we were celebrating a victory of life.

I was glad I had the strength to get through all of it. But by seven o'clock that evening, I'd hit my limit. I hovered back and forth over an air conditioner vent and tried to push a little further, but I was out of "juice." Mike and I said our goodbyes and headed for our hotel. From the reception to the hotel parking lot, we counted ten more "Just Married" vehicles. Mike honked, and we waved at each couple as we drove by.

We got to our floor of the hotel, and stood outside our hotel room. I could not wait to get into the room, out of my dress, and to just lay down for a few minutes. However, our key didn't work, so Mike had to go back to the front desk. I sighed heavily and waited outside the door in the hallway. I could not keep my eyes open, and my left leg was shaking from fatigue. I slid down the wall in my very beautiful, white wedding dress, and I sat down in the hotel hallway, on the floor. When Mike came back, he laughed and said, "Are you ok?" With my eyes closed, I slowly nodded. He helped me up to my feet, lifted me in his arms and carried me into our hotel room. "Whew;" and Mike helped me undress.

Although we were exhausted, later that night we couldn't sleep because we were hungry. They had served a great dinner at our reception, and the few bites of strawberry cake we had were delicious, but there was very little opportunity for us to eat it! Whenever Mike and I'd sit to eat, someone would come up and want to visit with us, or we'd get called away to do our obligatory first dance, cake cutting or any number of other things. With all the excitement of our wedding day, we hadn't had much time to eat, all day.

So, with our bride and groom caps on that I'd received from one of my friends at a shower, we walked to the nearest McDonald's and had our fill of burgers and fries. Then, we were finally able to sleep, and we slept well!

The next morning, we slept in and took our time getting ready. We were destined for Sarasota, Florida for our honeymoon, but we were smart and booked an afternoon flight. Once we'd checked out of our hotel, Mike drove me to my salon, and I got my hair cut. The wedding was over, my days of long hair were too. I thought Mike was going to cry when the stylist took a pair of scissors and cut right across my curls and I could hear the crunch of the hair spray as she cut. Bird seed fell out of my hair as she shook out my curls and pulled out bobby pins Mike and I had missed (there were over 50). She must have cut a foot of hair off my head. Mama had helped me manage my long hair after I'd had my March bleed and surgery, but I wasn't about to ask my new husband to do that for me; especially not on our honeymoon! I needed easy-to-manage hair. We then stopped by Mama and Dad's to open our gifts from the wedding and open our cards. Any checks or cash we received, Mike gave to his dad for safe-keeping until we came back. He told his dad to deposit half the money into his account for us to spend in Florida, and then we were off.

It was my first time flying since that horrible flight back from Phoenix. I was nervous and worried about my head. Mike held my hand and blew cool air down on me as I laid my head down at take-off. He was doing well with this husband thing so far. We had some problems getting there (we had to spend the night in Atlanta), but we made it safe and sound to Sarasota, Florida, just a day late.

We stayed at the Lido Lounge. The beach was in our backyard! It was so beautiful and relaxing. We went to the beach every day, ate lots of really good food (including seafood! Yum!), did some shopping, and even went parasailing! Half-way through our trip, Mike called his dad and told him to deposit the other half of our money, and we spent it all. After all, who knows when we'd ever get to do something or be somewhere so wonderful again?

It was a wonderful vacation and treat after having been through some hellish months. Neither of us were terribly eager to fly back to Kansas; we even casually entertained the thought of staying and moving to Florida, but we knew we needed to get home. Only Wichita wasn't my home anymore. The moment I said "I do," I agreed my home would be where Mike's home was, and his home was in Garden City.

10

After a very relaxing and beautiful honeymoon in Sarasota, Mike and I both left for Garden City to begin the next chapter of our lives *together*. From the time of Mike's proposal, I daily longed to be with him in Garden City. I began detaching myself from my family in Wichita. I invested more time and energy into my relationship with my fiancé, in anticipation of spending a lifetime with him. I looked forward to the day that I would no longer need to be dependent on my parents, financially or otherwise.

However, after my surgery, I became entirely dependent on my parents again. Rather than feel angry and embarrassed, as I did with my bleed in 2000, I welcomed their help. I realized I needed them and dearly loved them. I was not in a hurry to get away from them; I longed to be with them. I grew especially close to Mama and found a new level of appreciation, love and respect for her. Mama had become my best friend, and I knew it was going to be hard to be away from her. Mama and I worked very hard to get me ready and well for the wedding day and move. But I was still resting a lot and relying on Mama to help me with many things, just before I left.

There were still many things I could not do well for myself. I was excited to marry Mike, and move on, but as the day had drawn near, the harder it seemed to swallow what I knew lay ahead; I would be leaving my family and friends, who had become my avid support group, and I was still recovering from brain surgery. I knew the transition would be bittersweet.

Mike was eager to get me to Garden City and embrace me as his wife, broken or not. Adapting from being a long-distance girlfriend to a wife and from a student to a housewife was strange. So much had changed. I frequently had this daunting feeling like I should be studying for a test or writing a paper. I even had recurring dreams that I was in school and kept forgetting to go to class or would show up to a class completely unprepared for a test. After being a student for eighteen consecutive years, I suddenly wasn't anymore; I was a housewife. Well, what was a housewife supposed to do? Cook and clean? To imagine a life of simply cooking and cleaning seemed fruitless, lonely and boring, but I got to work. I was a straight A student, and even with my physical limitations, I had hoped to also be a "straight A" wife.

Unfortunately, I quickly learned that I hated to cook with one hand. It was very difficult and frustrating to cut and chop meat or vegetables, try to hold a bowl and stir ingredients, crack open eggs, or measure anything. Washing any pots and pans by hand when I was finished attempting to cook was a terrible feat too! I felt cooking a balanced meal with the use of one hand was impossible. I realized I'd truly taken Mama's daily dinners for granted. A lot of thought and effort went into preparing a meal. When I went grocery shopping, I didn't know what I was doing, and it was difficult to push a shopping cart anyhow. So, with all the frustrations cooking caused, I didn't cook much. Instead, we went out for dinner or brought fast food home. It was expensive, but I wasn't crying and cursing over making dinner, or needing to wash dishes with one hand, and Mike and I enjoyed finally dating more regularly by going out to dinner together. It was fun, but we really ate out much more than we should have. Mike was already overweight, and I had gained a tummy and extra weight from the steroids I took post-surgery. I would have preferred to have kept the weight and lost the gut. I believe I would have had a better chance of losing my protruding belly had we not eaten out so much in the first year of our marriage.

Cleaning was hard for me to adjust to as well. I really appreciate clean laundry and did all the laundry once a week, but folding the laundry with one hand was ridiculous. And I only attempted ironing twice before I decided it wasn't worth the headache. We just wouldn't wear or buy anything that needed to be ironed. I used and wore out a hand vacuum instead of using a broom and dustpan. I liked the lemon or pine smell of Lysol on a freshly-mopped kitchen floor, but I couldn't squeeze out a mop, so Mike got me a Swiffer. I also had to be careful and not scrub too hard when I cleaned the tub and shower. Trying to navigate cooking and cleaning with one hand was frustrating and exhausting. By mid-afternoon, my right arm and hand were worn out. I didn't feel like I was even close to a straight A housewife. I was failing "housewifery!"

The most troubling and embarrassing defeat, however, was in our bedroom. The first time Mike saw me naked, I had a gut, a gait when I walked, and a stiff arm I had little control over. I desperately desired to be desirable, but I cringed and cried at the sight of my deformed, naked body. I used to look so thin, fit and attractive; it was so unfair. How could Mike possibly have thought me desirable when my body looked and moved so awkwardly? I wasn't very good at or reliable with cooking and cleaning, but I was going to be good at and always available for sex. But I never felt sexy; I felt awkward. I teased and said, "Mike, help me put on this lingerie, leave, come back and act surprised!" Mike said my broken body didn't matter, he was still attracted to me, but I wished Mike could have seen me *before*, and I was kind of mad that we had waited to see each other. I felt so beautiful before! Between cooking, cleaning and even sex, I felt I couldn't do any of the things a wife was "supposed" to do. I wanted to please, serve my husband and play an equal part; but, when I didn't feel as though I could measure up or keep up, I felt worthless. I really wanted to help and contribute something to our partnership, but I felt I didn't have much to offer.

I felt a little lost. I wanted to be good at something, truly exceptional! I'd always been good at something, but handicapped, I wasn't good at *anything*. I looked forward to and enjoyed spending time with Mike in the evenings and on the weekends, but I slept a lot during the day. I was depressed, and my body and brain still needed frequent rest, because I was continuing to recover from my brain trauma. Also, I felt I had no purpose, no reason to get up each day. I'd just wake up each day to another day of impossible chores. I wasn't accomplishing much. However, Mike worked very hard to provide for us. I felt guilty and ashamed when Mike would come home from work to eat lunch each day and find me still in bed or just getting up and dressed. Mike was patient with me for a while, but as months wore on, he grew aggravated and impatient. This wasn't the vibrant, ambitious lady he had dated and fallen in love with. It was often apparent that Mike was irritated with me; I appeared lazy and pathetic. It upset me that Mike was not pleased with me. His approval was very important to me. I wished I'd taken Mike's dad's advice, and post-poned the wedding. He was right; I needed to have given myself more time to heal at home. But, somehow, I thought if we post-poned the wedding, it wouldn't happen. Then what would I have done with my life? Live at home forever? I wasn't well enough to attend grad school, and I didn't think Mike would have been willing to wait for me, that he would have perhaps moved on. And who else would have even considered marrying me in the broken state that I was?

I had my regrets about getting married and moving away so soon after brain surgery, and I cried a lot. I resisted embracing Garden City as my home. I longed for the support I had in Wichita. I longed for Mama and my room and minimal responsibilities. I was tired. I had very few friends in Garden City and no family. I was so used to being busy, useful and fit. I wanted to rush my healing and get back to work! Feeling bored and useless was foreign and upsetting to me. Mike encouraged me to look for a low-key, part-time job, not just for my sanity, but also so I could contribute to our income. I applied for bank jobs, a position at the community college, and other secretarial jobs, but my experience in the work force was sparse and I had some obvious limitations I couldn't conceal when I got in front of an employer for an interview.

When they asked me about my disability and limitations, I insisted that I'd been able to adapt and could do many things with just one hand. Even so, I got turned down for job after job after job. I was unemployable. With no job, and no college classes to attend, I didn't know what to do with myself. I decided a decent alternative might be to try to grow my Mary Kay business and make money selling skin care and makeup. I had signed up to be a consultant when I was in college because I loved the product and jumped at the chance to get it half price if I signed. Working for myself of course meant I could schedule my own hours and work only as hard as I wanted to or could. So, I started to make phone calls, booked facials and parties and hoped to make friends along the way. Mike wasn't on board at first, but saw there was promise for good income if I could even just work part-time.

Eventually, Mike came around, and he fully supported me. He often had good advice to help me propel myself in my business, since he was in sales himself. Selling Mary Kay was a great alternative to an office job and a boss who would have set my hours for me. And, it was fun. I got to spend time with girlfriends, play in makeup, and get paid for it!

Soon after I was settled into my Mary Kay schedule, we also rescued a puppy from the pound. On the afternoons that I didn't host a facial, the apartment was often so quiet and I missed Mike while he was at work; but our little puppy, Rikki, provided companionship around the clock. I wanted a small dog like a Yorkie or a miniature poodle that was more "apartment friendly," but Mike didn't want a dog he could potentially accidentally step on. I was reluctant, but when we saw Rikki's picture on the humane society's page, we agreed he was the dog for us. Rikki Tikki Tavi was an Australian shepherd and lab mix and had a beautiful rust colored coat. He was rowdy and often piddled on the floor when he got excited, but he was so sweet.

Having Rikki with me during the day made the apartment feel less empty, and I wasn't as lonely. As my leg grew stronger, we took walks together daily at the dog park. Occasionally, I relaxed and watched a movie when I felt tired; and it was nice to have someone to watch it with. However, with no backyard or place to run, Rikki quickly outgrew our apartment, and Mike had already been itching to get out of the apartment and into a house. Our lease for our apartment was almost up, so it was an ideal time to look for our first house. Married three months, and we were already looking for a new home.

We looked for homes all over Garden. I longed to have a big backyard; Mike wanted a basement (a "man cave") and a sizable kitchen. Although Mike's modular and manufactured houses he sold were beautiful, we couldn't afford them in addition to the land we would need to put one on. So, we looked at established houses in town, nearly every night for weeks.

We found a house Mike loved that met our requirements of a big backyard, a basement and a decent-sized kitchen. We found another house that I loved that met our requirements as well, was cheaper, had a room that would have been perfect for a dark room, had history and potential! But Mike's house was more practical (needed less work), so we purchased the more practical house and moved in the next month.

We became residents in Garden City instead of tenants which made our stay in Garden City seem more permanent. It was exciting, but also a little unsettling. It was time for me to accept Garden City as my home and stop considering it as a place we were "passing through;" we were going to be in Garden for a while. I missed my friends, family and church in Wichita, but I was excited to get to know, and be a part of, the new church family that Mike had grown to love. Mike was excited and proud to introduce me as his wife to all his church friends. And as his friends introduced me to others, they said "This is Mike Wohler's wife, Megan." That was weird, and took some getting used to. Everyone was so friendly and welcoming. To get to know people better and on a deeper level, Mike and I took the opportunity to get connected in a small group. We were well received in the life group, but at a different place in our lives than the couples in the group. We were the only newlyweds in the group, and at that time the only ones in the entire church. All of the young women I met had growing families, with multiple children. They graciously invited me to their baby showers and sometimes even their play-dates with their children. I wanted to go out for coffee with some girlfriends, talk about marriage and to get to know one another better. But with their children, it was hard for them to get away to have coffee. Instead, they talked about and exchanged advice on how to deal with colic, breastfeeding, diaper rash, and potty-training. Uh, I had nothing to say on *those* topics. All my friends back home in Wichita were just getting married or graduating college, just like me. I missed my girlfriends terribly! I was open to making new friends, and I wanted to share with these young women in Garden City about my bleeds, my surgery and my growth in the LORD. I was so excited to share, but I wasn't asked very often, and opportunities really didn't present themselves to talk about it. Caring for their kiddos was number one priority. I didn't have much in common with the women my age.

"Older" women I met through church and my Mary Kay customers had more life experience and were easier to talk to. They asked me about my physical ailments and I eagerly told them my testimony. Many of them befriended me and I was able to connect with them easier. They cared about me.

I appreciated the kindness of the older women, but I still wanted to be among the young women. I wanted my body to be healed and to feel young again. I too wanted to have children and officially start our family, like all the other ladies had. However, I thought it'd likely be a long while before we had children, because I believed God would undoubtedly help me heal first; the goal was to be healed. Once healed, I could resume my life. Because I had been able to recover from each bleed prior to the bleed of 2007, Mike and I expected nothing less than a full recovery after surgery. Although my eyesight had been restored as a result of surgery, surgery in itself was a setback toward the recovery of everything else; there was more weakness to overcome. But with high hopes and high expectations, I began attending physical and occupational therapy at the Garden City hospital two to three times a week. I was going to work hard at regaining all physical mobility and strength.

I was most determined to get my left hand operational again. The training I received from the physical therapist was disappointing, but the hand was the greater struggle anyway, and I considered myself fortunate to find a great occupational therapist in such a small town. For several weeks, we tried to do exercises I'd done before: pick up items off the floor, pinch clothespins, touch my fingers to my thumb, open and close my hand, etc. I had relatively good sensation remaining in my hand, but still very little to no response when I "asked" it to move. I wasn't ready to give up, but after a few weeks in therapy and still no response from my hand, my occupational therapist began to work with my shoulder instead.

She said, "We'll do exercises to strengthen your shoulder and move down your arm to the hand, as you grow stronger." I was not discouraged, but certainly disappointed that I still couldn't operate my hand. I attempted to do certain tasks around the house with my left hand. With a lot of focus and concentration, I successfully taught myself to grip a can opener and open canned goods. That was a proud day. However, to do so, I had to pry my fingers open with my right hand to get a grip on the can opener and concentrate very hard to continue to grip so as not to let the can opener slip. Then, when finished, I had to pry my fingers open once again to let go. I was celebrating small victories and still attempting new tasks, but everything I was "able to do" with my left hand was greatly aided by the right, and very tiring. I kept trying and going to therapy, but neither my determination nor therapy were fixing my hand.

After three months of regular occupational therapy, and with minimal progress, my therapist said

"With as little progress as we've made, it would be unethical to continue therapy and charge you for it."

"What?"

I was of course very upset. I wasn't ready to give up, but my therapist had. It was disheartening that my therapist had given up on me. She had lost hope, but I *couldn't*! I believed that God wanted to, and would, heal me as he had many times before. But how was my healing going to come about if I wasn't going to therapy? Rather than look for another therapist right away, we reevaluated and prayed. Mike and I prayed fervently for healing. "What can we do, LORD, how can I or will I be healed?" If I couldn't get my hand to move, I didn't know how to strengthen it. I surmised that I would have to have some sort of divine, entirely supernatural healing; nothing of my own accord. In the meantime, I wore a brace on my hand in bed to at least get my fingers stretched out and a bit more comfortable. It was difficult to relax and fall asleep with a clenched fist. Wearing the brace each night was all I felt I could do to help my crippled hand. We asked our church friends to join us in prayer for my healing. Frequently our small group prayed for me. And feeling rather desperate, I attended healing conferences at our church and had "more important" people who perhaps had a greater authority or had the gift of healing lay hands on me and pray. I really sought after the LORD to be healed and whole. I began to get up with Mike each morning. He got ready and went off to work, while I read in my Bible, journaled and prayed lengthy prayers every morning before eating breakfast. Praying for healing became my purpose and reason to get up every day. I was sure it was what God wanted me to do, and I had to do, to be blessed.

The LORD again spoke to me through "random" scripture, and gave me the smallest amounts of hope for healing.

"But blessed is the man who trusts in the LORD, whose confidence is in Him. He will be like a tree planted by the water that sends out its roots by the stream. It does not fear when heat comes; its leaves are always green. It has no worries in a year of drought and never fails to bear fruit" (Jeremiah 17: 7-8).

"That's me, LORD", I thought. "I'm the tree planted by the water and although I might be in a drought, I still bear good fruit."

Then also, later in the same chapter of Jeremiah,

"Heal me, O Lord, and I will be healed; save me and I will be saved, for you are the one I praise" (Jeremiah 17:14). Amen!

Even though the LORD spoke to me frequently through scripture, I needed to know that He still loved me and cared about the condition of my hand. My leg was in bad shape too, but the debilitation of my hand troubled me more. One Sunday, Mike and I sat in church, hand in hand, as the announcements were made before service. An elder in the church shared that there would be a night of prayer held Tuesday night at the church. I'd already been attending a lot of church events recently and thought I ought to stay home to be with Mike. However, as Blaine shared about the prayer night, chills went down my spine and I felt the Holy Spirit stir inside me; something which I couldn't ignore.

I went to the night of prayer, in expectation but not exactly sure what *to* expect. I stood in the back, right arm held high in worship as I sang, "Oh how He loves us." I was bearing my soul before the LORD in song. I felt an immense amount of love and joy. As I worshipped, I humbly prayed aloud, "LORD, I long to lift also my left arm to You in worship, please!" I repeated the prayer many times over and then began to cry. In one corner of the sanctuary, curtains covered an area that was divided into three sections where hurting people of the congregation asked for healing prayers. I was reluctant to sit in the line to wait my turn for laying on of hands, but I felt the Spirit lead me to sit and wait.

When they called me back, Mike had joined me. I explained to my friends that all I'd hoped for was to be able to lift my hand in worship to our King and Savior that night. That night, I vowed to the LORD that whatever use He returned to my hand would be used to honor Him, and I wished to praise Him with lifted hands.

A team of five, including my husband, laid hands on my head and my shoulders. And one man clasped both his hands around my left hand. I prayed silently as they prayed, "Please, please, please, Father." They took pause for a second after praying and said, "Lift your arm." With absolute ease, my arm rose high in the air! I jumped in my seat as I put my arm down and said, "Keep going, keep going!" Not only was I talking to the group of pray-ers but to my God and Father as well. The group laughed and shared my joy. They bowed their heads again and continued to pray. As they prayed once more, I felt my pinkie finger twitch and move. The weakest finger on my hand, and typically the last to recover, was *moving!*

They finished their prayer and asked me to lift my arm again, but I couldn't. I shrugged my shoulders, and they readily tried to give me words of encouragement and hope.

"Don't despair, claim your healing, *declare* that you are healed."

I returned home feeling hopeful and refreshed, but a little troubled by the group's final words to me. What did they mean when they said "Claim my healing?"

The Sunday following the prayer night, I had a dear friend approach me to ask me how my arm was doing since my miraculous hand raise. I was genuine and honest and said, "It was really awesome! I needed that. I needed to know that God still cared about this, and me. He gave me a greater hope of healing. I know He can, and He will." I was delighted to share this revelation and good news with my friend, but he looked upset. He asked me to raise my hand. With difficulty, I raised it part way and awkwardly (embarrassed) dropped it back down at my side. He fixed his eyes on me and said, "You need to claim your healing, believe that you are healed, don't let Satan take that from you!" Flabbergasted, I said, "What?" He again said, "Claim your healing; declare that you are healed, in Jesus name." I felt uncomfortable; put off; sort of offended; but most of all, confused.

I continued to ask friends to lay hands on me and pray, but started to feel a little uneasy with their changing approach to how they prayed for healing. They started to approach the "format" of prayer a different way. After they'd prayed, they would ask me if I felt any different; puzzled and discouraged I always told them the truth, "No." They looked defeated and deeply disappointed. In me, or God? I couldn't tell. I always felt sad for them. I often prayed as they prayed for me, "LORD, they desire to know You are present and still heal today. Will you give them a sign?"

They quoted scripture, "By His stripes we are healed." Their prayers didn't reflect a manner of humble expectance, but a testing of God's power and *my* faith. It was weird, and certainly not of God.

I agree with Philip Yancey in his book, *Prayer*, when he says,

"Somehow we must offer our prayers with a humility that conveys gratitude without triumphalism, and compassion without manipulation, always respecting the mystery surrounding prayer."

But as people prayed over me they prayed as if God was "supposed" to heal me. So, when the unceasing prayers for healing "didn't work," they reasoned that it must be my fault, because God desires and promises us healing and wholeness. It is not His will for us to be broken people. Fellow Christians, people I'd looked up to and trusted, reasoned that I lacked faith, or that I was being disobedient and therefore punished for my sin, or that somewhere in my lineage someone else had gravely sinned and I was paying for it (alluding to a generational curse), and another suggested that something within my own heart was keeping me from receiving my healing; that God wanted to heal me, but deep down I didn't want it. Of course, I had faith in God's insurmountable power; and I knew that He would heal me in His fashion and perfect timing. Of course I was sinful, just as the believer who accused me of such, but so was she! Even so, I didn't completely dismiss it. She was just certain that I wasn't yet healed because I was being disobedient, and she said God told her so. I considered, perhaps God *was* punishing me, and I needed to repent of something. I lay prostrate on my bedroom floor and prayed. I asked the LORD to reveal any wayward way in me. Was my disability punishment? Was there something specific I should repent of? I was still and waited to receive an answer. I received a clear word from the LORD, "If that were so, I would have revealed that to *you!*" In other words, my disability was not God's punishment. As far as a generational curse was concerned, I could not accept and believe that God would be so cruel as to punish me for any of my ancestors' sins! And I found scriptural grounds for that (Ezekiel 18). The God I know is merciful and loving. And as for not wanting to be healed, that was unfathomable and ridiculous. Of course, I wanted to be healed! I knew all these theories were bogus, but I was still confused and angry.

Why had I been healed from all the bleeds I'd had before in 2000 and twice in 2002, but not this one? What was different about this bleed? What should I be doing differently? "Are you mad at me, God? Don't you love me and desire for me to be healed?"

The fact that I remained disabled and unhealed was frustrating and confusing; and I still wanted to be healed. But I decided not to bother people with it anymore. As long as I remained anxious and desperate for healing, my debilitation was something seen in me that others desired to fix. My suffering made others uncomfortable, perhaps because it made *me* uncomfortable.

I was weary of feeling beat down and let down. What I/they were doing, wasn't working. What I felt, Philip Yancey perfectly describes in his book, *Prayer.*

"Some have attended healing services, felt a sudden rush of hope, and kneeled for an anointing of oil, yet still they live unhealed. For them, divine healing feels like the cruelest joke of all, a taunting accusation that in spiritual, as well as physical health, they do not measure up."

And because I had begun to feel like a nuisance, I resonated with this quote from Yancey's *Prayer*, even more so:

"Because of a weak theology of suffering, many churches tend to view unhealed people as an embarrassment, a token of failure." We had tried, and failed.

I believe that God was trying to speak to me through my pain, but unless He brought healing, I didn't want to hear it. I needed something more from God, or he needed something more from me.

I was angry, hurt, and confused. But I was beginning to see that the desperation and "need" to be healed was making us all a little weird. My desperation needed to be for Him, not for what He could offer me. As Lynn Austin says in her novel *Faith of my Fathers*, "True believers don't try to bargain with God; instead, they are willing to bend to His sovereign will."

God was changing my mind about the matter of healing and destroying my limited image of Him. I needed to ask God to help me be patient, with Him and myself. However, Mike was not at the same place. Mike loved me, and his deep desire was for me to be fixed. He believed God's will just *had* to be that I be healed. He was still assertively seeking my healing. He wanted to keep trying, and be open to trying new things.

In February of 2008, we were invited to attend a volunteer appreciation dinner. Mike had been helping at church on Sunday mornings in the sound booth, we both helped with youth group on Wednesday nights when we could, and I volunteered in the nursery during the week (however, I refused to attempt to change dirty diapers with one hand). It was really nice to be invited by the church leaders to a catered dinner to show their appreciation for our church service. Mike and I dressed up for the occasion. Someone at the door took our coats, they had a professional photographer take our photograph, and then another gentleman ushered us to our seats. I was surprised, and frankly a little disappointed, to have been assigned seats. We sat with another couple in the church, a little older than ourselves, who were strangers to us.

We sat and talked about how we were impressed with the formality of the event, and how delicious the food was. They talked to us about how they met, their lives together in Garden, and their two children. Mike told the story of how we met, and our journey of love. We told them that we didn't have kids, but we hoped to someday. Then the matter or question of my disability came up. They were more interested in my day-to-day struggle than in my story and testimony. I felt slightly uncomfortable somehow, being vulnerable and sharing my limitations with them. I would have rather told them about my journey of faith in the process and how all of it unfolded. I gave rather short answers to their questions, but Mike freely elaborated.

Then excited and passionately they told us about their personal experience with miraculous, supernatural healing. When they prayed, healing occurred sometimes instantaneously. They believed themselves to have the spiritual gift of healing. Mike was captivated by their stories, in awe of the power at work in their lives. They felt that they'd been gifted with the gift of healing, but I'd felt long ago that the LORD gave me the gift of discernment. Something about them seemed unsettling. I didn't doubt that they were genuine and kind, but I suddenly didn't feel comfortable discussing supernatural healing with them, so I changed the subject.

Mike was very excited on our short car ride home and continued to talk with great enthusiasm when we arrived home. He said, "We need that couple to pray over you. I think *they* are the answer!" I could see that Mike's intentions were good and he deeply desired for my healing at that moment, more than I did. I silently listened. He stopped talking for a moment, raised his voice and said, "Why are you not excited about this?!"

I said, "I don't know, Mike." He was testy and said, "What don't you know?" I replied, "I think we've been a little consumed with my healing." He sighed and rolled his eyes. I said, "No listen, I think it's time we take a backseat on this and let God drive." "What the hell does that mean?" he said. I cautiously continued, "Just that this, my healing, has made us act kind of weird and desperate for God's blessings rather than desperate for God. This feels wrong." (Mike was shaking his head.) "Seriously Mike, there isn't some formula we need to follow to receive my healing; we don't need 'the right words' or to go to 'the right people.' God will heal me when He's ready; not when you or I feel we're ready. I don't think we should forcefully pursue my healing anymore." Mike pleaded, "Megan, what would it hurt to go have that couple pray for you? God could *want* to use them to heal you!" I said, "I don't know, it just doesn't feel right."

Mike said, "I don't know where that's coming from, but that's bullshit, and you know it!" I said, "Mike, please..." But he threw up his arms, said "Nope; I'm done" and descended the stairs to the basement. I felt sad and confused like I had when I said to Nate in 2002 in pottery class that I'd soon be in a wheelchair after my episode on the wheel. Where was that coming from? Was it truly a discerning word from the LORD, or was I scared of what in fact may happen? Mike and I didn't talk about it again that evening. The issue wasn't resolved, but I thought he had let it go and we'd move on.

However, a few days later, Mike called me from work and was eager to tell me he'd written me a letter and left it in the mail bin on top of the fridge. I love letters, especially love letters, so after I got dressed, I tore open the envelope and eagerly read.

He opened his letter with sincere admiration and gratitude. He said some sweet funny things like "Thanks for making me meatballs," and "You're such a beautiful person." But then he said, "I think you need to give Mr. and Mrs. 'healing' a chance. I feel like you're giving up and not trying anymore. I'm disappointed in you."

I was angry. He hadn't been listening to me. He doubted I'd heard from God. I tore up the letter and buried it in the trash. When he got home, he asked me if I'd got the letter. I said, "Yes, but I'm not giving up; I'm giving in!" He rolled his eyes and said, "That's stupid." And we didn't talk about it any further. So, Mike seemed to think I'd given up and resolved to be handicapped (accept it, and deal with it), but actually, I'd resolved and desired to learn God's way for me instead of mine and trying to "force" God's hand; *that* was stupid.

Mike couldn't and wouldn't accept that. He, and many others, insisted that God's will was to heal me. "Scripture says so, name it and claim it!" Well, I said, "No." I want it God's way, in His perfect timing, or not at all. For the LORD says, "My thoughts are not your thoughts, neither are your ways my ways. As the heavens are higher than the earth, so are my ways higher than your ways and my thoughts than your thoughts" (Isaiah 55:8 ESV).

When I was outside the will of the LORD and actively seeking the blessing of healing, I had many people who shared a common goal with me. They surrounded me in prayer and supported me in my pursuit, as they too looked for solutions to fix me. When I finally discovered that it was not God's will for me to seek after my healing, the LORD showed me that I was to instead seek after Him. So, I did. Seeking after the LORD was fruitful and rewarding, but often lonely.

I didn't feel I could be honest with anyone about my physical day-to-day struggle, not even to my husband. Mike was disappointed in me and mad at God. I felt estranged from my husband and no longer had a common goal with the friends I'd made. They needed to grow in the LORD too. I felt so alone, and somehow ashamed. Perhaps I should have let that couple pray for me, just to appease Mike. But it was just so clear to me that it was not God's will. I had to be faithful and obedient to God, first and foremost. I had regretted getting anyone else involved in the pursuit of my healing. I felt like my disability was the big elephant in the room that everyone was painfully aware of but wanted to deny.

I had to remind myself to be patient with the process and with others as I sought Christ through scriptures and prayer. "Draw near to God and He will draw near to you" (James 4:8 ESV). I was not in command of God; He was *my* commander. Not why, but what? "Ok God, what is it you want me to learn through this trial? How can this be made for good and bring You glory? You've allowed my body to break for a reason. I don't need to know right now what that reason is, but I trust You and Your plan for my life. I surrender to You and yield all delusion of control I thought I had; control of the situation, and of You. I acknowledge that You are in complete control, and my life is wholly and completely in Your hands. You've captured my attention, and my heart. Help me to forgive those who have wounded me. I suppose I need to also forgive *You*! Please forgive me, Father, for I have sinned."

February 14th, 2008

Dear LORD Jesus,

Well, today is Valentine's Day. Today has never been a real big deal for me until I fell in love with Mike. LORD, I want today to be a day in which I can not only lavish my husband in love and appreciation, but more importantly, to You. I've decided that for my devotional today, I'm going to write You a love letter like King David did so beautifully and often in the Psalms.
So, here goes:

LORD Jesus,

I hope it's obvious enough by now that I love You! I love that You loved me before I loved You. Jesus, You not only gave me my life, but You also sustained my life, which strengthened my love for You. You are more forgiving, loving and gracious than any other. You allowed me to be tested and challenged, but have carried me through all of it with mighty hands. You've given me dreams of things to come, and whispered sweet words into my ears to comfort me when I doubt or am afraid. You've given me people here with me on earth to also love me and uphold me, but I recognize they're not perfect. I forgive their imperfections and will always turn back to You. I know I do things that disappoint You and I disobey Your written and spoken word. And yet, You still love me, protect me, and even bless me. Now this love letter isn't perfect, but it's the only way I know how to say thank You and I love You, in words.

Yours Truly,
Meg

"Rejoice in the LORD always. I will say it again: Rejoice! Let your gentleness be evident to all. The LORD is near. Do not be anxious about anything, but in every situation, by prayer and petition, with thanksgiving, present your requests to God. And the peace of God, which transcends all understanding, will guard your hearts and your minds in Christ Jesus" (Philippians 4:4-7).

I was truly entering Christ's insurmountable peace, and as I prayed through February, I got a word from the LORD that my body was going to go through a change. "Wow!" Excited and hopeful for healing, I trusted God with His perfect timing and plan, and waited for the miraculous change. But the change I had in mind was not what God had in mind.

11

After nearly a year of being in Garden City, I still frequently visited Wichita. I visited my family, my college girlfriends that I still missed so much, and I sometimes needed to go to take care of business. In late March of 2008, I travelled to Wichita to spend several days there for business and pleasure. My Mary Kay director lived in Wichita and held weekly unit meetings in her home. It was beneficial for me to occasionally check in with the unit and attend her meetings in Wichita to learn about new products, new sales ideas, and get other training. I had been working hard to grow my Mary Kay business in Garden City and I was doing very well. One of the reasons I'd travelled to Wichita was to ride with my sales director to Tulsa to attend my first career conference. We were going to ride in her beautiful pink Cadillac we'd all helped her earn from the company. I was very excited to ride in her new Cadillac, get some more individual attention from her on our trip, and to learn and celebrate our successes together at the conference.

During my Wichita visit, before we'd travel to Tulsa, I also had a medical checklist to address. I had just celebrated my one-year anniversary since brain surgery, so I was due for a one-year follow-up MRI, and an appointment thereafter in which I'd discuss the results with my neurologist. Although I'd graduated from pediatric care, I still consulted with Dr. Shah because he'd known all my history and I didn't think I'd be lucky enough to find a good neurologist in Garden City. Mike was working through the week and into the weekend (as he always did), so I drove myself into Wichita.

The day I drove in I had nothing scheduled, so I had a relaxed day at Mama and Dad's house. I unpacked my bag, settled in, visited with Mama and read while she worked. Before Mike went to sleep, I called to say goodnight. But as we did on all my visits, Mama and I talked late into the night. Although Mama and I could've conversed longer, at midnight I forced myself to go to bed. I wearily walked to my old room. Mama and Dad had rearranged my room enough since I'd moved that it didn't feel like my room anymore. The bed was moved up against the opposite wall, my Titanic posters and giraffe pictures had been taken off the walls and all my stuff had been packed up and sent with us to Garden City which was then sitting in a closet in our basement. I felt nostalgic and strangely sad that it was so different. I stared at the familiar wallpaper that used to be covered with giraffe pictures as I tried to fall asleep; but such a violent wave of nausea came over me that I couldn't settle down. I worked my way downstairs to grab a bowl in case I couldn't make it to the bathroom later and needed to throw up. I lay back in bed, but the nausea wouldn't let up. I slowly slinked down the hallway to the bathroom and sat in front of the toilet, convinced that I'd throw up at any moment. I wished I would, so I could get it over with and go back to bed. Nothing came, so I lay on the floor a while and quietly moaned. My parents were asleep in the very next room, so I hadn't turned on any lights. I tried to be quiet; there wasn't reason to cause any alarm. My first thought was that I was getting sick, but it didn't feel like a "stomach bug getting sick" feeling.

Pretty soon, Dad was up and came into the bathroom. I looked up at Dad and said, "Sorry I woke you, I was trying to be quiet." Dad said, "What's wrong, can I get you anything?"

I moaned and said, "I'm so nauseous." And without thinking, I said, "I think I might be pregnant, Dad, and I don't think I'm ready for that." This was yet another moment I felt terribly ridiculous and foolish to so quickly jump to a crazy conclusion. I had no other indication that I might be pregnant; I wished I could retract the statement. However, Dad very calmly said, "Oh." Then he smiled and said, "I didn't think I was ready either, but God knew better and you came anyway. If you are pregnant, it will all be fine. Let's get you back to bed." Dad helped me back to my room, and my nerves and stomach relaxed enough so I could sleep.

The next morning, I felt better and felt more stable in every way, but seeing as I had an upcoming MRI, I didn't want to take any chances and went into my previous primary care doctor's office to have my blood drawn to see if I was in fact pregnant. I felt silly and frustrated when I called and even sillier yet as I sat in the chair to have my arm prepped to draw blood. The nurse said to me, "So, you think you're pregnant?" I said, "No. I don't know." When it was over, I was glad to have it over with and when I gathered my things, the nurse said "We'll call you with the results as soon as we have them. It could be later today or tomorrow morning." On my way back to Mama and Dad's, I ran several errands and didn't really give another thought to my visit to the doctor.

I went to Friends University to talk to one of my professors in the psych department. She had taken a liking to me early in my college career and I knew she would be pleased to see me and willing to indulge me in my possible endeavor. I had really been enjoying my Mary Kay business, but it wasn't fulfilling; the work I was doing in Garden City was not what I'd longed to do with my life. For many years I aspired to be a marriage and family therapist or an art therapist. I genuinely grieved and went through a time of depression when I realized that dream quite possibly would not become a reality. My brain was damaged and I wasn't as sharp as I once was. I grew tired easier and was more forgetful, couldn't retain information as well. Grad school would likely be demanding and challenging for me, but I'd worked so hard through college and wanted to actually use my degree. So, I was entertaining the thought of going to grad school. I loved to learn and grow in education and missed growing. I had requested information and even applications from schools throughout Kansas and some other surrounding areas that I'd considered. I looked through brochures I received in the mail and dreamed of getting my master's in marriage and family therapy, art therapy or even photography. If there was a way to do it from Garden City, I knew my professor would help me find it.

We met in her office and discovered I had limited opportunities in Garden, but came up with a few options. To get a master's in Marriage and Family Therapy, or Art Therapy, I could commute to Dodge City to take classes via satellite, take classes at Emporia online and travel to Emporia on weekends. It was a possibility. I hadn't discussed my interest in furthering my education with Mike, because I wanted to present a plan first, and all the facts. I left her office with some ideas and viable options. All options we came up with seemed like they'd be very difficult to manage, but I wanted to try.

After having left her office, I went to visit old friends at the school library. I was well loved there, and it was nice to see everyone again. I took some time to pick up a book to read a little, and then left to make one last stop before going back home to Mama and Dad's. I stopped by the grocery store within a few blocks of my parents' house. I forgot my tweezers at home, in Garden, and some stray eyebrow hairs were driving me bonkers; they had to go! As I got back into my car, bag with tweezers in hand, my phone rang. I shuffled through my purse, where was that blasted phone? I found it just in time to answer before the caller was sent to voicemail. "Hello?"

"Is this Megan?"

"Yes, this is Megan."

"Hi Megan, this is Sandra from Hillside Medical. We got the results of your blood work. Congratulations, you're pregnant."

Stunned, all I could say was, "Wow, ok. Thanks."

I hung up, and slowly put my phone down. I was in shock and unable to start the car. I needed a minute to process the news just given to me. "Wow, I'm pregnant." I suddenly felt the "glow" that expecting mothers seem to emanate. I teared up, patted my belly and said, "I love you so much." An overwhelming sense of joy and love enveloped me. I felt startled by my own response. I didn't realize how much I'd longed to be a mama. The LORD was fulfilling the second part of His promise, already! I was going to be a mom. I started the car, and drove back to my parents' house. My body was trembling; I was smiling and crying. My legs were stiff and rigid as I walked up my parents' walkway to the front door. I was still trembling with excitement as Mama greeted me at the door. She looked at me a little puzzled, awkwardly smiled and said, "What's going on?" I knew I couldn't hide this kind of news for another minute from Mama. Before she even opened the screen door, I said, "Are you ready to be a grandma?" The color left her face and she slowly said, "No." I laughed and said, "Well, too bad. I just found out that I'm pregnant."

Mama certainly didn't seem as elated as I was. She feared for my body, immediately worried about the toll a pregnancy would take on me, especially when I honestly had yet to fully recover from my previous bleed and surgery. She said, "Aren't you worried?" With full confidence, I said, "I probably should be, but I'm not. God said I'd be a wife and a mother. The promise to be a wife has been fulfilled, now I'm going to receive the promise of motherhood. I trust God's timing. I'm so happy, Mama."

Mama had a hard time sharing my enthusiasm, but as we began to talk more about it, she warmed up to the idea. Mama said, "How far along do you think you are? Do you think we'll have a Thanksgiving or Christmas baby? Oh, wouldn't that be so fun?" Mama soon shared my joy in the anticipation of welcoming a baby into our family. Mama and I got so wrapped up in the excitement and then she suddenly said, "Did you tell Mike? What did he say?" I laughed and said, "I was going to tell him first but I couldn't hold it in, and not tell you." Cool, calm and collected, I dialed Mike's number at work. "Hi honey, how's your day going?" He said, "Fine. What's up?" I said, "Well, I'd rather tell you this in person, but I can't contain myself. Mike, I'm pregnant!" He said, "Wow, are you sure?!" "Yes, I had my blood drawn; I am definitely pregnant." Mike just repeatedly said, "Wow, wow, wow." Then he pulled the receiver away from him and said, "Hey Jay, I'm going to be a dad!" Then I could overhear his coworker Jay say, "Well congratulations! Your whole life is about to change!" Mike laughed and said, "I know!" He came back to the phone and said, "Wow, we're having a baby. I love you so much, hot mama." I giggled with tears of joy in my eyes, and I said, "I love you too, Dad." Mike and I both knew a baby would change our lives. Having a baby was going to be good for us; draw us closer together. Although it seemed fast, and Mike and I had only been married eight months, we had been together for four years and had been eager to start a family. We were equally thrilled to become parents.

I called Ellen to tell her the news, and she screamed. She was excited too. I told Ang and she hugged me and said, "That's awesome." I told Dad when he came home from work. He smiled and said, "Well you had a feeling, didn't you?"

I called each of my girlfriends and asked them if they'd meet me for lunch at Olive Garden the following day. I didn't know how far along I was yet, but I at least wanted to tell all the people I love most in the world this news in person. I really wanted to tell Mike's family too, but didn't want to deprive him of that joy. I'd let him tell our news to his siblings and mom and dad.

The very next morning, I was scheduled to have my MRI. I prayed as I fell asleep that night and cradled my tummy. "Thank You, thank You, thank You LORD, that You gave me the premonition or direction to get a pregnancy test before this MRI!" Unprotected, the magnetic radiation could have done harm to the newly-formed life in my womb. I informed the technician right away that I had just found out that I was pregnant and wondered if it was safe to undergo the MRI. He said, "Yes, we'll put a shield over your abdomen and we won't do the images with the contrast (which they had to inject into my vein.)" "Ok good, thanks."

Trembling, I said quietly again, "Thank You, thank You, thank You LORD that You showed me before I potentially could have done this baby any harm." I put the earplugs in, the technician laid me down, put the heavy shield over my abdomen and slid me into the machine. Having omitted the images with contrast and with the baby on my mind, the MRI was done before I knew it.

Afterwards, I met my girlfriends for lunch and joyfully shared my news with them, to which my friend Joy said, "Aww, I knew it, I knew it!" We dined together and celebrated.

The following day, I had my neurology appointment with my neurologist's assistant, Kathryn. I was fond of Kathryn. She was personable and easier to talk to than the quiet, reserved, and often brief, Dr. Shah. Dr. Shah would make his appearance during my visit, but I actually preferred to visit with Kathryn. She asked me how life in Garden was treating me. All I said was, "It's hard." Without me going on further, she nodded and seemed to understand. She asked me to squeeze her hands, pull and push against her with my legs and had me follow her finger with my eyes. And my least favorite part, she tested my mental math skills. After three wrong answers in a row, I had to say, "Ok, obviously I'm not good at mental math anymore. Do we really need to keep doing this test?!" When we finished, I felt about two inches tall because that stupid test exposed all my mental and obvious physical weakness that I retained from my massive bleed. I didn't like those painful reminders. Shortly after, Dr. Shah came into the exam room to view the images on the CD from my MRI. Dr. Shah visited quietly with Kathryn as he opened his computer. The radiologist had already called me with the results of the scan to tell me my mass in my left hemisphere that was just above my ear was stable, no change. And no other news to report. The right hemisphere where my mass had been removed looked all clear too. I eagerly waited for Dr. Shah to echo the radiologist's report. Dr. Shah sat down and started to open the images on my CD. He said to me (his eyes never leaving the screen), "They removed the left cav mal through a resection, yes?" I said, "Um, no; the thalamic hemangioma on the right." I thought to myself, "Wow, you have to ask?!" I thought maybe he would have read my chart, expressed some concern, showed any sort of emotion! I went through hell with that surgery. He scrolled back and forth silently, looking at my images. Finally, he looked up from the screen and said, "Everything looks stable." Then he ran through the same tests Kathryn had. I didn't have any specific questions for him, but anyway he said any concerns could be discussed with Kathryn. So, he moved toward the door, nodded and said, "Thank you." Once he'd left, Kathryn and I talked. She asked me if I'd had many headaches over the last year and asked about what changes my body had been through since surgery. I told her once they'd removed the mass, I developed a healthier appetite and quickly gained weight; as she could clearly see. A twenty-pound weight gain had helped me "fill out." Then I paused and slowly but excitedly said, "And I recently found out I'm pregnant." Rather than share my joy, she frowned and looked concerned. She said, "I wish this wouldn't have happened so soon after surgery. Your body hasn't had enough time to recover. But, what's done is done. Was it planned?" I sheepishly said, "No." "Well, were you using contraceptives?" "Again, no." I could tell she was disappointed and thought me to be awfully foolish and careless. She sighed deeply and said, "You need to take extra care of your body. Manage your weight; carrying a lot of weight can do damage to your hip, your already shaky balance and your brain. You need to have a C-section. Going into labor and pushing is not safe." I said, "Oh, trust me, I know." She finished with, "You'll likely need to be on bedrest the last few months of your pregnancy." "Ok," I said. She smiled and said, "Check in if you need anything." I gave her a hug, "Thank you. And, I promise I won't do anything to jeopardize my health or the baby's."

I was sorry that my news upset Kathryn, but I felt like skipping (if I physically could have) out of the office. I got a clear bill of brain health and Kathryn expressed a genuine concern for me and my baby. She'd be there to help me if I felt anxious about medicine and any brain hiccups I might have as a result of the pregnancy.

The last matter of business on my Wichita trip was Career Conference. Mama dropped me off at Regina's house. Before we loaded my luggage into Regina's pink Cadillac, I said, "I have news." A wide grin spread across my face, and I said, "I'm pregnant." Regina smiled and said, "That's wonderful; congratulations." Never having been to a career conference before, I was very excited to go. I brought several bottles of water to drink in the car. I promised Kathryn and Mama that I'd take good care of my body and baby; staying well hydrated, I thought, was very important. I drank so much water, we had to stop two or three times for me to go pee on just a two-and-a-half-hour drive. We talked about Mary Kay sales ideas and funny encounters we'd had with different customers. Regina had a lot of laugh-out-loud stories to share about awkward Mary Kay parties she'd worked.

We arrived at the hotel late in the afternoon and unpacked. Regina went down to a recognition dinner and party with some of her recruits who'd qualified to join. I didn't qualify for the dinner, so I stayed behind, watched TV and journaled. I had difficulty sleeping that night because I was so excited about the day ahead full of training, with times for me to be recognized for the growth in my business. When alarms went off in the morning, I could barely lift my head off the pillow. I was enormously fatigued and had one of the worst headaches I'd ever had (aside from the pain I'd experienced after brain surgery). I sat on the bed, quietly crying and cradling my head in my hands. I was scared. It was a Saturday morning, so I called the emergency number to reach Dr. Shah. I left a desperate message, and Dr. Shah called me within a few minutes. He said the best thing I could do was rest, and I could safely take Tylenol to subdue the pain. I called my cousin, who lived in Tulsa, to please come get me from the hotel so I could rest at her house. I sadly left the hotel and said goodbye to Regina. She said, "I'm sorry; I hope you feel better after some rest. We'll call when the conference is over so you can meet us back at the hotel to go home." Dang it, stupid, weak and fragile body. I missed out on what would have been my first career conference.

I tried to be very restful while in Tulsa and then all the next morning once back in Wichita. After a long week of joy and trauma, I left Wichita Sunday afternoon to drive back to Garden City. I beamed as I drove home thinking about my baby and Mike and I celebrating our news together. Of course, I was excited to share our news with folks at church too. But, after the weirdness of the church, and their approach to my healing, I had distanced myself a little from the friends I'd had there. I was more actively involved in my Mary Kay business, so I was around people, but had no true friends—until the LORD put Scott and Linda in my life.

Scott and Linda attended our church, and were the parents of our life group leader. I only knew of them, I hadn't personally met them. Scott worked at a small business, his assistant had recently quit, and he was looking for a new one. I wasn't looking for another job, but Scott's son told Mike of the opportunity, and Mike encouraged me to apply for the job. Since assistant and secretarial work is what I did best, it did sound perfect for me. So, to appease Mike, I decided to call Scott and set up an interview. Scott worked in a small office on his own. His job involved septic tanks and wells. I went in to the interview pretending to know what a septic tank was and how it worked. Something to do with waste, right? I was a city girl; I didn't know anything about septic tanks. I figured I could learn in time if I was chosen for the job. It seemed more important that I was familiar with Quicken, Microsoft office, Adobe and other computer software—which I was. I think he was also pleased that I could speak Spanish, since Garden City's population is primarily Hispanic. Even though I didn't know what a septic tank was, of all the people Scott interviewed, he liked me best and hired me as his assistant. I worked for Scott part-time at Southwest Kansas Environmental Planning Group.

The work wasn't exciting or challenging, certainly nothing like I'd hoped to do, but I liked working for Scott. Scott reminded me a little of Dad. He was very honorable, kind, caring and a gentle man. His wife, Linda, came into the office with their daughters to have lunch with Scott, at least twice a week. Linda was also very kind, caring and a gentle woman. They took a liking to me right away, and I to them. I knew they would be thrilled that I was going to have a baby, and would be very supportive. I couldn't wait to tell them.

Mike and I celebrated the good news by going out for a steak dinner. Mike and I were very excited, but we weren't completely naïve. We knew carrying a baby would be hard on my body, and that I'd need to be careful and prayerful.

I got set up with an obstetrician right away. My OB was very nice. He was a big guy, had a good sense of humor, and was very easy to talk to. He projected that I was roughly five to six weeks along in my pregnancy and the baby would be due around December twelfth. I told him about my condition and that I'd have to have a C-section. He said, "No problem; and we'll treat you as a high-risk pregnancy" (which I think meant I'd get special attention and more sonograms).

I was expectant and eager for my healing when I got the word from the LORD that my body was going to go through a change. But the change that God had in mind clearly was for me to have a baby instead.

I laughed as I also threw away my applications and brochures to the colleges I was considering in pursuit of a graduate degree in my career of choice. It was clearly not God's will for me to go back to school yet either. The strain of a pregnancy would be tiring enough for my broken body; maybe I'd go to college later.

I was excited to be pregnant and to have God's promise fulfilled that I'd become a mother; however, I worried too. Like Mama and Kathryn, I worried for my body or more specifically my brain. Would the hormonal changes with my pregnancy be taxing on my brain? Could I have a bleed while pregnant? What would happen to the baby if I did have a bleed? Would the excess weight be too much for my already weak and unstable leg? And more worrisome to me was, how was I to take care of a baby safely with the use of only one hand? That terrified me more than anything. I prayed God would heal me in time for my baby. Every day I prayed, keep my baby safe and healthy. LORD, keep me safe and healthy too. My number one priority was to protect myself and my baby from harm. I listened to my body, heeded my doctor's advice and rested more.

It was hard for me to do, and I had to let go of my pride a little, but I listened to the LORD's prompting in the early part of May 2008 by taking some steps back. I relaxed in my Mary Kay business and worked less hours for Scott. The LORD also called me to a spiritual rest. For a year, I'd been so eager for my body to be healed, the pursuit of my healing was making Mike and me a little crazy. I caught myself chasing after Christ's blessings instead of chasing after Christ. The LORD revealed to me that I needed some restoration and healing on the inside, so I entered my time of rest.

I devoted more time and thought to eternal things rather than temporal.

"Therefore, we do not become discouraged (utterly spiritless, exhausted, and wearied out through fear.) Though our outer man is (progressively) decaying and wasting away, yet our inner self is being (progressively) renewed day after day. For our light, momentary trouble (this slight distress of the passing hour) is ever and more abundantly preparing and producing and achieving for us an everlasting weight of glory (beyond all measure excessively surpassing all comparisons and all calculations, a vast and transcendent glory and blessedness never to cease!) Since we consider and look not to the things that are seen but to the things that are unseen; for the things that are visible are temporal (brief and fleeting), but the things that are invisible are deathless and everlasting" (2 Corinthians 4:16-19 AMP). Amen!

I wanted to learn about God, know God deeper, the character

of God, the love of God, the peace that surpasses all understanding. What's the meaning of suffering and how does God use it for good? Also, I asked the LORD to guide me through my pregnancy. "Instruct me, LORD. Use this time to help me grow and mature. I want to be an example of unwavering faith to my child. Prepare my heart and mind to become a parent."

12

Many women complain while they're pregnant about their aches and pains, nausea and discomfort; a friend of mine even equated it to having a parasite! I, however, *loved* being pregnant. What little nausea I had didn't last long, and watching and feeling my belly grow as my baby did was phenomenal. It was truly amazing, and I considered it a miracle that my broken body could carry a child. I thanked God every day that He gave me the gift of experiencing life forming within me. I sang to my baby every day and read the Bible aloud. I felt my first flutter from my baby at nine weeks, while I was working for Scott at the office.

At sixteen weeks, I had a sonogram, and we found out that our baby was a boy. Mike and I discussed biblical names for our baby, and after much deliberation, we settled on two: Luke and Jeremiah. We decided that once we'd met him, we would see which name suited him best. My cesarean was scheduled for December first. In the early months of my pregnancy I continued to work for Scott part-time, and as my belly began to grow, so did my breasts, my feet, my appetite *and* my Mary Kay business. I had Mary Kay sales parties and held multiple facials each week. I didn't slow down for long. I was making a decent amount of money, having fun and was going to provide nice things for our baby boy. I was wrapped up in the excitement and joy of being with child. I was taking excellent care of my body by getting plenty of exercise, drinking more water, eating better and getting better-quality rest. I was so happy and thankful, and kept myself very busy.

While I was bettering myself and my business, and working for Scott, I seemed to have forgotten that the LORD said He needed me to need Him, be desperate for His light, and allow Him to teach me. I was just enjoying the fact that He was blessing my business and work, and had blessed me with a baby. Although I was thankful, my image of Him hadn't changed. I was still more interested in His blessings than I was in knowing Him fully.

One morning, before I went to Scott's office, I was journaling and thanking God for all the blessings that each day held. I thanked God for my baby, and our good health, for my job with Scott, and for the success in my Mary Kay business. And I prayed for continued good health and financial success. I was genuinely thankful, and loved God deeply. However, while in mid-sentence, the Holy Spirit stirred within me and said, "Slow Down!"

I wasn't sure what that meant except that I should probably lighten my load. I was stretching myself thin and figured God was telling me to give something up. In response, I decided that of everything I was doing, I could quit working for Scott. However, I was afraid to tell Mike. I was certain he wouldn't support my decision. I expected he'd be quite angry with me. Mike liked that I worked for Scott. I didn't think we really needed the extra income, but it seemed Mike was a little happier with me when I brought a regular paycheck home. Somehow, I felt I wasn't worth anything to Mike unless I brought home a steady paycheck. As I expected, Mike didn't like that I quit working for Scott; it was a good job and although the income was small, it was steady. I didn't stop working altogether, I still worked my Mary Kay business; it was a better alternative for work at least while I was pregnant. I could rest when I needed to and continue to take care of my body. I was really happy that I had something that I could do to continue to work and help.

I was only uneasy about my decision because Mike didn't agree with it and was upset. Mike and I had actually begun to fight a lot. We were beginning to realize that we were more different from one another than we thought. We had different values and were quite often not on the same page. I seemed to frequently irritate Mike. With the exception of what we had for dinner each night, everything became a power struggle with Mike: spending money, earning money, housework, church and even sex. When we met together to discuss an issue, we'd start out expressing our ideas and feelings and listening to one another, but every conversation turned into an argument and debate. Mike often told me my ideas, input, and advice didn't make sense and were stupid. He said his choices and decisions made perfect sense and were always the clear choice. He wouldn't back down or give up until I'd wear down and give in to what he wanted. And when it boiled down to it, he'd use his power of "head of the household" to always have the final say.

Ultimately Mike didn't like sharing *his* money, *his* time, and *his* stuff. Mike had lived on his own for several years before we were married and had been managing his own money and time himself. He wanted to continue to dictate his own time, finances and agenda and answer to no one. I felt like a bystander expected to follow suit and do as I was told. I was deeply hurt when he said my ideas and input were stupid, and it didn't appear he wanted to make room for me in his life. I wanted to be treated as an equal, be valued and cherished as his wife. Mike was so eager to marry me, but as time wore on, I concluded that Mike didn't actually like being married! Where was the man that had doted on me for over three years, who had driven over 400 miles every weekend to visit me, who had spent hours each night on the phone with me, who spent entirely too much money on me, who traveled to Phoenix with me and who couldn't wait to marry me? Where was that guy?! I was so confused. I felt blindsided, like I'd seen the best parts of

Mike on the weekends we'd dated, and I'd been charmed into his arms, but he didn't really love me. The man I was living with seemed fearful and mad and was often mean, neglectful, dismissive, irritable and demeaning. And he even seemed to *enjoy* fighting with me and putting me down! What was I doing being with him in Garden City? I was scared and lonely, but I couldn't leave him; we were having a baby together. Things would get better, they just had to. God was blessing us with a child; we would eventually work things out.

In the meantime, I remained hurt and mad and felt helpless. I frequently traveled back home to Wichita, and my Mary Kay profits financed every part of my trips. I signed up for two credit cards without Mike's knowledge. I used one for my gas to get to and from Wichita, and the other exclusively to pay for Mary Kay supplies and products. I had my own checking account for Mary Kay purposes and to pay the occasional medical bill. I also made it my responsibility to pay the monthly payment toward my student loan debt. Mike said it was money wasted since I wasn't using my degree. I got tired of hearing that; each time he griped about paying my student loan, he rubbed salt into my wound. I *wanted* to use my degree. Instead, I made decent money in Mary Kay and it provided a small source of income and support. I didn't want Mike to try to dictate my business and tell me how to spend the money I made. Sadly and selfishly, the more Mike and I fought, the more he demeaned me and discounted my part in our marriage, the more money I spent on myself. In addition to my trips to Wichita, I shopped for clothes for myself, bought stuff for the baby, I got massages, haircuts, and pedicures. I was taking care of me. If Mike was going to be selfish with his time and money, then with what little I had, I would be too. Although Mike often said, "We don't have any money," and that we needed more, Mike's income provided more than enough money to pay for our basic needs, and then some. Mike was not depriving himself of luxuries either.

Mike and I watched TV shows and movies together at night,

but I felt like we were worlds apart. And if he wasn't happy with me, I didn't know how to genuinely connect with him, nor did I really want to. I didn't really trust him not to hurt me further. He didn't appear to love me as sincerely as he once had. At times I wasn't sure if he even *liked* me. I tried to put on the façade that I didn't care what Mike thought or did, but my dreams revealed to me that no matter how hard I tried to fight against it; I truly longed to be touched, loved and adored. I began to dream of other men and woke up feeling gross and distraught. Many tears were shed each morning as I reflected and prayed. Sadly, the temptation to seek comfort, love, validation and even intimacy from someone else was strong. The LORD gently reminded me that He was and is my first love and that the comfort, love, and validation I needed could always be found within His arms. The LORD asked me to be patient with Mike and to be faithful to him with my heart, mind and body. He asked me to honor Mike and value him even when I felt devalued and mistreated; that was not an easy thing to do. I prayed that Mike could truly and deeply love me; that he would desire to share his life and his heart with me. He chose me many years ago, but seemed to have changed his mind. I prayed for a softening of my heart too, because I was angry. "LORD, help me to see Mike the way You see him." I prayed for God to move, but in the meantime tried to distract myself so I wouldn't hurt so much.

I made some lofty goals for myself in my business, and two months prior to our son's birth, I earned a Mary Kay car! I was so proud, and looked forward to bringing my baby boy home from the hospital in my brand-new car. We stayed in Garden City for Thanksgiving because it was too close to the baby's birth for me to travel. We had some friends over and ate steaks instead.

Through November, the baby's kicks were more pronounced. As Mike and I watched TV together, I'd lift my shirt, and we'd watch the baby kick and punch my stomach. Mike would rest his head or arm on my belly as our baby boy moved; it was the closest

I'd felt to Mike since our wedding day. I was expectant and hopeful that our baby would knit us closer together.

December first 2008 arrived and it was time to finally meet our baby boy. I was so excited to see him. I never had need to be on bedrest; I worked and walked clear till the end. So, I thankfully and proudly walked myself into the hospital wearing one of Mike's shirts (I had outgrown my own). They had me lay down and got me ready for surgery. After having had brain surgery, I figured a cesarean would be a piece of cake. However, when they put the catheter in, I felt so uncomfortable. My bladder felt like it was going to explode and I wanted to get up to use the bathroom. My nurse assured me that the catheter was working properly and draining my bladder as it should. But I couldn't sit still. I hadn't eaten or had anything to drink since evening snack the night before. I was instructed not to eat any breakfast that morning. My belly was empty and I was beginning to feel faint. My baby and I needed some food and water. The doctor was running behind, so our scheduled cesarean time came and went. In the meantime, I had passed out and was frustrated with my doctor. "Where was he?" When they wheeled me into the operating room, I was uncomfortably rolling side to side on the bed. That stupid catheter was driving me nuts; my body was shaking and I felt short of breath laying on my back.

The anesthesiologist sat me up to give me the anesthesia in my back. He poked me once, and I started to sit up. He yelled, "Don't move; I'm not done!" Oops, how was I supposed to know that he wasn't done? Once he'd finished, they laid me down on the operating table and tried to position my body. The anesthesiologist asked me to spread my arms out. I said, "I can't spread out my left arm." He yelled again, "Why not?" Mike kindly responded that I had a crippled arm, to which he curtly responded to Mike, "You'll need to hold her arm down then." They put a curtain up in front of me, so I couldn't see what my doctor was doing through the surgery. "Thank God!" Even talking about blood made me queasy. However, Mike was fascinated with all of it and wanted to watch my doctor perform the cesarean. Once my southern region was numb, I could no longer feel the catheter, but I still couldn't calm down. I was uncomfortable on my back, nervous, cold, and my left arm hurt as it stiffened up and tried to resist Mike holding it down. I tossed my head back and forth, "Jesus, Jesus, Jesus." The anesthesiologist yelled, "Don't say that; what's wrong?" I said, "I'm just so uncomfortable and now my left arm is feeling numb." He said, "You need to calm down, or we'll have to put you to sleep." I said, "Yes, yes, do that; put me to sleep, please!" He said, "We will if we have to, but it's not good for the baby." And with that statement, I managed to find the strength and peace I needed to calm down. I hated to be awake during the operation, but I did it for my baby.

My doctor jostled me, and I felt pressure as he cut me open and he tore through my muscle. Mike said, "Whoa, you can't feel that? Ouch!" He made comments about what different organs looked like and the amount of blood I was losing. Finally, I said, "Stop Mike, you're not helping!" I thought I was going to pass out again, until I heard the sound of my baby boy cry. I started weeping. "Oh, my baby; he's here." The nurse held him up for me to see, and I said, "Oh, why is he covered in white stuff?" The nurse laughed and said, "That's the vernix. He's beautiful, mom. Good job. We'll give him to dad and you can see him when you get back to your room." Mike and my baby left me laying on the table while my doctor finished up the surgery. He vacuumed me out, sewed and stapled me up, and gave me something to help me settle down and sleep.

By the time I awakened, my family had seen my baby boy, Mike had helped give him a bath, put a diaper on him, and swaddled him. He was the most beautiful baby I'd ever seen. Mike lifted him up and said, "So what do you think; is he a Jeremiah or a Luke?" I smiled and said, "Luke." When I ignored the word I thought I'd heard from the LORD that it was not His will that I marry Mike, and I married Mike anyway, I wondered if the

LORD would still bless a marriage that was possibly outside of His will. But the LORD *did* bless Mike and me; He gave us Luke.

Luke Alan was born at 7:43 a.m. and weighed seven pounds, seven ounces. He was perfect. My heart was full of joy and love for Luke. I had never felt such an unconditional love for anyone before. Mike was in awe, and in love with our baby boy too. It was such a joy to watch Mike dote over our son, and hilarious to watch him change his tarry black diapers. And each time Luke and I slept in the hospital, Luke slept right beside me. I nuzzled him close, felt his soft skin against mine, and cried tears of joy. I had to "fall in love" with Mike, but I fell in love with Luke from the minute the nurse said, "You're pregnant." What a sweet cuddly baby he was! He instantly seemed to love me too, and he mutually enjoyed being close to me.

I was excited to get Luke home. Mike drove us home in my brand-new Mary Kay Pontiac Vibe; but just as I had feared, the LORD had *not* healed my hand. I dreaded having to change Luke's diaper, and his clothes, and was even afraid to hold him. Nursing him was very difficult, but I was determined to do it. It was better for him and myself. The day we got home from the hospital, Mike left to get some things at the store. He said he would be "right back." I was very nervous to be with our newborn baby by myself. I begged Mike not to leave me alone with Luke, but he said, "You'll be fine, he's asleep anyway." Luke lay on our bed, sound asleep. I snuggled in next to him and hoped he'd stay asleep the entire time Mike was away, but he didn't. Twenty minutes went by, and Luke woke up crying. I was afraid to pick him up, so I just rubbed his tummy and tried to calm him down. But Luke's cries grew louder. "What do I do?" Mike finally came home an hour later, and by that time, Luke and I were *both* crying. Mike said, "What's going on; what's wrong?" I said, "Please don't leave me alone with him again; where were you?" He said, "I went to Dillons for groceries, and went to Walgreens to fill your prescriptions; calm down." Mike picked Luke up off the bed, coddled him, and got him ready for me to nurse him. I couldn't hold Luke up to my breast by myself; I needed help getting him into position. Mike pushed my "boppy" pillow up against my belly, put pillows on top of that, wedged Luke in, turned his head toward my breast and Luke and I both calmed down.

Within a few days of having Luke home, Dad (Pappy to Luke) came to visit and help out. Mike had to go back to work, so Dad changed Luke's diapers, and he laughed out loud the first time he changed Luke's diaper and Luke started peeing on the wall behind him. Dad also helped me feed Luke, change his clothes, burp him, and swaddle him. I wasn't terribly comfortable with Dad seeing me bare chested, but I didn't feel I had a choice; I also needed his help to nurse my son. Nursing my tiny newborn was such a challenge. I thought it came naturally to babies to know how to nurse, but it was not as simple as I thought it would be. I was so glad to have Dad with us. He stayed with us for five days and was a huge help.

Before Dad left, he encouraged me to try to change Luke's diaper by myself. I said, "With one hand? Nope, no way." Dad said, "You'll need to learn to do it eventually." Of course, I knew Dad was right, but I was *so* nervous. Luke was so little; I didn't want to hurt him. The next morning, Dad was cleaning up the kitchen for me, and Luke had just woken up from his morning nap. Instead of calling Dad to my room to change Luke, I thought I'd try to do it myself. I carefully thought it through. Ok, lay out the diaper first, carefully unzip his clothes (Oh LORD, please don't let me pinch his skin!), pull one leg out at a time, unfasten his diaper, slide the diaper out from under him, wipe him, slide the new one under, lift his legs with my right hand and slide him into place, pull tabs, and done. Whew! Putting clean clothes on him was a bit trickier, but I did that too! I was so proud of myself, but a little disappointed too. LORD, I wanted to be healed for my baby, not need to learn how to adapt! But I did; I learned how to adapt. By the time Mama came to help, I was changing Luke's diapers and clothes myself, and felt more comfortable holding him, even while standing up. Mama helped me get a better handle on nursing Luke, and by the time she left, I needed less assistance. Mike went off to work each day, Luke slept, ate and pooped. And per everyone's advice, I slept when my baby slept; we often napped side by side as we had in the hospital.

Luke became my reason to get up each day. I loved him more than words can possibly express. I still tried to work my Mary Kay business, but I was losing interest. I enjoyed meeting with people, but doing facials seemed less important and more like a waste of valuable time. As Luke grew and we got him into a workable eating and sleeping schedule, we were both happier, less tired, and I had regular time to journal again. I thanked God every day for Luke. I recognized that Luke was God's child, and that God had given me the privilege and honor of raising Luke and loving him. I prayed that God would direct me and guide me to be a mother full of grace, love and patience. I prayed I could always be an example of faith to Luke and that he would grow to love the LORD very deeply.

I had a vision of Luke when I was pregnant with him. He was standing on a stage, speaking to a mass group of people about Christ. I wondered if he'd shared my testimony, or if he was sharing one of his own. The vision filled me with hope and joy. I prayed that I'd be there to see that come to pass. I knew that the LORD had a grand purpose for Luke. I thought Luke was really special, and set apart from other babies. I learned to adapt and adjust to caring for Luke with just one hand, and carefully carry him with an unstable leg. But Luke learned to adapt and adjust to me too! Mama was always so impressed that he sat still for me when I changed his diaper and his clothes. He didn't squirm when I held him, and he learned how to safely cling to me when I carried him, put him in his car seat, the stroller, or nursed him. My son and I, and our connection, were a marvel to many of the people around us. My aunt called him my miracle baby; I did too.

When Luke was two months old, we took our first extended trip to Wichita. We had been to Wichita briefly when Luke was just four weeks old because my grandpa Mitchell had passed away. I was glad my grandpa had come to Garden City with my parents and got to meet Luke the day he was born, but I was sad Grandpa wouldn't get to see Luke grow. I desired for my family and even my extended family to fall in love with and get to know Luke. On our extended trip to Wichita, we introduced Luke to extended family on all sides and showed him off to some friends. Everyone thought he was gorgeous, and such a happy baby. He had begun to give big goofy smiles; I loved it.

While in Wichita, I got my yearly MRI and we had the images sent to Dr. Spetzler for review. I was still debilitated from the bleed two years prior, but I was healthy enough to have a baby and care for him. I felt awesome and had full confidence that I'd get a good report.

After being in Wichita with family it was difficult to come back home to Garden City. I loved seeing Luke be loved and adored by our families. Luke and I both needed that. We were both a little grumpy when we came home, and it took us a while to get back to our schedule and routine, but we were moving along smoothly again within a few days. In the next few weeks, I received a phone call from Dr. Spetzler's office. They called to talk to me about the images from the MRI I'd had done in Wichita.

I had just finished eating lunch, and sweet little Luke was laying on his Thomas the Train blanket on the kitchen floor. I suspected I'd had a very small bleed while I was pregnant and wiping down our sliding glass door (something I probably shouldn't have been doing). So, I wasn't terribly surprised to get a personal call. The doctor on Spetzler's team introduced himself as Dr. Wilson. He sounded concerned when he asked me if I'd been experiencing any new symptoms, to which I replied, "No sir." He quickly began to give me a full report of the condition of my masses. I waited patiently for a pause, and finally said, "What do you mean *masses*, as in more than one?" Perhaps I'd grown another?! Dear God in heaven, no! He continued to report that the mass in the left hemisphere of my brain had bled a very small amount. "Yes, I suspected that," I said "but my only symptom was a headache." Then he seemed pleased to report that the mass in the right hemisphere of my brain was stable. I was confused, "I don't have one in my right hemisphere anymore. Did I develop another one?" I held my breath as I awaited his answer. He said, "The cavernous malformation that Dr. Spetzler resected in 2007 was not completely removed. A small piece remains." I froze in shock and terror. I didn't know what to say; I was completely caught off guard. "A piece remains?" I told him I had no further questions; I hung up the phone and simply fell to the floor. I crawled on the floor to my son and wept. God had gifted me with this perfectly precious baby boy, I anticipated a complete healing to follow, but I was in fact not healed at all!

Luke was an immediate comfort and smiled at me as I wept in anger and fear. I was so mad at God; absolutely heartbroken. What was His plan for me? Was it actually "plans to prosper me and not to harm me?" Or would there be more heartache ahead; more debilitating bleeds? Mike was distraught and confused too. When Mike and I were able to kind of gather our thoughts and questions, we called the doctor back. We wanted to know if what was left could bleed or if the mass could have the potential to grow back. Unfortunately, Dr. Wilson had no definitive answers for us. His repeated response was, "We don't know." Mike's and my search for answers and peace was in vain. We grew angrier, sadder, more confused, and I fell into despair. There's a fragment of my hemangioma left, it might have the potential to grow back, it might bleed again, but no one knows for sure.

That year, I experienced for the first time in my Christian walk, a season of dryness. I felt God had broken my heart, and Mike's unhealthy response to the news also shattered my heart. Mike distanced himself from Luke and me and hid in the basement. He spent countless hours in front of his computer every night after work and often didn't make it upstairs to sleep next to me in bed; he regularly slept on the couch. Mike had already been pulling away from me, neglecting me, fighting with me, but it was heartbreaking that he also began to neglect Luke. Luke was such a beautiful boy, a joy to be around. I loved watching my little man grow and change. I begged Mike to give him attention, spend time with him, but his response was "He can't do anything yet. What am I supposed to do with him?" I urged Mike to cuddle him, play with his toys with him, and he did once in a while, but more often chose not to. I knew someday he'd regret not spending time with our son; it grieved me and angered me that he likely wouldn't realize that until it would be too late.

I felt like a single mama most days. But even if I wanted to, I couldn't completely care for Luke on my own. I couldn't change Luke's crib sheet, give him a bath, or trim his fingernails and toenails with one hand. I had to ask Mike for help. I hated asking him for help, especially when he acted burdened to or just refused to. One evening, I had just finished nursing Luke and was getting him undressed to get ready for bed. I considered just putting him into his jammies for the night, but Luke was in desperate need of a bath. He had a nasty poop earlier in the day, and although I'd wiped him up well, he needed some warm water and gentle soap to clean his bare bottom. He also needed his hair washed after getting a little breast milk in it. Mike was playing his game on the computer in the basement. I left Luke in his diaper, in his crib upstairs (I didn't always feel comfortable and safe, carrying Luke downstairs. I let people with better balance and two strong arms do that.), while I ran downstairs to ask Mike to give Luke a bath. Luke was still so tiny, I didn't feel he'd be safe if I bathed him. Mike said, "He's fine, just put him in bed." I pushed, "Mike, he needs a bath, he had a nasty poo and has milk in his hair; he needs to be washed." Mike sighed, "Fine, I'll be up in ten minutes." Twenty minutes went by and I returned downstairs to find Mike still on the computer. "Mike, ten minutes has passed; it's been twenty now. Please, Luke needs to go to bed, but he just needs a quick bath first." Mike said, "Just put him in bed, I'll do it tomorrow." Angry and hurt, I went back upstairs. I prayed and brought Luke with me into the bathroom. I wasn't going to put my dirty baby in his pajamas and let him sleep in his filth and just get dirtier all the next day. I cried hot, angry tears and I trembled with anger and fear as I filled Luke's little blue tub with warm water and removed his diaper. He smiled at me as I very carefully lifted him and put him in his tub. He slid over to the side a bit when I took my hand off him to get the soap. "Oh LORD, please help me." I was so nervous as I washed his body. It wasn't difficult to get him into the water, but he was going to be slippery when I got him out. When I was finished washing his body and hair, I drained his tub and prayed, "LORD, don't let me drop him, LORD don't let me drop him." I leaned forward, scooped him out, and quickly pulled him up against my body. I did it! I swayed back and forth with him a while before I laid him down on his towel to dry him off, while saying "Thank You, thank You, thank You, Jesus!" I smiled at Luke and sang, "Jesus loves you this I know, for the Bible tells me so." I carried him back to his room, wrapped up in his towel, and got him ready for bed. I kissed my sweet baby goodnight as I laid him in his crib, shut his door behind me, and cried. I was so proud of myself, and thankful God helped me safely wash my baby, but I was furious with Mike. "I hate him LORD, I hate him!" I wouldn't ask Mike for help with Luke again.

I could have used a close companion, my husband, to talk to when I felt shattered from the news the doctor had given me, that I may not actually be free from my mass, but I didn't trust him not to wound me further. I withdrew. As Mike continued to neglect my needs, my fury and fear grew. One night when we were in the heat of an argument, I said, "I can't do this anymore. What am I doing here; why did you marry me? You were so excited to marry me and have a family, but you treat me like dirt and don't spend time with your son. I'm leaving you." Mike snapped, "Oh yeah, what are you going to do, move back in with your parents; let them take care of you? You don't work, do you expect your parents to support you? And what about Luke; do you really think you'll be seen fit to effectively care and provide for your son? You'd lose Luke. You need me, and you know it." Would Mike really be so cruel as to fight for full custody of Luke? Would I lose custody of Luke because I'm disabled and unfit to provide for him? It was a chance I wasn't willing to take. Luke was my world! And so, I'd stay with Mike. I wanted to be financially independent from him, but I couldn't afford to be, and that really bothered me. I *did* need him. Sadly, I felt trapped. Mike and I were kind to each other and almost loving when we attended life group together, and for a while, Mike was sweet and kind after meeting with his account-ability group on Sunday nights. I looked forward to accountability group and life group nights. We were good together for a while.

I prayed for Mike's and my marriage regularly; I prayed for his heart and mine. I wanted to choose to love Mike, and keep trying, even if he didn't. I put a lot more of my energy, however, in caring for Luke. When Luke was just four months old, I seldom sold Mary Kay. My team's production slowed down too, and a few had already given up and quit before they even got started. Just a few months later, my Pontiac Vibe was repossessed. I didn't find joy in Mary Kay any longer and didn't see that it had any eternal value anyway. The days all seemed to run together, and I lost track of time. But I still got up and around each day to continue to care for Luke, and I didn't let my despair affect how I loved and parented Luke. Luke needed me, and I needed him. Mike bought me a camera as an early Mother's Day gift, and I took hundreds of pictures of the buds on the trees in downtown Garden City, and thousands more of our son. Photography was enjoyable and comforting, but it didn't dissolve my pain. When the LORD had told me to stop and rest, I didn't for long. I quit working for Scott, but went full throttle with my Mary Kay business and filled my time with that instead. Also, God blessed me with the privilege of carrying a child, and I was so happy, enjoyed the blessing, did my daily devotionals, but still missed God's point. I needed to heed His advice and truly yield. God desired my heart, not just my time. I didn't know how to do that, or what that looked like anymore, until the LORD allowed my heart to be broken. When the doctor told me part of my mass still remained, I accepted the hard truth that my journey of pain and suffering likely wasn't over. And I felt I had lost my husband. I desperately needed Jesus.

When I'd read scripture before, it generally was for a specific "purpose." More often than not, I was looking for answers to questions and I read stories in the Bible that inspired me. However, I then started to read and pray simply to draw closer to God. I wasn't looking for answers, had no preconceived notions or purpose; I just needed, and deeply desired, to draw nearer to God. No more distractions, no more "random" passages; I was digging in. I read the Psalms out loud, I read through Job, Jeremiah, Philippians, Romans, Colossians, James, Hebrews, all four gospels, Daniel, Genesis, 1st and 2nd Peter, 1st Corinthians, Philemon, (most of the New Testament) and more. And although I wasn't searching for it, when I read scripture God revealed His heart to me in regards to healing, His people and for *me*.

"You will seek me and find me, when you seek me with all your heart. I will be found by you, declares the LORD" (Jeremiah 29:13-14).

13

The LORD spoke to me through scripture and prayer and led me to authors with sound wisdom and a solid understanding of the scriptures. I started going to a Bible study outside of the Cornerstone group when I was pregnant with Luke. I needed a break from Cornerstone and to meet new people. The women were so nice and welcoming. One of the young ladies threw me a baby shower a few weeks after Luke was born and the ladies provided extra diapers and nursing supplies. It was very thoughtful. I'd only been a part of their group for a short time but had already felt so deeply loved.

Our Bible study leader introduced me to the written work of Warren Wiersbe. Warren Wiersbe has written a commentary on every book of the Bible. In the Bible study, we'd first studied the book of Philippians (my favorite book of the Bible). Philippians 4:13 "For I can do everything through Christ, who gives me strength" was the verse I clung to through all my brain trauma; it gave me comfort and courage. Although I wasn't faithful with my reading of the study each week, I gleaned a lot from the scriptures, the ladies' insights, as well as Wiersbe's, on the book of Philippians. Next, we read the book of Romans, along with Wiersbe's commentary. I read that book more faithfully and I sometimes even read ahead of the group. I was learning a lot. As I reread other books of the Bible (James, Hebrews, Job, etc.) I read Wiersbe's commentary on each book. The words of the Bible made more sense and brought forth life.

When news of my latest MRI results spread to my family and friends that part of my mass still remained, I received encouraging letters from home, phone calls and prayer for restoration of my body and the healing of my heart. I was very open and had shared that the news shattered me and broke my heart. My cousin prayed for me over the phone and said she was mailing me a book. She had read it and mailed me her copy to keep. She sent me the book *Where is God when it hurts?* by Philip Yancey. Yes, I thought, "Where is God in my hurt?" I loved *Where is God when it hurts?* so much that I asked for several more of Yancey's books for Christmas. I made many highlights and notes through Wiersbe's and Yancey's books. I thanked God that such brilliant men decided to write books and share their insights with others like myself. During Luke's morning nap and often after he'd gone to bed for the night, I journaled and prayed and I grew in my understanding and love for God. And through these authors and scripture I learned how God feels about suffering and healing, all validating my views and contradicting the belief that I was being punished for sin, that I was afflicted because of a generational curse, or that healing was being withheld for a lack of faith. I realized that these accusatory Christians had a limited/narrow understanding of suffering and how God actually uses it for His glory and also for our benefit. Until Jesus told them differently, the disciples had a limited understanding of suffering too.

"As he passed by, he saw a man blind from birth. And his disciples asked him, 'Rabbi, who sinned, this man or his parents, that he was born blind?' Jesus answered, 'It was not that this man sinned, or his parents, but this happened that the works of God might be displayed in him'" (John 9:1-3 ESV).

Several more verses tell us how suffering can be used for our benefit and growth.

"Praise be to the God and Father of our LORD Jesus Christ, the Father of compassion and the God of all comfort, who comforts us in all our troubles, so that we can comfort those in any trouble with the comfort we ourselves receive from God" (2 Corinthians 1:3-4 NIV).

"We can rejoice, too, when we run into problems and trials, for we know that they help us develop endurance. And endurance develops strength of character, and character strengthens our confident hope of salvation. And this hope will not lead to disappointment. For we know how dearly God loves us, because He has given us the Holy Spirit to fill our hearts with His love" (Romans 5:3-5 NLT).

Paul talks about present suffering and future glory in Romans 8: 18-30 and a very encouraging and uplifting passage it is, especially for those who chronically suffer. There is a hope of heaven and the redemption of our bodies.

Paul begins with: "I consider that our present sufferings are not worth comparing with the glory that will be revealed in us" (Romans 8:18 NIV). Hallelujah!

"And the God of all grace, who called you to His eternal glory in Christ, after you have suffered a little while, will Himself restore you and make you strong, firm and steadfast" (1 Peter 5:10).

The following verse felt impossible, insulting and appeared to minimize my pain. However, I see James' point now, agree with him and appreciate his wisdom.

"Consider it pure joy, my brothers and sisters, whenever you face trials of many kinds, because you know the testing of your faith produces perseverance. Let perseverance finish its work so that you may be mature and complete, not lacking anything" (James 1:2-4).

"Blessed is the one who perseveres under trial because, having stood the test, that person will receive the crown of life that the LORD has promised to those who love Him" (James 1:12).

Wiersbe and Yancey penetrated my heart through what they

said concerning suffering and healing across several different books that I read when I was confused and in pain.

In Wiersbe's commentary on Philippians, the first of his "Be" series that I read, he commends Paul for setting a good example of what it looks like to be joyful even when life deals a difficult hand. Wiersbe says, "The secret is this: When you have the single mind, you look on your circumstances as God-given opportunities for the furtherance of the gospel, and you rejoice at *what God is going to do* instead of complaining about *what God did not do.*"

Furthermore, in his commentary on James, Wiersbe discounts the belief that the reason for an individual's suffering is because of their sin and disobedience.

Wiersbe exclaims, "Satan tells the faithful Christian that his suffering is the result of sin or unfaithfulness, and yet his suffering might well be *because of faithfulness*! 'Yea, and all that will live godly lives in Christ Jesus shall suffer persecution' (2 Tim. 3:12). We must never think that obedience automatically produces ease and pleasure. Our Lord was obedient, and it led to a cross!" Yes, the spotless lamb of God died on a cross!

In his book *Where is God When it Hurts?* Yancey uses Job as an example to express a similar sentiment.

"The book of Job should nail a coffin lid over the idea that every time we suffer it's because God is punishing us or trying to tell us something. Although the Bible supports the general principle that 'a man reaps what he sows' even in this life, the book of Job proves that other people have no right to apply the general principle to a particular person. Nobody deserved suffering less than Job, and yet few have suffered more."

Wiersbe and Yancey also have much to say contradicting the belief that people remain afflicted and suffer hardship due to a lack of faith. I highlighted and underlined this next quotation from Wiersbe in my book and even wrote, "Yes; thank you!" at the end of it. I was weary of fellow brothers and sisters telling me I just needed to pray more and have more faith to receive healing.

"We must never conclude that the absence of deliverance

means a lack of faith on the part of God's children. I know that God can heal. But I also know that God *does not have to heal* in order to prove that I have faith. The writer of Hebrews recorded the fact that many unknown men and women of faith *were not delivered* from difficult circumstances, yet God honored their faith. In fact, it takes more faith to *endure* than it does to *escape*. We should trust God and obey Him *even if He does not deliver us*."

In his own words, Yancey echoes Wiersbe.

"The very tedium, the act of waiting itself, works to nourish in us qualities of patience, persistence, trust, gentleness, compassion —or it may do so, if we place ourselves in the stream of God's movement on earth. It may take more faith to trust God when we do not get what we ask for than when we do."

Another influential writer, Lawrence Crabb, wrote an entire book (*The Pressure's Off*) about abandoning the pursuit of blessings (or my healing) rather than pursuing the one who blesses. Our pursuit should be for Christ and His presence, not His blessings or what He should do for us to make our lives "better."

"God first plants a desire in your heart, a longing that actually values His presence over His blessings; then He invites you to live out that desire, to abandon yourself to what you most want. It takes you out of control, but it sets you free." Yes, relinquishing control and yielding truly sets us free.

The scriptures and these various authors gave me a lot to think about and process. I reflected and prayed as I absorbed this information and gained knowledge of the Spirit working in and through me and my circumstance. I felt I'd never experienced such immense growth in the LORD and an outpouring of compassion and love from my dear heavenly Father. I had a much greater appreciation and understanding of the Word and even my suffering. With my growing love for the LORD and for my son, my heart was full. Oh, how I wish Mike would have grown with me, that we'd draw closer to the LORD together. We had lost touch with each other as Mike neglected both Luke and myself. The chasm grew wider as months passed. However, we began to have regular coffee and cupcake dates on Thursday afternoons at our local coffee shop. We sat and played chess and talked. No computer, no TV, just us together. We still occasionally attended life group on Monday nights and church on Sunday mornings, but I still didn't feel we were connecting spiritually. I longed for Mike and me to walk together in faith, to run the race that Christ had called us to, to ask for spiritual wisdom we needed to handle our situation with grace and in a way that furthers the Immanuel Agenda. I had learned to be content and patient with myself and the LORD in regard to my healing, but it seemed that Mike was still mad at me for having done so and perhaps mad at God too. It was heartbreaking.

In my loneliness I was especially blessed and thankful to have true beloved friendship with Scott and Linda. Scott and Linda took Luke and me under their wings. They loved me and supported me as if I was their own daughter and they doted on, loved and cared for Luke as if he was their own grandson. In fact, they called themselves Grandma Linda and Grandpa Scott. I thought it was very appropriate. They had had more than their fair share of trials and knew they would struggle with many more. But they clung to Christ, trusted Him with their circumstances and were great examples of unwavering faith. I considered these great giants of faith and generosity my Garden City parents. They were a godsend. I knew they would always uphold me in prayer whether I asked them to or not and would always be there for me in my times of need. Luke took his afternoon naps under Grandma Linda's watch while Mike and I had our Thursday afternoon coffee dates and when Mike and I had an evening date. I always knew that Luke was in capable, loving hands when he was with Grandpa Scott and Grandma Linda.

When I quit working for Scott the year prior, he hadn't hired anyone to fill my position. He was doing his job and the work he'd usually assigned to an assistant. When Luke was roughly three months old, Scott asked if I'd come back to work for him; even if I could just devote a few hours a week, he'd be thrilled to have me.

He missed having help and I think missed me. I enjoyed working for Scott and had missed seeing him on a regular basis, so I came to work for him again for seven to ten hours a week. I'd quit selling Mary Kay, so it was nice to have a little extra income again. My precious Luke came with me each day that I worked in the office. He took his afternoon nap behind me in his pack n' play and played while I worked. He was so very patient and sweet.

Mid-April, I got a phone call from Dr. Spetzler's office. I braced myself anticipating more bad news. We had talked many times shortly after I'd received the initial bad news phone call from Dr. Wilson. I frequently called to ask more questions and ask for advice. The phone call I received from Michelle in mid-April, however, was of a different nature. She said, "I have an opportunity for you to apply to a program called Dream Street. I think you'd really enjoy it and benefit from it. I don't know why I didn't think of you before!" She was so enthusiastic as she briefly described what Dream Street was. She said Dream Street was a weeklong camp in Tucson, Arizona. She said I'd travel to Arizona in early August to Canyon Ranch, a spa resort where celebrities like P!nk had stayed! I would stay there with many other young adults who had experienced physical traumas too. It was a place that we could connect, empathize with one another, share together in group "therapy," while also enjoying beautiful scenery, great food, and some of the spa services. It all sounded wonderful but I had a son that I was caring for, I was his food supplier, and wasn't I too old for camp? I had wanted to nurse Luke for a full year. If I decided to go, I potentially could pump prior to going and pump while at the camp, to keep up the milk supply; but that would undoubtedly be stressful to try to keep up and pump while away. I didn't like the idea of weaning Luke so soon and I felt guilty and sad about leaving Luke for a whole week; he'd only be eight months old when I would leave. But Mama and Mike strongly urged me to at least apply to be accepted. So, Michelle mailed an application upon my request, to my house. I thumbed through the brochure to the spa and read through the description of the camp.

The brochure displaying pictures of the spa was beautiful and very inviting. And after reading about the camp, I agreed with Michelle and thought it would be good and therapeutic for me to go. During one of Luke's afternoon naps, I eagerly filled out the application and was honest, vulnerable and thorough in my answers. I prayed and had Mama pray that I'd be accepted. A few weeks later, I received a letter that I'd been accepted and would fly out on August 2nd. I was so excited but still had mixed feelings about leaving Luke. I'd have to start to wean him in the summer. I loved nursing my baby boy. It was so hard to wean him before he or I felt ready; I hated it. But I started to wean Luke in June by skipping one feeding a day. Sadly, weaning Luke didn't take near as long as I thought it would. By late June, Luke was down to just one breast feeding a day.

Sunday, June 21st : it's Father's Day. Mike, Luke and I walk into church. I'd fed Luke his one breast feeding for the day, so I was fairly certain he wouldn't need me through service, but Luke was still a little unsettled when we dropped him off in the nursery. It was a very busy morning in the nursery. I soothed Luke until he seemed to be more comfortable and Mike and I proceeded to the sanctuary. The worship that morning seemed louder than usual and head pain ensued. As our pastor shared his message to the church, I took notes to stay focused, but my head was burning. I gripped the back of my head and winced. I was in so much pain, I couldn't sit still and keep quiet. I decided to get up to walk around a bit in the foyer. I'd go to the bathroom and get a drink. I had to get up and move about. The longer I sat, the more my head burned. I walked down the center aisle of the church, making my way to the door. My leg dragged as I walked, and I felt incredibly awkward as I faked a smile to the people I passed to get to the back of the church. I thought to myself, "Why did we decide to sit so close to the front?" While I was out in the foyer, I peeked in on

Luke to make sure he was doing alright in the busy nursery. He was sitting off by himself, quietly playing with some toys. I used the restroom, got a drink, rubbed my head and moaned aloud as I headed back toward the sanctuary doors.

When I came back into the sanctuary, I was trying to make it back to my seat quickly, but my weak heavy left leg was slowing me down. I slid back into my seat feeling embarrassed that I'd drawn so much attention to myself. I occasionally rubbed the back of my aching head as I patiently waited for service to end.

I tried to focus and take notes, but I didn't receive any of the pastor's message. I was relieved when service came to an end and I made a beeline to the nursery to get Luke, leaving Mike behind. Mike came in shortly after with a fellow congregant named James. Mike said James approached him after service and asked if he could pray for me. James said, "Megan, I saw you struggle to walk and felt the LORD prompt me to pray over you for your healing." I thought to myself, "Oh good grief, not again." But something about how James approached me was different. He somehow seemed more genuine. So I thought, what the heck, sure; go ahead and pray for me. I sat down and James placed his hands on my head, and prayed aloud. He paused part way through his prayer and said, "Do you feel any different?" I said, "Sorry, no." He nodded, closed his eyes and humbly closed his prayer. He smiled as he stood up, and said he'd continue to pray for me and my healing. I was pleased that he didn't seem disappointed. He was the first person from Cornerstone who'd prayed over me that I felt prayed with a humble expectance. There was no pressure on me, or on God. I appreciated that. I sincerely thanked James for his prayer and concern. Mike scooped Luke up and talked with James awhile as I walked across the nursery to put Luke's toys in his diaper bag. As I walked across the room, I noticed something was different. I wasn't struggling to walk! I was a little confused at first; did I feel that right? James left and Mike walked after him ahead of me as we made our way back out to the foyer. I walked down the hallway still with no foot drop or difficulty. By the time we reached the foyer, my left leg felt strong and restored; it didn't feel heavy or drag. I didn't need to lift my hip up for my foot to clear the ground! What was happening?! Mike and I took a minute to say "hello" to our friends serving at the welcome center. I wanted to grab my friend Roz by her shirt collar and scream, "I'm walking normal, Roz! James prayed for me and I can walk; I feel incredible!" But, I decided to keep still while in the church building. I didn't want to be put on display. I was going to enjoy this miracle myself. I was inwardly ecstatic at what was happening, but also in a state of shock! Mike, Luke and I made our way out to the church parking lot. Mike headed toward the car, but I stood still. He said, "What are you doing, aren't you coming?" I smiled, handed him the diaper bag and said, "I'm going to walk home" Mike nodded. He seemed to understand that something was happening and didn't question me. I walked through the parking lot with a *perfect* set of legs. Several people leaving the parking lot asked me if I needed a ride home. "Nope," I said, full of joy, "I'm walking." I turned the corner to walk the few blocks to my house. I belted out praise to God as I walked home. I walked as if I had never had a brain bleed in my life! It was glorious. I cried, as I sang, enjoying the beautiful weather the LORD had provided, and I walked all the way home. I didn't know if I'd been healed for good or momentarily, but I wanted to walk on my perfect leg as far as it would carry me. My left leg held up so well and felt so strong all the way home. As I approached our driveway, I saw Mike and Luke sitting on our porch waiting for me. Mike wanted to know what was going on. Why did I want to walk home? As I walked up our driveway, my left leg returned to its broken condition, but I was still overjoyed. I was beaming as I told Mike the story of that miraculous experience.

I went onto the back porch and sat on our bench to enjoy the fresh air. And Mike and I thanked our Father for the glorious gift of healing and the beautiful day that allowed me to walk home and enjoy my perfect leg. It was a treasured gift my Father had given me on that Father's Day. I was maturing in my faith and resting and I knew God was honoring my obedience by imparting understanding and wisdom and showing more of Himself to me. My inner being was healing. That Father's Day, the LORD showed me that He was also caring for my body and would not neglect my physical healing. The perfect walk home encouraged me to hold on to hope; to not give up the dream and desire to be healed.

"He delivers the afflicted in their affliction and opens their ears to His voice in adversity" (From Elihu in Job 36:15 AMPC).

August 2nd rolled around and it was time to fly to Arizona to attend Dream Street. I waved goodbye to my husband and eight-month-old baby as I walked out to board the plane to fly from Garden City to Denver. I was very excited to attend Dream Street at Canyon Ranch and meet a lot of other young people who had also had some "hard knocks" at a young age. It would be good to share with people who could relate. I needed and had been praying for a reprieve but I felt torn. I didn't want to leave my son behind. Oh, how I wished I could have taken him with me. I cried a little as I waved goodbye to my sweet, toothless, towheaded boy. I prayed Mike would take good care of him and take the opportunity to have some quality bonding time with his son. I wouldn't be there to fill in when he didn't feel like it.

I rode from Garden City to Denver with nine other people on a prop plane. I got to bring my camera aboard with me on the plane and took pictures of the plains, clouds and reflection off the wing of the plane. The ride was bumpy and loud but I enjoyed the scenery. I liked riding in the smaller plane. I was worried about flying alone but even when I had to change planes in Denver I did just fine.

I arrived in Tucson midafternoon. Dream Street camp counselors picked up myself and twelve other young adults in a couple of mini vans and drove us out to Canyon Ranch. I immediately befriended the other passengers in the van. There were two from

California, two local to Arizona and several others from the east coast. I was the only one from the plains. Most of the other young adults had fallen victim to cancer and were either in remission or still fighting to survive. I did meet one other patient of Dr. Spetzler's; that was a nice surprise. She too, of course, was a huge fan of Dr. Spetzler's; he had operated on her brain more than once. All campers were friendly and nice and I looked forward to hearing each of their stories. The camp counselors kept us very busy; I didn't have as much time to journal and be alone as I thought I would. We attended classes at the spa, we had a few spa services (I had a massage and it was wonderful), we played tennis, went on hikes, had group exercises and therapy, and ate great food. It was difficult to sleep at night, sharing one big room with several other girls, but the experience was well worth it. I could catch up on sleep at home.

I think the most beneficial part of the experience for all of us was to be able to share our heartaches with one another. We didn't know each other prior to Dream Street but we each understood what it was to hurt, to not be as healthy as our peers, and to value life after having survived something so horrific. Something we all had in common was feeling misunderstood and alone in our suffering. It was so nice to have people to talk with who understood.

One evening in a group discussion, one of the young ladies was talking about potentially having children in the future. She said she had pretty well decided that she would never have children. She wanted to have children, but she couldn't possibly knowingly risk passing on to a child the cancer gene she knows she has. She said, "I would never want to cause anyone else to go through the horror of what I've had to go through." I teared up as she continued talking about risk of inheriting such a horrible disease. "I couldn't do it," she kept saying. I couldn't hold back any longer; I started sobbing. I wanted to yell, "Please stop!" Someone shut her up!

A counselor noticed me crying, broke away from the group

and pulled me aside. "You miss your son?" she said. "Yes, but that's not why I'm crying." She started rubbing my back and pulled in closer. "Then what's wrong?" I said, "There's a possibility that what I have is hereditary. Although I'm the only one in my very large family who knowingly has hemangiomas, I could have inherited them from someone in my family. If they're in fact hereditary, I could have passed them to my son." By this time, I'm so badly choked up that I struggle to breathe and talk. No one else in my very large family has had a bleed, but what if they are in fact hereditary and not spontaneous? It's a fear that had been in the back of my mind even before I'd become pregnant. The thought of Luke going through what I'd gone through, or *worse*, just shattered me. I couldn't think about it. The fear, anxiety and grief were just too overwhelming.

The counselor said, "Don't you love your son? Are you glad you had your son? Are you saying you wish you'd never had your son?" I understood what she was getting at, but I felt selfish. I did love my son more than anyone and anything, but was that enough?

Luke is God's child first; He called Luke's life into being. Whether he has hemangiomas or not is in God's hands, not mine. I had to pray, "LORD, please, help me to not carry any guilt or fear over this matter." The LORD loves Luke much more than I could ever dream and He has a plan for him. I was able to calm down and dry my tears, but after that meltdown, I was especially eager to get back home to Luke.

The next morning, all of us Dream Street campers and counselors packed up, said our goodbyes and promised we'd keep in touch. I was excited to get back to my baby, to get a good night's sleep, and to share about my Dream Street experience with Mike and Mama. I was glad that they encouraged me to go and I was eager to tell them so. I was incredibly nervous about flying to and from home by myself. I hated flying and had never flown without someone I knew. Flying to Tucson went smoothly, but flying home, I encountered some problems. I made it to Denver but flights to Garden City were canceled, due to storms. My anxiety was building, I called Mike frantically. "Mike, what do I do? Will you come get me?" It was late and Denver is a five-hour drive from Garden, but even so Mike considered coming to get me. In the end, he decided I should instead take advantage of the hotel and dinner vouchers the airport provided and come home on another flight in the morning. I didn't know where to go or how to get to the hotel. And what if I missed my flight tomorrow too? "Oh LORD, help me please!"

When I got off the phone, I spotted someone in the airport that I knew; it was a miracle and answer to prayer! Someone I knew from Cornerstone church was also flying home to Garden City and also stuck in Denver for the night. "Oh, thank you Jesus." With my new-found friend's help, we made it to the hotel, I stayed in my own hotel room, took a nice long shower and got a good night's rest before returning home. My Garden City friend and I made it in time to our flight the next morning—barely.

My fellow traveler's car was left at the Garden City airport while he was gone, so he gave me a ride home. Once home, I jumped straight into my car and drove to Luke's babysitter's house to pick him up. I was so excited to see my sweet boy and never again wanted to be apart from him for so long. When I arrived, his sitter said he'd been napping. I slowly opened the door to his room and he woke up. He gave me a big grin and stood up in the crib! Wow, he wasn't doing that before I left! Luke learned to stand up while I was gone. I picked him up, squeezed him tight and kissed his forehead. I was home to my baby.

I felt refreshed after just a week away and empowered. I was encouraged by the people at Dream Street. I decided to be proactive and take better care of myself. I'd started to think it wasn't worth the time and effort, that *I* wasn't worth the time and effort, but after a week of caring for myself while away, I felt differently. Things were going to change at home. I couldn't be afraid of being dejected and ridiculed by Mike anymore and needed to stop hiding from him to protect myself and Luke. I had started seeing a counselor and she advised that I stop taking my monthly trips to Wichita without Mike. Avoiding him and leaving wasn't a solution to the problem. Although I was more vocal with my needs and desire for our relationship and Mike's relationship with Luke, things didn't change overnight. The counselor I was seeing challenged me and was helping me heal. I talked to her about my grief, my anger at being handicapped and feeling trapped in a loveless marriage. When I first talked to Mike about attending counseling together, he said, "I don't have a problem, we don't have a problem, if you think there's a problem it must be with you. *You* need therapy; I'm fine." So, for several months, I went alone but eventually I coerced Mike into coming with me to see my counselor.

She discussed with Mike some of the issues I had shared with her and asked his opinion on such topics. When Mike would try to change the subject, she'd get back to the root issue and ask further questions. I don't know exactly what it was that made Mike uncomfortable; perhaps he was uneasy because she was speaking hard truth that Mike didn't want to hear. In any case, he was getting angry and short with my counselor. Mike stepped out before the session was over and accused her of not listening to him, painting him out to be a bad guy, and said she was a "feminist." I apologized to my counselor and said I'd see her next week. Mike was clearly still upset on the drive home. He didn't tell me not to see her again, but he said he wouldn't be back.

Although Mike wasn't receptive to therapy, changes were made at home. Mike more faithfully attended his accountability group on Sunday nights. Mike shared with me that one of the men in the group said to Mike that I looked like a wet puppy dog every time he saw me: sad and dejected. I thought I'd been successfully concealing my feelings well in public, but I was glad his friend noticed and made Mike aware. The accountability group suggested Mike limit computer-gaming time. So, Mike played computer games one night a week, instead of five to seven nights a week. It was a start, but I still prayed he'd tire of his computer games and have no desire to play at all. He replaced some of the game time with watching television, but at least part of the time, I could do that with him.

When I returned to therapy, my counselor was distressed about the visit that Mike had joined. She said, "I don't condone divorce, and I'm not saying you *should* get divorced, but don't think you have to stay in an abusive relationship because you have no other options." The truth of it was, even though at times I would have liked to divorce Mike, I felt I couldn't and that I also shouldn't. I felt I couldn't because we had a child together, but I felt I shouldn't because I hadn't heard the LORD tell me anything other than to pray for Mike, and to pray also for the restoration or rebuilding of our relationship. We needed to demolish whatever shaky foundation we'd laid and somehow "start over." I had struggled through so much physically and dreaded ever having to fight through more, but the emotional uphill battle of fixing our fractured marriage seemed like too great a weight to bear and I wasn't sure I was up for the task. "LORD God, why this struggle, too?"

On top of everything else, in early fall I started to get sick. I had a very hard time getting up each morning to care for Luke and struggled to stay awake throughout the day. I couldn't stomach much food without feeling nauseous, so I often didn't bother. I was depressed and chronically tired. Feeling discouraged, I called Mama; she suggested I call my doctor, but I didn't want to unnecessarily accrue another medical expense. Mike was always stressed about money and griped about medical bills. I wasn't having headaches or added weakness in my extremities, so it couldn't have been that big of a deal; I decided to wait it out. However, after more than a week of feeling incredibly lethargic, I relented and called my local PCP. I couldn't effectively take care of Luke and I needed to remedy that quickly. My doctor said to come in for labs. They were going to test me for anemia and for a thyroid imbalance. I rolled my eyes as I said, "Oh, I talked to my mom, and she thinks I might be pregnant." The doctor said, "Ok, we'll check for that too."

After labs, I had a strong cup of joe to make it through the rest of the day. I went in for a few hours to work for Scott that after-noon and Luke played in his pack n' play behind me. As I was packing up to leave, I got a call from the doctor. She said, "Well you're not anemic and your thyroid is fine, but you better call your mom because she was right—you're pregnant!" I said to my doctor, "What, are you sure?" My doctor chuckled and said, "Your HCG levels are higher, which is a pretty good indicator that you're pregnant. So yeah, I'm sure. Now give your mom a call and schedule an appointment with your obstetrician." I was absolutely stunned when I hung up the phone. Pregnant? It just wasn't possi-ble! I hadn't even had a period since before Luke was born!

I turned around, looked at Luke standing in his pack n' play, giving me a big goofy grin. "Hey buddy, are you ready to be a big brother?" I choked up and said, "I'm not ready to be a mommy again." I cried and wanted to apologize to Luke. Luke was still a baby himself and I was going to have another one? Already? I wasn't ready for Luke to be a big brother. I especially wasn't ready to have another baby with Mike! It seemed like horrible timing to be pregnant. Scott walked in to the office from being out at job sites. He saw me packing up and wiping my eyes. He said, "You need some help?" I was sure not to make eye contact with him. I just might burst into tears again, "No thanks," I said. "I've got it; see you tomorrow." I wanted to tell him. I wanted to tell Scott that I was pregnant and that I was anxious and scared about it, but I kept still.

On my drive home, I heard a song come across the stereo that reminded me of my friend Denae. I called her and she said, "What's new?" So, I decided to share the news of my pregnancy with Denae. She said, "Wow, how old is Luke?" I said, "I know, Luke is still a baby himself." When Mike arrived home from work late that evening, I'd ordered pizza to surprise him. He was pleas-antly surprised to find pizza on the table and as he went in for a bite I said, "Mike, I'm pregnant." Mike was stunned, but excited. Mike is the second of five kids in his family. His older sister is only fifteen months older than himself and his brother born just after him is only eighteen months younger. Having two kids so close together didn't worry Mike like it did me. He only seemed slightly worried about the need to financially provide for another baby. Otherwise, he genuinely seemed excited. Mike was excited about baby number two and excited that Luke was going to be a big brother and soon have someone to play with. I however was afraid another baby could potentially destroy our already fragile marriage. I was praying for Mike to change, I prayed for him to grow up and to love both Luke and me as we deserved. But I was still impatient and mad. I had so much hate and sadness in my heart. *I* needed to change. Our relationship, our marriage needed to be repaired and restored by the LORD Jesus Christ before another baby was introduced into our family. As long as I harbored hate, I knew nothing I could say or do would be helpful. I needed the LORD to help me learn to love Mike unconditionally and to forgive him. I had felt justified hating Mike and being passive/aggressive because he'd wounded me so badly. But as Paul addresses the Corinthians in 1st Corinthians 7

"Marriage is not a place to 'stand up for your rights.' Marriage is a decision to love and serve the other." When mad at Mike I'd read a scripture, hear a sermon and think to myself, "This is Mike. He needs to hear this or read this;" instead of receiving it for myself, personally surrendering and taking responsibility for my own heart and actions. I had grown so much in my understanding of scripture and the LORD's heart for me during my time of reading, studying and praying, but as long as I was still harboring bitterness, resentment, fear and hate for my husband I couldn't fully receive the inner healing that God desired to lavish upon me. The journey to forgiveness and unconditional love for someone I deemed unlovable, I knew was going to be hard!

I had to humble myself, repent, and ask the LORD to show me *His* eyes and love for Mike. As I prayed, the LORD repeatedly asked me to trust Him with Mike. I would be obedient and choose to love. Over time my heart softened for Mike. He was still abrasive, but as I remained home and stopped traveling to Wichita and chose to love rather than retaliate, I saw evidence of growth in both Mike and myself. Perhaps there was hope for us and our baby after all. I began to dream and hope for a brighter better year in 2010.

January 1st, 2010

Dear LORD Jesus,

Today begins a new year. What must I seek and gain from You this year, LORD? I pray fervently that this second child I carry is also Yours, Father. I pray that this new life will be a new addition to Your Kingdom, Father. I pray that even as we name this child You, LORD, will direct us. I pray You guide and direct us as we parent two children. Give us strength and wisdom to carry out this job You've assigned to us. I'm more joyful and excited as I feel kicks and punches and jabs within my womb. I'm excited that we don't know whether we're having another son or a daughter. I pray that even Luke, as young as he is, is kind, obedient, loving and interested with his baby brother or sister. I pray against complications with the pregnancy and delivery and I pray that the baby will be beautiful and healthy. I sincerely, incessantly pray that our children will grow to know You and love You deeply as I have and deeper still. I want to be able to share my experiences with my children and tell them what I've learned about You, how I've grown to love You as the all-powerful, merciful, compassionate, loving God. I have no idea what's in store for my life ahead, but I humbly pray and ask that You please prolong my life on earth so that I may help guide and teach my babies about You. In this new year I pray that Mike and I's and even little Luke's understanding of You and Your love for us grows. I pray we more regularly take time to seek You and Your wisdom through prayer and scripture and that we readily open our hearts to You. Make 2010 radically new for us Jesus.

-Megan

"I will not die but live, and will proclaim what the LORD has done" (Psalm 118:17). Yes, Jesus!

January 12th, 2010

Dear LORD Jesus,

This new year brings about a fresh start, a new dawn. New life groups have started and I'm attending two. I couldn't decide which one to go to, so I thought why not attend both? I can't get enough of You, Abba Father! I want more of You! I don't know what's awakened this desire within me, but I love it! I've struggled to find my place recently. What is Your will, what is my purpose? It seems there's a time to learn and soak in Your goodness and Your word, and the commission is to share that love and knowledge by teaching and serving. I get upset when chores and other mundane responsibilities get in the way of reading Your word and serving the community, but I must remember You've called me to a different service. I attended a conference at Cornerstone Church and a small group prayed over me. They prophesied healing and other things I thought were bogus, that they hadn't truly heard from You, but there was a lull of silence, and quiet thoughtful Craig, who had been silently praying over me said "What you're doing is enough." That's all he said, but I knew exactly what You were telling me. Serving my husband and my family for right now is enough. I softly cried; I needed to hear that and I received it. I turned to Matthew in my devotion today in which You confirmed Your word spoken through Craig. "Whatever you do for the least of these, you do for me." I render my service to Mike and Luke and this baby I carry as to You, LORD, until You call me to something different or somewhere else.

I've been learning from Beth Moore's study to be patient with the journey and to accept where You've placed me for this time. And LORD, I say this with little hesitation, because I do trust You; I am ready for whatever comes next!

Amen and Amen.

Megan

"Because you love me," says the LORD, "I will rescue you, for you acknowledge my name. You will call on me, and I will answer you; I will be with you in trouble, I will deliver you and honor you. With long life I will satisfy you and show you my salvation" (Psalm 91:14-16).

14

I nitially I wasn't too eager to have another baby so soon after Luke, but the further into the pregnancy I got the more excited I was to meet baby #2. The pregnancy, however, proved to be a greater strain on my body. Luke couldn't walk yet, so I still picked him up and carried him from room to room, I loaded him in and out of his car seat, stroller, high chair, pack n play, and organized exercise was more challenging; taking care of Luke *was* my exercise. I took short walks outdoors with Luke, but as my baby inside grew, walking became more difficult and uncomfortable. I was hurting my hip and my left leg. Mike and I had discussed long before Luke was born that we'd probably just have two kids. I'd heard two cesareans aren't so bad, but the more you have, the harder it is for the body to recover. My body had already been through enough and two kids sounded just right. Our decision to be done after our second was an easy decision, especially considering that the second one was much more difficult for my body to carry. I should have been resting more at home, especially toward the end of the pregnancy, but I felt sad that Luke's and my one-on-one time was going to be cut short. So, Luke and I had a fun outing together every day. I craved cinnamon rolls, so we made regular visits to McDonald's to get their cinnamon melts. I got one for me and one for Luke. I often ate mine and most of Luke's. We went to the park, the zoo, the grocery store, the library for story hour, had playdates with friends or just went for a drive. I was going to miss being able to give Luke my full attention. I had a feeling he would miss it too.

I walked into the hospital on my scheduled cesarean date, April 16th. Mike and I were excited to meet baby number two. I had been so antsy the night before and had an adverse reaction to a medication that was supposed to put me to sleep; I'd only had two hours of sleep. I looked forward to that time after surgery when they'd give me something to settle down and finally sleep, as they had after Luke was born. I knew when baby number two made its debut, we'd suffer sleep deprivation all over again.

I laid in the hospital bed as they prepped me for surgery. I laid there wondering if we were going to have another son, or if we would instead have a daughter. When I had sonograms, we told the technician that we didn't want to know what we were having; we wanted to be surprised. Mike and I were convinced, however, that we were having another boy. We had a strong biblical name for a boy: Jeremiah Paul. Just in case we were wrong and we had a girl we agreed on the name Natalie McKay. I'd always liked the name Natalie and McKay is a family name that is also my middle name.

I was eager to go and was much more subdued for the second cesarean. We knew better what to expect and what to request, not to mention I was unbelievably tired. The procedure seemed to move quicker and I think I might have fallen asleep at one point. I "came to" when the doctor pulled out my baby and said, "Ok Dad, what is it?" Mike hesitated so I said, "What's wrong? Is he ok?" Mike finally said, "Oh, it's a girl!"

I choked up, "Oh, a girl. Natalie, let me see my Natalie." They laid Natalie on my chest for just a moment and a tear slid down my cheek. I beamed at Mike, "We have a girl." The nurse took

Natalie from me and Mike followed as the doctor got ready to tie my tubes. My doctor said, "Now, are you sure you want to do this? It's not too late to change your mind." "I'm sure," I said. "We have a boy and now a beautiful baby girl. We're done having babies." So, my doctor proceeded with the tubal ligation. My doctor pulled and yanked me around. "My God, I'm glad I can't see what's going on down there!" I thought. The tubal procedure seemed to take forever and I was getting terribly impatient. I wanted to see my baby and get some rest.

I was looking forward to resting for a little while before visitors came and anything else was required of me. However, shortly after they rolled me into my room, they put Natalie at my breast and expected me to nurse. Natalie wriggled and cried. She did not like being messed with and she wanted to sleep. The nurse was having a difficult time keeping both Natalie and myself awake. Natalie must have been up with me last night!

When Grandma Linda came to see me, I couldn't keep my eyes open long enough to greet her. She admired Natalie as I struggled to stay awake. The nurses kept prodding me; they wanted me to get up and walk. The birth was a lot less traumatic with Natalie than it was with Luke, but I was failing miserably with the afterbirth. I was so tired. I also had a greater amount of pain because I'd had the tubal ligation done too. My insides burned and I couldn't stay awake and when Natalie wasn't sleeping, she was very cranky and screamed. I missed Luke, wished I could be in my bed at home, and waking to him stumbling around the living room playing with his indoor basketball goal that Mama and Dad had recently bought him. I was already in over my head with baby number two. I tried to cuddle Natalie for naps in the hospital as I had with Luke, but she stiffened up and screamed when I tried to pull her close. She was so uncomfortable. When I tried to nurse her, she either fell asleep or stiffened up and frequently pulled off to cry. When Luke came to see us at the hospital and meet his baby sister, he seemed confused and shy. He put his fingers in his mouth and felt his hair to comfort himself. Mike held Natalie to show her off, but Luke wasn't interested; he was more concerned with me. Why was his mama here at the hospital and not at home? My parents took turns holding Natalie while I had a little mommy-son time with Luke. He reluctantly crawled up in my lap on my hospital bed; I held him tight and kissed him. He laid his head on my tummy (Luke's way of giving hugs). I read him a short book before my parents took him back home, and when he left, I cried a little. I felt sorry for Luke. My little buddy had been pushed out of the nest too soon. Natalie would steal a lot of my attention away from him. I was thankful Luke was old enough to walk and could talk a little, but he still was dependent on me and needed a lot from his mommy.

When we were able to bring Natalie home, I thought she'd be more settled and less agitated, but when Natalie wasn't asleep, she was screaming and crying. Many times, when I tried to console her and failed, I'd wished I could put her back and have a few more months with Luke. I felt guilty for not loving her as naturally as I had Luke. I'd get frustrated with her and her screaming. If anyone, I should have been the one who could console her and comfort her, but I couldn't. She struggled to nurse and that frustrated me. I had a lactation consultant come to the house to help me. Natalie wriggled and screamed so much, even while nursing, that I nearly dropped her out of my arms. I wasn't bonding with Natalie and didn't feel I could help her or safely take care of her with one arm. She was too restless and Mike had to help me. One night, late into the night, I was in the bedroom below ours trying to calm Natalie down after nursing so we both could go back to sleep. She screamed incessantly and was giving me a headache. The blanket I'd swaddled her in was coming unwrapped and her little arms and legs were flailing about. I laid her a few feet from me on the bed and I cursed aloud and cried. "Shut up, Natalie, just shut up!" Mike heard me and came downstairs. He wrapped Natalie tight and gently said, "Megan, go back to bed; I got this." Mike stepped up and gave Natalie the firm hold that she needed. He was oddly patient with Natalie and I couldn't make sense of it. He pushed her legs up to relieve her of the gas that made her so uncomfortable. He wrapped her up tight each night and held her while he played his computer games and she screamed. It was perplexing to me that it didn't bother him, but he was a huge help caring for our colicky baby. Thank God for that.

As Natalie grew bigger and older, she outgrew her colic. She cooed, smiled, nursed better, slept better, and was much less restless. Luke grew to love her; I was better rested and relaxed and able to love and care for her better too. She was such a beautiful baby and admired her brother so much. Although I'd initially felt she was brought into the world too soon, now I can't imagine what our family would be like without her. Once again, God had a better plan. She was a lovely, perfect addition to our family.

It was physically more trying for me to care for two babies. I didn't get to nurse Luke nearly as long as I wanted to, but I had determined to nurse Natalie until she was a year old. Because I was her only food source, I was up with her at night to feed her and then up with Luke in the morning to feed him breakfast and care for him too. I had very little time or energy to care for myself, so I was still in my time of "rest" that the LORD had called me to. It was my time to care for small children and I was Ok with that. I had to be patient with my limitations and do the best I could do with what the LORD provided me.

It was too difficult to wrangle two kids with one arm to various places, so we left the house less. I took lots of pictures of the kids indoors, caught Luke climbing into Natalie's crib multiple times in the morning and took pictures of him playing with her in her crib. Natalie was born in the spring, and even though it was often smelly because of the feed lots, we spent a lot of time outdoors in the back yard in the warm sun. Luke and I learned to be content at home with Natalie and enjoyed her company. We needed to learn to be content to stay in Garden City with Mike too. Even if I had no desire to fight for my marriage, my therapist advised that I not run away from Mike anymore, but learn to connect and grow stronger together at home. With less time in front of the computer, and my presence, we were beginning to connect.

In the summer of 2010, Mike brought to my attention that one of his cousins wanted to move out to Garden City from Wichita. Mike wanted to offer our home for him to stay for a few weeks, just until he found a place of his own and could get settled. I readily agreed. We had a spare room in our basement and I was happy to help a family member in need. I thought it would be good for Mike to take his cousin under his wing and nurture him. He would come to church with us and eat family dinners with us. It was going to be great. It was nice at first, but Mike felt torn between being a friend to his cousin and a husband and dad to his family. Mike chose to be a friend and I lost him all over again.

Mike's cousin's two-week stay, turned into several months. Mike and his cousin lived together in the basement. Every night after work they ate dinner at the table, but talked about their computer game and then went to the basement to game on the computers late into the night. Often, Mike came up to bed just hours before he had to get up for work, or he slept downstairs. I complained to Mike that his cousin's presence was tearing us apart and things needed to change or his cousin needed to go. Mike told me I was being selfish and that it was important for him to be a friend and a witness to his cousin. I did my best to clean house, make dinner and care for my children; I tried to make the best of the time that Mike did give me and his kids, but that time was rare. I wasn't going to leave Mike, but I wasn't going to fight with him either. I was too tired to fight. I'd live life upstairs, while Mike and his cousin would have their own lives and agendas downstairs. Mike's cousin successfully obtained a job, but did not have a car. One afternoon, Mike called and asked if I'd drive his cousin to work. Usually I napped with the kids in the afternoon, but instead, we all loaded up, I got a coffee to keep me going, and we drove him to work.

At the end of the day, once the kids were in bed, I was

exhausted; even so Mike and I had decided to watch TV together. I didn't want to miss out on an opportunity to have quality time with my husband. Mike was in the kitchen popping a big bowl of popcorn for us to share while I was in our bedroom getting ready to change my clothes. I got my pajamas out of the drawer, laid them on the bed, then suddenly my right thumb went numb. Very quickly the rest of my hand went numb. I ran to the kitchen, frantic. "Mike, I can't feel my right hand!" As I was standing in front of him, the rest of my arm started to numb. By this time, I'm freaking out. I'm having a bleed? Mike told me to go out to the car and he'd tell his cousin that he was taking me to the ER. While I waited in the car, I had numbness in my face and my tongue went numb. I lost control of my tongue and kept biting my cheek. Mike got into the car and said, "Ok, my cousin is going to stay with the kids. Let's go." He turned to me as he backed out of the driveway. I was crying, opened my mouth to say "I'm scared," but all that came out was a moan. I couldn't talk! Mike's eyes grew wider, but he stayed calm. He drove like a madman to the ER, but calmly placed his hand on my leg and prayed for me. As he prayed, my speech returned and I slowly started to feel my right arm and hand. I was better, but we still proceeded to the ER to find out what the heck had happened to me.

The Garden City ER staff checked my vitals, had me do a head scan, but found nothing wrong. I decided to call my neurologist in Wichita. He said if the scan was clear of bleeding, I'd probably had a seizure. A what?! I'd never had a seizure before! Why did I have a seizure? We had tried a new recipe for dinner that night, Mike proposed that maybe it was a spice in the meal. "What?" I said. "That's absurd!" The ER staff agreed with my neurologist's diagnosis, and since the symptoms had subsided, they sent me home and said to be restful.

The very next morning, Mike and his cousin were scheduled to leave for Colorado. A large group of men from Cornerstone were going up to the mountains to have a retreat. Although the seizure had shaken us, I insisted that Mike and his cousin still go on the retreat. One of Mike's friends suggested that the seizure I'd had was Satan trying to keep Mike from going on the retreat. Although I wasn't certain that it was true, I really needed Mike to go on that retreat. He needed some godly counsel! I needed him to come back enlightened, repentant, transformed, even just a little bit and to get away from his computer! His cousin needed it too. So, Mike and his cousin left the next morning for Colorado and Scott and Linda were on call if I needed them. While they were gone, I was going to be restful. I didn't want to experience another seizure; that was frightening. Mike and his cousin came back from their retreat refreshed and inspired. Mike told me they'd been told to wash their wives in the Word. I was excited to hear this and looked forward to it, but it was never put into practice. Nothing changed. I deeply longed for Mike to become the spiritual leader in our home. He didn't seem to be ready to take on that role yet. I'd continue to be patient and pray.

In December, Mike, his cousin, and I, all got horribly sick. We all had fevers, aches, vomit and diarrhea. I had never been so sick. Mike and his cousin were sick together downstairs. I stayed upstairs with the kids. Weak as a kitten, I still tried to care for the kids and prayed they wouldn't get sick too. Thankfully, Luke and Natalie stayed healthy, but we grownups were in bad shape. After a rough night of being in and out of the bathroom and shaking from fever in my bed, Natalie woke me early in the morning to nurse. I must have only had three to four hours of sleep. I heard her crying from her crib in the other room. I sat up in bed, pushed back the covers and slowly stood up. I felt very faint, and as I approached her crib, I realized I couldn't feel my right hand. I stood in front of her crib scared and reluctant to pick her up. My left hand AND right hand were unreliable. I was unable to feel my right hand, but I could still use it. I watched my hand carefully as I lifted her out of her crib and I quickly made my way to the couch to nurse her. Luke followed us with his blocks and train. Luke sat on the floor and played as I pulled Natalie up to my breast to nurse. As she nursed, I felt my tongue go numb again. I remained calm and talked to Luke as he played. The sounds from my mouth didn't sound much like words, but rather like moans and groans. I was definitely having another seizure. I kept trying to talk through it and Luke looked at me with concern and confusion for a moment, then smiled and laughed, thinking I was trying to be funny. Thankfully, even before Natalie was finished nursing, feeling returned to my hand and tongue and I could talk normally again. I picked Luke up off the floor and got him breakfast. I nibbled on an apple and crackers and called my neurologist in Wichita. "It happened again. I had another seizure."

I told Mike about my incident. He seemed sad and burdened. Once we adults all felt better, Mike took me out, and we talked. Mike said he'd been very thoughtful and prayed with his account-ability group about what to do. He had come to the conclusion that we needed to be in a place where I could get better healthcare and help. I could tell he was sad as he said, "I think that means we either need to move to Phoenix or Wichita, what do you think?" I was ecstatic! Finally, finally, we can get out of this stinky city and move home!! I was completely overjoyed that this had been Mike's idea and suddenly wasn't sorry I'd had the seizures. Thank You LORD for seizures! But, in the car with Mike, I hid my enthu-siasm because although it was his idea, I knew he would be sad and disappointed to leave. He loved Garden City and was very successful at his job. I said, "Healthcare would be best in Phoenix, but all of our family is in Wichita. I want to move to Wichita." Mike agreed, and sympathetic to Mike's sorrow, I put my hand on his and said, "Thank you. I know this is hard for you." The rest of the car ride home I couldn't contain myself. I smiled as I looked out the window and, in my head repeatedly said, "Thank You God, thank You, thank You." I was thankful it was night time and dark, so Mike couldn't see my expression of pure joy. I was completely overjoyed; we were moving home. I was prayerful then that Mike wouldn't change his mind. Just a few days later, however, I drove to Wichita with the kids for my appointment with my neurologist and I didn't return to Garden City.

Mike stayed behind for a while, put in his two weeks' notice at his job, put the house on the market and had friends come over to help him pack up our stuff. I went to my appointment and my doctor said he wasn't surprised that I was having seizures. He said, "Most often when there is an abnormality in the brain, something there that's not supposed to be there, you'll have seizures. I'm actually surprised that you'd not had any before now." Well darnit, I thought. I'd gotten away with not needing to take daily medication for several years. I occasionally took a vitamin, when I remembered to do so, and some mild pain medication when I had headaches. But the doctor advised I start taking seizure medication, or I'd likely continue to have seizures. I was extremely disappointed, because taking the seizure medication meant I couldn't nurse Natalie anymore. I tried to wean Natalie first before I started the medication, but every night I was having tingling in my hand and face as I laid down to fall asleep. I couldn't prolong starting the medication; I needed to do it right away. So, I had to stop nursing Natalie cold turkey, which was painful for both of us. Natalie didn't like drinking from a bottle at first and had trouble digesting formula and my breasts got engorged and very painful. Stupid meds. I wanted to nurse my baby until she was a year old and not ever have to give her formula. Yuck! I moaned as I watched Natalie drink from a bottle. I didn't even get a chance to pump for her before I had to quit. I just wanted to give her the milk that my breasts were engorged with. We both liked it better, but Mama said "No way." Not while I was on seizure medication.

That New Year's Eve, my sister Ellen married her high school sweetheart and moved to Kansas City so her husband could go to medical school. Mike moved to Wichita a few months later, and for six months the four of us lived with my parents, in my childhood home. One daughter out, and another daughter moved back in. The LORD brought me home.

"Keep me safe, O God, for in you I take refuge. I said to the LORD, 'You are my Lord; apart from you I have no good thing.' LORD, you have assigned me my portion and my cup; you have made my lot secure. I will praise the LORD who counsels me; even at night my heart instructs me. I have set the LORD always before me. Because he is at my right hand, I will not be shaken. Therefore, my heart is glad and my tongue rejoices; my body also will rest secure" (Psalm 16: 1-2, 7-9).

15

I loved being back home! Mama was home a lot during the day, so we spent a lot of time together talking to each other and playing with the kids. Although she had come several times to visit, and we talked on the phone nearly every morning, I had missed Mama so much while in Garden City. The additional help I got from Mama and Dad in Wichita was wonderful, and I felt like I could be a better, more available parent. Luke and Natalie were also developing closer relationships with their grandparents. Also, while we lived with Mama and Dad, Mike and I were able to save money to have a considerable down payment ready for a house of our own someday. I thought living with my parents was a huge blessing, and I was very thankful they were so patient with us, generous, hospitable, sacrificial and loving.

I loved living with Mama and Dad, and the kids seemed to as well, but it was hard on Mike. Mike took a lower-paying job when we'd moved to Wichita, and he felt like he was a failure for not being able to provide a place to live for his own family. My parents loved him, but he felt out of place living in their home. Often after dinner, we all congregated in the family room. Mama and Dad had a wide variety of children's books they'd saved from our childhood, and lots of toys for Luke and Natalie to play with in the family room. Mike often played his game on his computer in the corner, while the rest of us talked to one another, read books to the kids and played with them. Mike and I had my sisters' old bedroom to ourselves. It was our own space in the house. We had hard conversations about money, and how close are we to having our own place? And we watched TV. Living with my parents also afforded Mike and me more occasions to have date nights. We went out together to have dinner and reconnected with old friends. We returned to Asbury church for Sunday morning services, but so much had changed since we'd been away. Many of the couples we'd grown to know and love had moved on to other churches or cities. The pastor moved on too. Asbury didn't feel like our home church anymore. We would begin looking for another church.

After having a seizure, I was suspended from driving until I'd been one-year seizure free. So, in the meantime, Mike sold my car, and Mama became my driver. Mama drove me to doctor's appointments and therapy. I started to attend both physical and occupational therapy again. Living back home, and having extra help from my parents, allowed me to better care for myself and my health. I had opportunity for better healthcare in Wichita, so took advantage. I returned to my favorite therapist, even though her specialty was pediatrics, to get some therapy help from her. I went once a week and loved seeing her again. My pregnancies had taken an extra toll on my body and my gait was worse. I wanted to strengthen my hip and improve my walk even just a little bit, so I wouldn't be in pain or cause further damage to my body. I did occupational therapy too because my arm and hand were causing me pain at night and gave me a nagging, constant discomfort throughout the day. And over the years, the muscles in my arm had atrophied a lot. My arm was very skinny and awkward, and I often felt uncomfortable wearing short-sleeved shirts. I wasn't sure that I'd regain any use of my hand; I had just wanted to alleviate pain in my arm and hoped to not lose more muscle or motion than I already had. Each time I went to therapy or to an appointment, the kids had nature walks with Granny. I was thrilled that Mama was imparting upon them a love for nature and that they were getting some valuable quality time with Mama. Therapy was great.

Both Mama and Dad love to explore and hike. They both have a deep appreciation for nature and all of God's creation. In July of 2011, Mama and Dad rented a cabin in Colorado for us to go on a family vacation all together. Mama, Dad, myself, Luke, Natalie, Ellen, Paul (Ellen's husband) and Angie all went to the mountains together. Mike didn't have vacation time so stayed behind alone at Mama and Dad's house. I didn't mean to punish Mike or disregard his feelings, the way he often had mine; I just thought it wouldn't make much difference to him whether we were there or not. Mike often neglected the kids and me, and he was gruff. The kids hid from him nearly every time he came back to Mama and Dad's from work. It made me feel sad and angry that the kids didn't feel loved and safe with their dad. In hindsight, we probably should not have gone without him, but it was good to get away.

When my parents vacation someplace, they don't sleep in and relax; they get up early, plan a full day of activity and head out to explore. My parents rented backpacks for the kids to ride in as we hiked. Mama, Ellen and Paul took turns carrying Luke and Natalie on their backs. We hiked every day for several hours. I brought and wore my custom-made brace for my left leg. It was uncomfortable but stabilized my ankle and leg to help me be able to walk further distances than I would have been able to walk without it. Dad and I walked behind the rest of the pack at my pace. Mama, Luke, Natalie, Paul, Ellen and Angie walked far ahead of us, and much farther. I brought my DSLR camera along everywhere on our trip and stopped to take photos each time I needed a break. I was so happy to be around so much beauty, and to have been strong enough to hike over rocks, hills, uneven ground and through creeks with Dad every day. It was immensely refreshing to be outdoors and fulfilling to be with my family sharing some adventures together. Even after a long day in the mountains each day, and I'd tucked the kids in for bed, all us grownups played games together late into the night. I loved it. The kids really liked spending time with my family too. Each night, Luke requested that we make popcorn to share together. It wasn't until the third night that we realized Luke wasn't actually eating any of the popcorn; he only requested it because he liked having us all together.

I wished I could have kept up with the rest of my family to be able to experience more with them and to see some of the amazing things they saw, but I couldn't have walked as far as they did. But the longer further hikes with the rest of my family allowed my kids to bond even closer to my sisters, their uncle and to their dear Granny. Since I'd been married to Mike, moved to Garden City and had children, I'd grown apart from my sisters, and I missed them. Especially when Mike was distant and I was lonely in Garden, I needed their love and support. It was important to me that my kids and I were close to them now.

Late one night, Ellen and I stayed up together long after the others had gone to bed. I had just got off the phone with Mike, and we'd had a fight. I was visibly agitated when I got off the phone with him, and Ellen urged me to talk about it. I hesitated to be vulnerable with my sister. Ellen was my *younger* sister. It was my job as the older sister to comfort *her*. I felt a little embarrassed but shared my heartache with Ellen and how Mike and I had grown apart; I didn't know how to connect with him, the kids were afraid of him, and I often was too. "I know I should miss him, but I don't. It's a relief to be away from him." Ellen patiently listened, held me as I cried and comforted me. "Ellen, Garden City was awful, Mike and I were awful; I felt trapped for three years! I'm with family now, and I'm better. But I don't think Mike and I are better." Ellen and I were up together well past midnight when Ellen finally said, "We need to go to bed. We're going to help you, Meg. You're not in this alone." I embraced my sister and had never felt so thankful for her love and support.

First thing the next morning, Ellen told everyone we needed to have a family meeting. I tried to dissuade Ellen from drawing attention to me and my problems, but Ellen said they were going to help. I felt embarrassed and sat mostly silent as my sister repeated what I'd said to her the night before. Luke and Natalie, oblivious to what we were discussing, were playing together on the floor with a bag full of toys. Oh, how I deeply loved my children. I was watching them play when Mama said, "Meg, are you wanting a divorce?" I thought of Luke and Natalie, the commitment I'd made to Mike to stay married through "better or worse," and said, "No Mama, I think I still love Mike, but I need your help." I wasn't sure what that help looked like, but I knew I just needed their undying support, their prayer, for them to hold Mike to account, and me too. They all made me promise to talk to Mike when we'd be back home. I uncertainly said, "Ok, I promise." For the remainder of our trip we continued to hike, and I took hundreds more pictures. On our last day, I was relieved to leave, get back home and into our regular routine, but I wasn't looking forward to having a talk with Mike.

Before I lost my nerve, I pulled Mike aside as soon as we returned home and told him we needed to talk. Mama and Dad watched the kids while Mike and I went out to dinner together and I told him how I'd been feeling wounded for a long time. My family's support had given me confidence and courage to talk honestly with my husband. I'd been too cowardly and tired to confront him before. When we'd lived in Garden City it didn't seem to do any good, and he would wound me deeply with his words and actions. At first, Mike accused me of attacking him, but when I didn't back down, he admitted that he'd felt unhappy living in my parents' house and wished we could have a place of our own. He didn't feel needed or wanted in my parents' home. I sympathized and agreed we needed a place of our own. So, we looked at affordable apartments to move in to.

Mike and I moved out of my parents' house and into an apartment nearby, just two weeks later. I was in charge of cleaning and cooking and caring for my kids by myself again. I was exhausted each day by mid-afternoon and napped with the kids, but we were all functioning better as a family. However, it was challenging for me to care for little miss Natalie on my own. Unlike Luke, Natalie had grown accustomed to having several other adults diaper her, change her clothes, and hold her as a baby on a daily basis. She did not learn to adjust to me. She was used to having many able-bodied adults with two working hands and legs to care for her. It was a bit of a nightmare caring for Natalie each day by myself. She didn't sit still during diaper changes and would fling herself backwards. I cried in frustration as she wiggled and squirmed, and I got impatient with her. Because I couldn't change her diaper and hold her still at the same time with just one arm, I used my right hand to diaper her, and I firmly put my right foot on her tummy to hold her still. The first time I did that she looked scared and screamed. I wasn't hurting her, but she didn't like that one bit. I didn't know what else to do; I wasn't about to let my one-year-old run around without a diaper on! Natalie would have to get used to having my foot hold her squirmy body in place.

Natalie was very sweet and beautiful but could be a handful. As Luke got a little older, he started to get naughty too; they were runners and would run away from me as soon as we got outside. I couldn't manage them myself outside of the apartment, so unless another adult was with me to help out, Luke, Natalie and I stayed inside. At night, when Mike was home, we were able to walk together around the pond at our apartment to feed the ducks and turtles. The kids loved that. Although Mike wanted better than an apartment for our family, Mike was clearly more relaxed once we were in our own place. We grew tighter as a family. It was Luke and Natalie's relationship and bond that truly blossomed while we were on our own. They were developing a stronger love and dependence on one another. Big brother Luke so naturally and protectively held Natalie's hand as we walked around the pond or ventured out to a busy park, or he just sat close beside her on the couch as they quietly watched TV. Both kiddos sucked their middle two fingers on their left hands when they were tired, nervous or shy. They almost always instinctively did it at the same time. Luke and Natalie shared a room together, played together and they functioned better together than they did when they were apart. When we were out, many people mistook them for twins. Besides twins, I'd never seen two siblings so close and dependent upon each other for love, comfort, support and friendship. God knew exactly what He was doing when He gave us Natalie so soon after Luke. Luke needed Natalie and Natalie needed Luke, and they would need each other for things to come.

It was often just the four of us at night or on weekends, when Mike was home from work, and the kids and I spent a lot of time together alone, but the kids and I still saw Mama a lot throughout the week during the day.

I was eight months seizure-free by the end of the summer; just a few more months before I could drive again. I'd gained some independence once we'd moved into our apartment, and it wouldn't be much longer before I would be able to drive myself to therapy. In the meantime, Mama continued to drive me and brought the kids along. Even in the hot summer sun, Mama spent time with Luke and Natalie outdoors. They continued to walk the trails of the nearby nature parks, while I exercised indoors.

I was afraid to admit it to my therapists because I had been doing so well, but I had started to have unbearable pain in my left bicep and shoulder. I thought to myself, "Good grief, what now?" I wanted to ignore it, and hoped it would go away on its own, but the longer I waited to do something about it the more aggravating the pain was. My therapists tried each week to alleviate the pain with stretching and other techniques. I also went to a massage therapist, and even to a chiropractor. The pain would lessen for a short while, but return even angrier than before. After weeks of aches and pains, my therapist ordered an x-ray and an MRI of my shoulder. The MRI for my shoulder was much faster and easier than any of the scans I'd had of my head. I got to wear headphones and listen to music.

The MRI revealed that I had avascular necrosis on my left

shoulder and I'd need surgery to correct the problem. My shoulder surgeon said taking steroids at age sixteen, and then more recently in 2007, was likely the cause of the avascular necrosis of my shoulder. Ugh, stupid steroids. So, it seemed, the steroids had very annoying side effects both short term *and* long term, but I've been told they were a necessary evil. I could have had more swelling and bleeding without them.

I had shoulder surgery in August 2011 to clear away the damage to my shoulder and to keep the necrosis from spreading. My bone was so soft that they had to be very careful when scraping and cleaning my bone. My shoulder would be much better for a while, but my surgeon predicted I'd need to come back in five years to have a shoulder replacement. I had some shoulder pain, post-surgery for several weeks, and slept on the couch a lot. I couldn't be a mom to my kiddos, but Mike took some time off work and was full-time dad to Luke and Natalie for several days. He took good care of me and helped me change the ice for my shoulder, helped me get up to use the restroom and brought me food to eat. I was immensely grateful for his selfless love and support. I was too sleepy and sore to do anything for myself. I needed him and loved him more sincerely for coming to my rescue.

I had to wear my arm in a sling for several weeks and go to therapy for my shoulder, exclusively, for several months. Physical therapy, and occupational therapy for my left side, were put on hold. I was extremely frustrated, because I was enjoying therapy for my leg and my core, and was starting to see results. The shoulder surgery was a setback. I was so tired of delaying my recovery and the healing of my left side! I had been through so much already, I just wanted my suffering to be finished. I wanted to be allowed to heal what was broken and never break again.

I was tired of struggling and fighting. I wanted more progress and victories rather than more brokenness and heartache. I was such a mess. This hemangioma mess was too much. It caused so many problems.

Although through my trials I'd experienced great growth in my faith and in my relationship with the LORD, I pleaded and begged the LORD that the hemangioma mess be my burden, and my burden alone. Hemangiomas can be inherited or develop spontaneously. I chose to believe and trust that mine had been a spontaneous occurrence because no one else in my large family had any history of bleeds. In good faith, trusting the LORD that the hemangiomas were not hereditary, Mike and I decided to have children; but that decision was not made lightly. I believed I was finally on the road to healing, and I needed it to be once and for all. No more bleeds, no more setbacks. No one else afflicted with the mess the hemangiomas had caused me.

My youngest sister Angie, however, started having some alarming and concerning headaches. She said her head hurt so bad, it hurt to lay down on a pillow. Lots of people have migraines without anything seriously wrong with their head, but because of my history, Dr. Kim advised that Angie have an MRI just to make sure something more serious wasn't occurring. I lost sleep praying for Angie. Dad had migraines in young adulthood, maybe it's just a coincidence. Or maybe Dad has hemangiomas, that's why he had migraines, and he passed them to us! I nearly drove myself mad fretting about the "What ifs" and was scared for my sister. "Please LORD, tell me these are just mine and that Ang is ok. Give me rest and peace. Tell me she's ok." I didn't get any such word from the LORD, except that He asked me to trust Him. "I don't like that answer, LORD!"

I went with Angie to her MRI and placed my hand on her leg as I prayed for her. She didn't ask me to, she didn't need me to, but *I* needed to. I shook and perspired as I prayed over my sister. "Please no, LORD, please no." Once Angie received her results from the MRI, she called me and asked me to meet her at Mama and Dad's to tell me in person. I thought, "That can't be good." Once at Mama and Dad's, Angie and I went to the backyard and she said very matter of fact, "So, I do have hemangiomas in my brain. I have four of them, and the doctor says one of them has a "slow leak," which caused only some facial weakness. It explained why Angie had often talked out of the side of her mouth. Ellen and I suddenly felt really bad for making fun of her for it all those years. Angie said, "Otherwise I'm fine." I shouted some curse words, embraced my sister, started to sob and said, "I'm so sorry Angie." She clearly was disappointed, but was of sober mind and calmly went back inside while I stayed outside a little longer to cry. Once Angie had gone inside, I fell to the ground. I pulled at the grass, shouted to the heavens and cursed at God. Never before had I been so angry! "These were supposed to be mine to bear, no one else's. This cannot be part of Your good and "perfect" plan (I said sarcastically and mocking.) Why would You allow this? They're hereditary? God, You gave me children! Must I live in fear and with the guilt that they could have these nasty beasts too? Either Mama or Dad have these, my aunts, uncles, cousins, my cousin's children, and my grandma could have these too? So much pain, so much sorrow could lie ahead. No God, no! I hate You right now, I hate You!" The Holy Spirit tried to comfort me and speak to me and kept saying "Trust me." I covered my face and screamed, "No, I don't! Leave me." I seethed in anger, and just as I'd asked Him to, I felt as though the Spirit left me alone to be angry for a while. I grieved for my children and worried for my extended family. I had been trusting Him with *my* life, but I needed to learn to trust God with my family's lives also, as He commanded me to do.

I needed to take care of me, listen to God's direction for my life, and pray that my family would submit to the LORD's will and that He would nurture them and equip them should they experience devastating bleeds as I had. I made a vow that I'd be an avid support to them if it came to that. I would set an example to continue to press on and not give up on God or themselves.

By November 2011, my shoulder had finally improved enough that I resumed therapy for my leg. Although I'd missed out on several months of therapy while trying to revive my shoulder, my physical therapist was pleased with the progress I was making. I was more determined than ever before and it showed. My gait was beginning to look better and both my therapist and I were excited to see hard work paying off. However, one morning in December, Mama dropped me off at therapy, I walked into the therapy gym and before I sat down on the mat, my therapist said, "What happened?" I was confused. "What? What are you talking about?" She said, "Something's not right. Your walk looks worse today." I thought, whatever, I'm fine. But my therapist sat me down and tested my strength then said, "Yes, you're definitely weaker today. Are you tired? Have you had any other symptoms?" I told her I'd had some headaches earlier in the week but I assured her that otherwise I felt fine. And yet, my therapist was concerned enough that she called my family doctor while I was at therapy with her and convinced my doctor to order an MRI. Earlier in the week, I thought I'd maybe overexerted myself with the can opener while opening a can of beans, but I felt perfectly fine! I hadn't noticed any additional weakness. Did she think I was having a bleed? No way! She couldn't convince me that something was wrong. Maybe I was just tired; I often didn't sleep well. But Jan was a skilled, experienced therapist, and my friend, so I trusted her judgment and didn't dismiss her gut feeling.

Mike and I weren't terribly worried, and Mike didn't think I needed to have an MRI if I wasn't feeling bad, but Mama was distressed by my therapist's concern and began praying. Eventually I agreed to have an MRI and Mama drove me. I was still at peace, and not at all worried. I was simply undergoing the test to put Mama and my therapist's mind at ease. I had since left Dr. Shah's office as a patient. I had long outgrown the need for a pediatric neurologist and felt silly going every six months to sit on a lion-shaped exam table, with cartoons on the wall and a crate of toys and children's books in the corner. I hadn't yet found another neurologist to go to, so I found a neurosurgeon in Wichita to read the results of my MRI. It was someone Angie had been referred to when it was discovered that she had cavernous malformations too. They of course told her that surgery was unnecessary, and they'd just keep a close eye on hers. The neurosurgeon I met with had actually been a fellow of Dr. Spetzler's! My brain was in the very best hands in Wichita! Sadly, it turned out that I *did* have a bleed! Although the mass that had been resected in 2007 was still stable, the mass in the left hemisphere of my brain had bled for a second time. I was confused, "If the mass on the left side of my brain bled, why did I have symptoms on my left, and not on the right?" The neurosurgeon said, "Yes, that is unusual, but sometimes damage to the brain, no matter where it is, can instead affect your body where it's already weakened." That didn't seem at all logical to me, but my belief was that it was by God's grace that my right side was not also debilitated. I would be helpless without function of both my left *and* right side!

The neurosurgeon, Dr. Spetzler's fellow, advised that I have surgery to remove the mass, but he wanted to get a better look at the mass to determine the urgency with which we'd need to address the matter of surgery. He said it's difficult to tell on an MRI if the mass is arterial or venous. I thought we were already certain that it was venous, but Dr. Sam said if it was arterial, it would be more serious and need to be addressed immediately. So, Dr. Sam ordered an angiogram to determine the nature of my mass. I fought him on it, but he insisted. In the days following, between my appointment with Dr. Sam and my scheduled angiogram, I was beginning to feel excessively tired. I was feeling the effects of the bleed. No matter what type of mass it was, it was decided that I was going to have surgery; so, I tried to prepare for the trip. I went to Target, and a few other clothing stores, to buy myself some sweatpants and comfy tees to wear while in recovery. I tried on clothes, compared prices between stores, and I was out for a couple hours, shopping. When I arrived back at our apartment, my brain felt like it was on fire, I collapsed on the couch while Mike watched TV, and I fell asleep. I had pushed myself too hard. Getting through the day, trying to care for my three-year-old son and twenty-month-old daughter, was scary exhausting. Each night, I went to bed when the kids did, and slept until they woke up. I napped when they did, and still dragged myself around.

I was very nervous when I went in for the angiogram. The kids stayed with Granny, while Mike and I went to the hospital. I'd never had an angiogram, and it sounded like it was going to be awful. I'd be awake for the test, but they offered to give me a little sedation since I was so nervous, and I couldn't keep my left arm and leg from twitching. I readily accepted the small dosage of anti-anxiety medication, and was prepped for the test. I laid down on a cold, hard table, staring up at the ceiling. They injected iodine dye into the blood vessels in my neck and head to get images of my arteries. I could feel the dye as it was injected into different areas of my neck and head. It was alarmingly warm, and uncomfortable. As they repeatedly injected the dye, they'd inform me where they were taking each picture as they took them and would tell me where I should feel the dye. As they injected, they asked me to confirm that I indeed felt the dye injected into the area that they said I would. I said," Yes, yes," but I felt one of the injections in a different area than they said I'd feel it, and it made the right side of my neck burn with excruciating pain! I screamed. "Ouch, no, wrong spot!" I held my neck in my right hand as it continued to burn and throb in pain. They stopped the test immediately, and I could hear technicians talking quietly to one another, but I couldn't understand what they were saying. A nurse came to my side, and I said, "What's going on? What happened?" She said, "Just relax; they'll come in and talk to you in a moment." From the technician's booth, I heard the words "Serious" and "ICU." What did they do to me? Still laying on the table, waiting for word from anyone about what was going on, I stared at the ceiling and said to the LORD, "God, I'm scared. What's happening? Am I dying?" The LORD responded, "This is the beginning of the end." Oh God, I *am* dying! I said, "Ok LORD, take me home. I'm ready." Then I immediately thought of my kids and that I couldn't bear to leave them behind. "No, no LORD, I take it back, I'm not ready to go home. I want to raise my children, watch them grow and learn, see them graduate high school, get married, maybe have their own children. I want to be a part of all that. I don't want to go home yet. But, if it's my time, please prepare my heart and my soul for eternity. Help me to be at peace and accept the end of my life." I tried to mean it, but I was in anguish and grieving the thought of not being there for Luke and Natalie. I couldn't die; not yet. Finally, a doctor and a nurse came to discuss with me what had happened, and what they were going to do with me. They said I had a dissection (small tear) in an artery in my neck. It was unclear if it had happened during the test, or if it was already there. They said they'd put me in ICU so I could rest and let it heal on its own. I had to be extra careful with my head and neck. Mike and I waited in the dark, outside the angiogram exam room, and waited for a room to be ready for me in the ICU. I told Mike about the word I heard from the LORD while waiting in the exam room, and we both began to cry. Mike prayed, and I asked him to call our pastor to come to the hospital to be with us. I suppose I wanted him there to usher me into heaven.

By the time Pastor Aaron arrived at the hospital, I had been put in a room, and a very handsome nurse tried to assist me with a bed pan, to which I kindly requested a female nurse to help me with instead. I had trouble staying coherent and awake, but when Pastor Aaron came to my bedside, I mustered all my energy to stay awake and alert. He listened carefully and thoughtfully as I told him about the exam gone awry and the word I'd received from the LORD. I said, "Aaron, I'm not ready to leave my kids." Aaron said, "I think your word could be interpreted two ways: that your life is truly coming to an end, or that your *suffering* is coming to an end!" He said, "I know I can be overly optimistic, but I have no check in my heart when I say I truly believe the LORD meant that this is the beginning of the end of your physical fight with this stuff!" He was very enthusiastic and excited. He prayed over me for strength and peace and thanked the LORD for the word He had given me. It was the beginning of the end of the turmoil the hemangiomas had caused me. I wanted to believe it and receive it. "LORD, if this is the interpretation of Your word for me, help me to accept it, and not doubt it."

I stayed in the hospital for a few days and nights and had lots of time to think and pray. I didn't do a lot of reading or writing, because it made my neck burn to position my head that way. I hated being away from my kids. I'd never been away from Natalie for more than a few hours at a time, and hadn't been away from Luke since Dream Street. Mama brought the kids to see me but couldn't contain their restlessness by herself, so they didn't stay long. Dad and Angie came to see me and friends from church too. Friends came to sit with me and read while I slept, others brought flowers or a gift, gave me a hug and left. My friend Nancy, who came from my church, read scripture to me to encourage me and give me hope, and she anointed my head with oil as she prayed for me. Each of them agreed with Aaron's interpretation of the word the LORD had given me, that it was the beginning of the end of my suffering.

Dr. Sam came in to see me the morning of my departure from the hospital. He reported that the angiogram showed that my mass was venous rather than arterial. I thought to myself and wanted to say, "Yeah, I already knew that!" Instead I said, "Ok, that's good, right?" He said, "Yes, it's serious, but not as serious as an arterial mass would be." We discussed continued rest, so my artery could finish healing, and Dr. Sam said he'd be contacting Dr. Spetzler and sharing all my information with him in pursuit of a second brain surgery. The word from the LORD I'd heard and didn't wanted to receive in 2007, that my first brain surgery would not be my last, was confirmed.

"Peace I leave with you; my peace I give you. I do not give as the world gives. Do not let your hearts be troubled and do not be afraid" (John 14:27).

"Have I not commanded you? Be strong and courageous. Do not be afraid; do not be discouraged, for the LORD your God will be with you wherever you go" (Joshua 1:9).

I was in sorry shape when I left the hospital. My neck burned, and my brain had been damaged again, from the bleed. I was too tired to function. Unfortunately, I needed full-time help, caring for Luke and Natalie. I felt sad for Mike. We had only lived in our apartment together for six months; he was functioning better, and happier in our own place. But, out of necessity, we had to pack up and move back in with my parents. Mama and Dad welcomed us back with open arms and admitted they'd missed the kids. Mama pushed me to be available to my kids as often as I could, but I slept a lot. Mama got up with the kids each morning to help them get dressed and eat breakfast, so I could get a little extra sleep. However, I set an alarm each morning so I wouldn't sleep too long. I too wanted to be available for my kids. I sat downstairs with them to read to them and play with them. Mama expected nothing more of me, and I'm eternally grateful to her for that. Doctors said I needed to rest for six weeks to recover from my dissection, before having brain surgery. In the meantime, during my afternoon rest, I often overheard Mike on the phone impatiently trying to get my brain surgery scheduled. It was like pulling teeth to get a date set, but Mike wouldn't let up. He was fighting for me, and called every day. Turns out there was a misunderstanding with insurance, Mike got to the bottom of it, figured it out, and thanks to Mike's persistence, my surgery date was scheduled for February 28th, 2012. Although I was ready for it to be over, I was so anxious about having brain surgery again. The recovery process from the first surgery was a nightmare, and I dreaded going through that again. And this time around, I had kids to care for! I knew I had to do it, but I didn't *want* to do it. I cried in anguish with my friend, Susie. "Susie, why did the LORD give me kids?" She said, "Well, because of them, you'll do what it takes to fight through this." I said, "Exactly; why did the LORD give me kids?!" The fellows at Dr. Spetzler's office understood my anxiety concerning another surgery. They told me however, that the surgery would be much less invasive than my first, less risky to operate and that I'd have a smoother recovery. The cavernous malformation in the left hemisphere of my brain was just above my left ear, and much closer to the surface of my skull. The pain likely wouldn't be as bad, I wouldn't need to take steroids, and would likely be home in less than a week. For some reason I just had a very bad feeling about this surgery. I had a feeling it wasn't going to be as easy as they made it sound. I couldn't shake the feeling, and I was afraid.

A group from our church invited us to the church office to lay hands on Mike and me, to pray.

They prayed for the full restoration of my body, for my suffering to come to an end, for the LORD to comfort us, give us peace and be with us. I prayed, "LORD, go before us, be with us and be behind us."

"God said, 'My presence will go with you. I'll see the journey to the end.' Moses said, 'If your presence doesn't take the lead here, call this trip off right now'" (Exodus 33:14-15 MSG).

My body trembled as they prayed. I was feeling very anxious, I couldn't keep my body still and relax. Luke and Natalie were playing in the nursery within earshot, but we couldn't see them. We all had our heads bowed as person after person prayed for healing, for peace and for strength; then my sweet daughter (who was not quite two years old) came out of the nursery and squeezed through the circle of people surrounding me in prayer, to get to me. She was confused, and didn't know what was happening, but she knew she wanted to be with her mama. I picked her up and put her on my lap. She squirmed and whined that she wanted to go home. I softly said, "Shh, Natty," and began to rub her arm gently. Within a few moments, she relaxed her body, put her fingers in her mouth to self-soothe and leaned into me. Every once in a while, she looked up at me with her sweet baby blue eyes, and I'd smile at her. My daughter's tenderness and need for me to comfort her and hold her was a great comfort to *me*. Tears ran down my cheeks as I squeezed her, and whispered, "I love you, my sweet girl."

"Ok LORD, I can do this for Luke and Natalie." Yes, I was going to fight and be strong so I could come back to my babies. I loved Luke and Natalie more than anything in the world. I needed to be brave and do this for them.

My college girlfriends came over to the house to pray for me too. We sat together on my bed and held hands as they each prayed. I said goodbye to each of my friends, and Becca said, "We'll see you again soon." Tears slid down my friend Joy's cheeks as I looked at her smiled and I said, "I hope so."

For several nights, leading up to surgery, I struggled to sleep. I tossed and turned in the bed, couldn't find a comfortable position to rest and couldn't shut off my mind. Night after night, I felt a pressing need to write "goodbye" letters to my husband and to each of my kids, but I couldn't bring myself to do it. It was too hard to face. I was scared of surgery, and didn't deny the possibility that I might die, but somehow writing letters felt like an admission of defeat, an acceptance of my end. My kindle was full of book samples concerning the afterlife and heaven. Although I was more curious, and wanted to be better "prepared," I was too tired, in a lot of pain, and otherwise couldn't bring myself to read about that either. I just hoped and prayed that I'd be back home again with all my family.

The night before we left for Phoenix, I tucked my sweet babies into bed, not knowing when or if I'd see them again. Mama, Ellen and I sat together in the dark in the living room of Mama and Dad's house. We talked, we prayed, and we cried. We could have sat there together all night, and part of me wanted to, but eventually, Mama said it was time for all of us to get up to bed; I had an early morning. Before I changed and got into bed, I went into my kids' room and kissed each of their foreheads as they slept. "I love you so very much." I choked back sobs as I said, "Oh LORD, please bring me back to my sweet babies." Ellen grabbed me, hugged me firmly, and said, "You *will* come home to them." Ellen sounded so sure. But, the LORD hadn't given me any such promise this time. The word He gave me in 2007 was that I'd be a wife and mother first, and I was able to cling to that. The word I'd received this time was "This is the beginning of the end." Everyone seemed certain that the LORD was telling me that my journey of suffering from these hemangiomas was nearly over, but I still wasn't sure. I wasn't yet convinced. The LORD hadn't validated that or given me any other word to cling to. I didn't get much sleep that night as I thought about our flight to Phoenix and the upcoming surgery. My brain and neck burned in pain the longer I was awake, so it became increasingly harder to sleep as the night wore on.

Even so, it felt like a very short night. We got up the next morning when the sky was still dark and left before the kids ever woke up. I hated leaving Luke and Natalie behind, not knowing what was going to happen to me. Luke had just turned three, and Natalie wasn't yet two. They were so young and didn't understand what was happening. I'm not even sure that they knew anything was wrong. They were still well cared for, loved and felt safe. They would be in Mama's very capable hands while we were gone. While my babies still slumbered, Mike, Dad and I headed to Phoenix to get reacquainted with Dr. Spetzler.

The few days leading up to surgery are a bit of a blur. Mike, Dad and my journal have helped me fill in some of the blanks. We arrived in Phoenix on Sunday afternoon. We arrived ahead of our check-in time, so waited around for a room to open up at the extended-stay hotel. Their waiting room didn't look too comfortable or inviting, so we waited outside. I was exhausted and very hungry. I laid on a sun chair with my eyes closed, while Mike and Dad discussed dining options for lunch. We were carless at the hotel, so unless we were willing to walk, we were going hungry. I'd grown so hungry that I felt sick. Mike searched on his phone for restaurant locations and found a Subway not far from the hotel. He took Dad's and my orders and started walking. I got quite testy while we waited for Mike to return. It was well past lunch time by the time he returned, and we ate lunch. He said he ended up having to walk a lot farther than he anticipated.

Once we were able to check into our rooms, I threw myself on the bed and took a three-hour nap. I'm not sure what occurred after that. We killed some time before getting back to bed. We wandered, connected with people back home, ate dinner somewhere and got a good night's sleep before my visit with Dr. Spetzler.

The next morning, before meeting with Dr. Spetzler, Mike, Dad and I went out for breakfast. I had the most delicious eggwhite omelet with spinach, cheese, mushrooms, peppers and tomatoes. Yum! Soon after breakfast, we went to the Barrow Institute for my appointment with Dr. Spetzler. My full stomach churned and my left leg and arm were stiff as we waited to see Dr. Spetzler. I was anxious and nervous to see him again. I'd hoped I would never have need to see him again, yet there I was, waiting to talk to Dr. Spetzler about my second brain surgery. I wondered if he'd remember us. It had been nearly five years since we'd seen him. Dr. Spetzler entered the room, and Dad reminded him of each of our names; but he didn't need to. Dr. Spetzler greeted each of us as if he'd seen us recently. It was clear that Spetzler remembered us. Just as before, Dr. Spetzler shared with us the process of the procedure. This time I knew what he was talking about, since I'd been through it before. I would have a resection of yet another one of my cavernous malformations. Then Spetzler said, "Any questions?" I thought to myself, "Oh dear, Mike, please be serious." However, it was Dad who asked a question that I wished he wouldn't have. The question had long lingered in my mind, but I didn't want to know the answer. Dad said, "We've recently discovered that Angela, Megan's sister, also has hemangiomas." I thought to myself, "Oh Dad, please don't." But Dad continued, "So, we know now that either myself or Cate have hemangiomas too, correct?" Dr. Spetzler quietly nodded. Dad said, "Megan has two children…" Although I was curious myself, I wanted to scream at Dad, "Stop!" But Dad finished, "What is the likelihood that Megan's children will have hemangiomas too?" Dr. Spetzler took pause, looked at me and surely could see the fear and anguish in my gaze. He seemed reluctant to answer but said, "One or both will likely have them too." I kept my composure until Dr. Spetzler left the room, then yelled at Dad for even asking, and cried. I didn't want to know! I already struggled with guilt and fear concerning the possibility that Luke and Natalie might suffer the same fate as me. To know the probability was 50/50 was hard to hear. "Oh LORD, let them be hemangioma-free! Please!" I had been emotional after the appointment and exhausted myself. I took another long nap after lunch. By the time I was up and around again, the sun was setting and Mike's dad, Tim, had arrived in Phoenix. We walked to the Walgreens across the street from our hotel, to watch for Tim. He rented a little black car. I was so relieved that we'd have a car for the night and would not have to walk to dinner. I was weary of walking. We waited on the corner, watching for Tim, as the sky grew darker and darker. It was getting late, and the dinner hour had come and gone. I was getting quite frustrated with these men. Then Dad spotted a black car in the flow of traffic that didn't have its lights on. He laughed as he said, "You s'pose that's your dad, Mike?" When the little black car with the lights off pulled into the Walgreens parking lot, we all laughed. It *was* Tim.

We all piled into the car, Mike told his dad to turn the car lights on, and we drove in search of a place to eat. Tim said, "Megan, what sounds good?" "Seafood!" It took us a while to find, but we ate a late dinner at Joe's Crab Shack in Phoenix. Another very tasty meal. It would be the last thing I could eat before surgery first thing in the morning. We left the restaurant and headed in the direction of the hotel. Tim said, "Anything you want to do before you go under the knife tomorrow?" I was teasing when I said, "Yeah, shopping for clothes!" Even though I was kidding, Tim then went in search of a store to take me shopping. He was bound and determined to take me shopping. However, it was so late at night by the time we left the restaurant that everything was closed. I laughed and said, "That's Ok. You can always take me any time after surgery." I thought it was very sweet that he tried. Before I went to bed that night, I sent an email to all my friends and family. I asked them to think of me, and please pray for me.

Dear friends and family,

I'm ready to be done with my pain and troubles from this mass, but I'm yet frightened, wondering what recovery will be like. I anticipate I'll be here for a shorter time than earlier expected, but that will be better known as the week progresses.

Please join me in praying against the risks of surgery and the possibility of paralysis, trouble with speech, and right-sided numbness. I turned to Colossians 4 in my devotions last Friday afternoon: "Continue earnestly in prayer, being vigilant in it with thanksgiving, meanwhile praying also for us that God will open to us a door for the Word to speak the mystery of Christ, for while I also am in chains, that I may make it manifest as I ought to speak." Please pray this for me in the duration of my stay in Phoenix and my recovery. The entire journey and battle is worth the suffering even to see just one soul come to know Christ as their Lord and Savior, as He is mine. I love you and dearly miss my sweet babies. This is the first time I will have been away from Natalie for more than 2 days. Fortunately, they are very comfortable with my mama and seem to be doing very well without me, but I am coming back!!! :)

Blessings and Thanks to you all,
Megan

Especially after seeing and visiting with Dr. Spetzler, I was beginning to gain confidence that I would survive surgery and return home. And I wanted my attitude to be different than what it was the first time I had surgery. With my first surgery I was always in survival mode simply enduring the trial and wishing it was over. With this second surgery I had been afforded an opportunity to respond differently to my pain and suffering. Since my first surgery, I'd grown in the LORD and in my understanding of suffering. I was going to *enlist* this trial rather than simply endure it and use this time to glorify God; I aimed to somehow share the good news of His salvation and grace with others.

Although I couldn't completely dismiss the nagging feeling that something awful was ahead, by the time they had prepped me for surgery, I felt more at ease and ready to go. Mike and Dad prayed for me before I disappeared into the OR.

Dr. Spetzler and his team again fit me into the 3-pin Mayfield holder, marked the area on my scalp where they'd make the incision, trimmed my hair around it, then applied a local anesthetic to the area and proceeded to make the incision. They elevated the muscle off the bone, a bur drill was used to create a circular bone flap which they set on the back table. Ha! My dura was tacked up to the bone, then they cut through my dura. For some reason, each time I read about cutting through my dura, I want to grip my head and I think "Ouch!" Once they'd cut through my dura, my brain was exposed. Dr. Spetzler was in my brain and ready to operate. As he had in 2007 with my first craniotomy, Dr. Spetzler used a microscope and wand guidance for the resection of my cavernoma/cavernous malformation/hemangioma/my beast. They had said that this surgery was much less invasive than my first and the risk for further damage was minimal; this cavernoma was much closer to the surface. But as I read through my surgery notes, I realize that this surgery was very delicate in nature also. Notes say the cavernoma was "very large" with blood around it and a large vein close by that Dr. Spetzler carefully navigated around. He removed my beast in two large pieces and sent it off for analysis. The beast was no longer my problem. Hallelujah! Another one bites the dust! Doctors put everything back in place, stitched me up, took me out of the Mayfield holder, and sent me off to the ICU to rest and recover.

When I woke up again in the ICU, I felt great! I thought to myself, "Huh, that's not what I expected." I felt very little pain and was completely coherent. I said out loud, "Thank You LORD; I was worried for nothing." I was so immensely grateful that I was Ok. I felt nothing like I did after the first surgery; what a relief. Mike, Dad and Tim came to see me and were pleasantly surprised as well. Before my guys left for lunch, I showed Tim my kindle and all the free samples I'd downloaded about eternal life and heaven. I said, "See what's been on my mind the last few months?" But I was fine; I survived brain surgery! Hallelujah, praise Jesus! I would have jumped out of the bed and sang for joy if I could have. Mike, Dad and Tim were in great spirits too, and obviously relieved surgery had turned out so well. The worst of it was over. They left for lunch while I drifted off to sleep.

"I lift my eyes up to the hills—where does my help come from? My help comes from the LORD, the Maker of heaven and earth. He will not let your foot slip—he who watches over you will not slumber; indeed, he who watches over Israel will neither slumber or sleep. The LORD watches over you—the LORD is your shade at your right hand; the sun will not harm you by day, nor the moon by night. The LORD will keep you from all harm—he will watch over your life; the LORD will watch over your coming and going both now and forevermore" (Psalm 121).

17

I slept for what seemed to be only an hour before I woke up
again. But when I woke up, I was no longer Ok; I no longer
felt great. I couldn't speak! I had somehow lost control of my
tongue and swallowing. I was biting my cheek and tongue, trying
desperately to catch my nurse's attention. She was right by my side
in a heartbeat. When I tried to speak to her, all that came out was
a moan. I couldn't form words with my mouth. I was confused
and frantic. I motioned to her to get a piece of paper and a pencil.
She quickly got them for me on which I wrote, "I could talk an
hour ago!" She calmly said, "I know, Megan. The doctor is
coming." I closed my eyes and felt very afraid. This wasn't like a
seizure; my voice did not return after a few minutes' time. In fact,
my symptoms grew more serious. I was losing my eyesight and was
in and out of consciousness. Dr. Moon (fellow of Dr. Spetzler's)
came to tell me they were going to do an emergency MRI. I don't
remember the MRI at all, but I kept wondering, "Where is my
family?" The nurse tried to explain what was happening to me and
placed a clipboard in front of me to sign something, but I wasn't
coherent enough to know what she was saying and what the form
was for. I held the pen in my hand but could barely feel it. She
said, "Just mark an 'X' Megan, you don't need to sign your full

name if you can't." But I couldn't steady the pen or myself even long enough to mark an "X." I couldn't verbalize any sort of agreement either! I didn't understand what was going on. Were they going to let me die because I couldn't give them permission to do what they needed to do? Didn't I already sign a release before I was admitted? Where the hell was my family? Help! Just save me, please. When my family finally arrived, Mike didn't ask questions, although Dad tried to. Mike said, "I don't give a damn, just save her before it's too late!" Dr. Moon was soon by my bedside. I could barely see him, but he calmly and clearly said, "Megan, you have another mass in your brain that we didn't see before; surgery aggravated it and it is now aggressively bleeding. We are going to have to do an emergency brain surgery." I felt for Dr. Moon's hand, put my hand on his and nodded as if to say, "Ok, I'm ready." The mass was bleeding so aggressively that I was close to death. I had never been so scared, and I was heartbroken that I couldn't talk to say "goodbye" to Mike, Dad and Tim. I was certain I was going to die on my way to the OR or during surgery. I wished I'd written my "goodbye" letters to my family after all.

I was brought back into the OR, intubated by the anesthesiologist again, put back into the 3-point head holder again, secured to the bed again, and they proceeded to remove the staples and undo the careful stitching they'd done to close up my head from the previous surgery only a few hours prior. The wound was fresh and to reopen my head only hours after surgery was risky. Blood oozed out of my dura, venous blood oozed out of my brain; my brain was still bleeding. Once Dr. Spetzler was in again with the microscope and wand guidance, he was able to resect a "very large clot," and he indeed saw that the bleeding mass was another cavernous malformation. Once he'd successfully resected the cavernous malformation, a fellow stitched me up once more; I survived the bleed and surgery. It was scary risky, but he did it; Dr. Spetzler stopped the bleeding and thus Dr. Spetzler saved my life.

I woke up once again after my emergency surgery in the ICU. I was thankful to be alive and I could see again, but I sadly was still unable to talk and swallow. I thought to myself, "Ok LORD, I wasn't worried for nothing after all." I nearly lost my life and now can't talk or eat. Disorienting drugs and trauma of losing my speech and swallowing made me feel very emotional. I was an emotional mess. I couldn't talk to my family or communicate my basic needs to the staff. The nursing staff had paper and a pencil that always sat next to me so I could communicate by writing, but I had tingling and numbness in my right hand after the bleed from the hidden mass. It was uncomfortable, nearly painful to hold a pencil and to try to write. Between my sloppy penmanship and the disorienting drugs and pain killers, much of what I wrote either didn't make sense or was illegible.

While still in the ICU an inpatient speech therapist visited me. I was excited to see her. She would help me jump start my recovery to speak, drink and eat again. She first asked me to press my lips together to form the word "Me." I struggled to keep my lips pressed together, but I tried. My brain thought "Me," but the sound that came out of my mouth was a loud moan, "Ahh." Each time I opened my mouth to speak, the only audible noise I could make was a moan. Only Chewbacca or Han Solo could have understood what I was saying. She kept repeating to me, say "Me." Repeatedly I replied with a loud moan "Ah." I wrote on a piece of paper, "I'm trying!" In my mind I knew the word, I could process what she was saying and asking of me, but my lips and tongue would not cooperate. I was getting increasingly frustrated.

The therapist handed me a mirror to look at myself as I tried to speak, as if that would help. I lifted the mirror to my face and looked back at my reflection for the first time since before surgery. I looked beat up. My mouth drooped and I drooled, my eye was black and blue, I looked dirty but pale, and I had big dark circles under my eyes. I looked terrible. But seeing myself for the first time was a comfort to me. I looked awful and beat up, but I was still me. I had survived not just one, but two surgeries that week, the second of which seriously threatened my life. I didn't feel like myself, I didn't sound like myself, but I was comforted to see me and know that I was still in there. I didn't lose "me."

I watched myself in the mirror now as I tried to say "Me." I cried when I watched myself helplessly moan, mouth gaping open and drooling out the side of my mouth. The speech therapist then said, "Ok, try to just say 'E.'" No success with that either but thinking about the letter "E" made me think of my sister Ellen. I hoarsely barked uncontrollably as I laughed. Dad and Mike looked at me like I was out of my head. "What's so funny?" I choked out laughs as I wrote down "E, for Ellen." Thinking of my crazy, high-energy sister made me laugh. I wished she was there to keep me laughing. The therapist sighed, changed directions and instead of asking me to speak, she asked me to hum. She said, "Hum a song you would sing to your kids." I took a deep, labored breath and hummed "Jesus loves Me." I sang this song to my children when they were in the womb, when I nursed them and rocked them to sleep, when I tucked them in for bed and sometimes at random when I snuggled with them on the couch. Humming "Jesus loves Me" brought back a flood of memories and precious moments with my children. I didn't make it past the first verse before I began to loudly sob. I missed my children so much and I worried that I might not be able to sing that song to them ever again. My kids were still very young and were learning to talk and would eventually learn to read. Would I be unable to teach them because I couldn't talk clearly myself? "Oh LORD," I prayed, "please fully restore my speech!" I want to talk clearly to my kiddos.

Later, Mike tried his hand at getting me to talk. I adamantly shook my head and tried to quiet him (that's not easy to do). I wanted him to leave me alone and let me rest, but he wouldn't shut up. He obviously wasn't going to stop until I tried. Mike tried to help me say "Mom." He worked together with me sounding out each letter. After many failed attempts, I shook my head, cried and wrote on my paper, "I can't." Mike persisted, "Yes you can, you're close! Try again." We sounded out the letters again and it was very hard work, but I successfully put the sounds together and said,

"Mom." I did it. I broke apart the one-syllable word and spoke it as two, but when I said, "Mom," Mike, Dad and Tim understood. It was the first word, the only word, I could say. Each of my babies' first word was "Mom," and as I was relearning to speak, it was mine too. I was so exhausted from trying to speak. I laid back in my bed, closed my eyes and patted my chest as I said "Mom, Mom, Mom." Dad said, "You miss Mom?" I shook my head no, Mike said, "Do you want to call your mom?" I shook my head again. Mike thought for a moment and quietly said, "Are you saying *you're* the mom?" I quietly and peacefully nodded. I had a moment of confidence when I spoke my first word. "I am the mom. I am Luke and Natalie's mom." I was in a more broken state, but I was thankful to have survived surgery. Ellen was right; I would get to go back home to my sweet babies, just not right away.

Dr. Spetzler and Dr. Moon came in to visit me before I made my transition from ICU to the inpatient therapy wing. I had made the mistake of coming home too soon after surgery last visit to Phoenix; I was not going to do that again. They weren't going to release me to come home until I could eat again anyway. We presumed that the staff at the Barrow Institute would be much better equipped to help me recover. I was never going to return as an inpatient to that rehab hospital in Wichita again! When Dr. Spetzler came in to see me to wish me well, I looked at him with desperation in my eyes. I wanted to ask him so many questions. I wanted to yell at him, "How did you not see the hemangioma hiding behind the other one while you were operating the first time? What am I supposed to do now?" I couldn't verbalize any of these things. I couldn't share my frustration. Instead, I wrote on a piece of paper, "Will I be able to speak and eat again?" I handed the paper to Dr. Moon and he sadly said, "I don't know, maybe not." Dr. Spetzler, however, contradicted him right away. Dr. Spetzler said, "Yes, you will; work hard and you'll get it back." He spoke as if he had no doubt that I'd fully recover my speech and ability to eat and drink. I should have been grateful for my life, but instead I was mad. How could he so casually say "Work hard?" I was so tired of working hard. I had worked hard before and not seen results. Dr. Spetzler was confident, but I wasn't.

"Oh LORD, I know I said I would respond differently to this surgery, but I'm so scared and mad." Several different times I sobbed as I struggled to communicate with the staff and my family. I bit my lips and my cheek and my tongue, moaned and drooled all over myself. It was too hard and seemed hopeless. I felt I was asked to fight another uphill battle and I didn't know if I had enough fight left in me. Despairing, I'd put my finger to my head as if to model the barrel of a gun and with another finger squeeze the trigger. I wrote on paper, "Please just kill me!"

Because I couldn't eat, I received my nutrition and "food" through a tube that went through my nose, and directly down my throat. They got me hooked up with tube feed but the tube feed gave me diarrhea, I also started my period, the pain pills I took made me unbelievably nauseous, I was really thirsty but couldn't drink yet without drowning myself, and my chin was chapped from drool; I was absolutely miserable!

The nurses had to hover over me each time I used the toilet, to make sure I didn't fall. When I stood up, I held on to the bar alongside the toilet, while they wiped me. With having diarrhea and being on my period, it was especially gross and embarrassing. They all said to me, "It's Ok, we're used to it." And I thought "Yeah, but I'm not!"

I had a tube in my nose to administer medications and to be able to hook up the tube feed each time I "ate." It irritated my throat, my nose and my ears. Although the food and meds went through a tube and bypassed my tongue, I swear I could taste all of it. Yuck!

I struggled a lot post-surgery with a vast number of issues, but my pain wasn't near as intense as it was post-2007 surgery. I was incredibly thankful for that. Even though they had to cut through and operate on my head twice, the surgeries weren't nearly as invasive as my first. I was on pain meds post-2012 surgeries, but I wanted to quickly wean off of them because they made me dizzy, nauseous, sensitive to light and sound and interfered with my ability to function physically; I needed to be able to put forth some effort and heal in therapy. I didn't want to, but like Dr. Spetzler said, I needed to work hard. And I would—for my kids. With the exception of weekends, I had therapy every day from morning to late afternoon. I saw a physical therapist, an occupational therapist and a speech therapist Monday-Friday twice a day for 30-60 minutes each. Every day was exhausting and I took a two-hour nap after work was done. It was hard work. Most of the weakness I still had in my left side was from my bleed in 2007. The 2012 bleed simply made my left side a bit weaker than it already had been. Therapists had me do balance and strengthening exercises all over again. My occupational therapist helped me get up out of bed, get dressed and bathed. She was quite impressed how I'd learned to do a lot of my care myself with the use of only one hand. I did allow her, however, to help me get dressed because I was tired, and frankly appreciated having someone assist me for a change. It was a little embarrassing to have her help me bathe. She was young and cute and fit. I sat in front of her with my awkward naked body slouched over on the shower chair, my bulging belly hanging out (from having babies so close together), small but saggy breasts, a tube hanging out my nose, and drool dripping out of the side of my mouth. Even as she washed me and cleaned me up, I felt disgusting. She tried to help me break up the tone or spasticity in my arm when we were in the gym and also helped me to improve balance. She was fun and the most personable and friendly of all my therapists. I could tell she thoroughly enjoyed her job, and even though they were with her sometimes for only a short while, I knew she loved her patients. That's as it should be.

In years past with my various bleeds, any speech therapy I'd had was easy and fun. Over the years with my six previous bleeds, I'd gotten a little slower to respond, and mental math was a greater challenge, but overall speech therapy was fairly easy for me. In Phoenix after I'd lost my ability to speak and swallow, speech was

NOT fun, nor was it easy. I hated the sound that came of my mouth when I tried to speak. I moaned and groaned in place of comprehensive speech. I hated it! I sounded dumb. Everything in my mind was intact in that I understood people and I still retained knowledge and memory; I just couldn't verbalize my answers to any of the doctors' or staff's questions and appropriately communicate. Instead of hearing my pathetic incomprehensible moans and groans, I made gestures and pointed with my good hand to communicate my needs and answer questions. I also used a dry erase board to "talk." During speech therapy, however, I couldn't get away with pointing and writing things down. I had to practice talking. My speech therapist said I was suffering from dysphagia and dysarthria. I cried through every session frustrated with the sound coming out of my mouth and frustrated with how hard it was to communicate. My personal speech therapy goal was to be able to read a children's book aloud to my kids, eat a cheeseburger and maintain a conversation even for just a few minutes. However, my speech therapist put lists of words in front of me to read. She had me practice moving my tongue side to side, pushing it against the back of my front teeth, holding and sucking on ice chips: textbook speech therapy stuff, I would imagine. She gave me homework to do, but I rarely read the lists out loud on my own. Speech therapy was incredibly mundane, exhausting, boring and disappointingly impersonal. Of all people, I needed my speech therapist to sympathize with my situation and comfort me. The loss of speech was so devastating; I longed to connect with people. But when I despaired, felt frustrated and cried she appeared impatient, uncomfortable and annoyed. My speech therapist wasn't necessarily unkind, but she was strictly professional, she didn't show much compassion, and I felt like I was just another patient to her; someone to fix. She made no effort to make any sort of connection. It was the most vital of all my therapies, I especially needed to be able to eat again; but I dreaded and hated speech therapy.

Once my pain was better controlled and I no longer needed pain medication as often, I started to feel better. The nausea subsided. The smell of food from the kitchen no longer made me want to hurl, and I was relatively less drowsy. I was genuinely fatigued only from the intensive therapy I received each day. Once the nausea had subsided, I began to get really hungry. I still couldn't chew and swallow or drink, but I was famished! The tube feed didn't give me proper nutrition. It was going straight through me. And to think, I was worried that I'd have to take steroids again post-surgery and suffer all the terrible symptoms of steroids, including massive weight gain! Instead, because I couldn't eat and the tube feed wasn't sustaining me, I was losing weight. It was a very unhealthy way to lose weight. I complained to my speech therapist that I was unbelievably hungry. I hadn't had anything to eat in over a week. Day seven in the rehab hospital, she decided I ought to have the barium swallow exam done to see if I could advance to a liquid diet, in addition to the tube feed.

I really wanted to pass her exam. I really wanted to be able to eat again, but I was afraid that I was still not yet ready. My therapist presented to me graduated amounts of liquid barium with varying densities of liquid. The barium mixed with the various substances allowed them to see on a screen how my tongue and throat responded as I tried to drink. Would I be able to safely drink the variations of liquid, keeping it out of my lungs? Claire gave me each variant in a small cup, had me tilt my head back and try to swallow. Every last one of them I failed to swallow. I choked it up, spit it out and let it drool out the side of my mouth. I was embarrassed and discouraged. Clearly, I wasn't ready for even a liquid diet, and was certainly far from being able to eat solid food like a big juicy cheeseburger. I was certain I failed the swallow exam.

When I next had speech therapy, I was surprised Claire said that I'd passed the swallow exam. "What?" It was the first time I'd seen her smile and get excited for me, having made some progress. Although I hadn't successfully swallowed much of the liquids presented to me in the barium test, none of it passed through my airways. I could feel the liquid as it went down my throat and I coughed it up, not allowing it to enter my lungs. I passed! Claire thus brought me cups of pear and peach nectar to practice spooning into my mouth and swallowing during our following speech therapy session. I was glad to have a break from her boring lists of words to read aloud. And although it wasn't real food, it felt good to put something in my mouth to eat. Mike and Dad helped me practice with swallowing nectar and continuing to manipulate ice chips in my time outside of therapy. Practicing eating was homework I didn't mind doing.

All the therapy I received was really important and the reason for my extended stay in the hospital, but the down time and rest was important to me too. Although I missed my kids, Mama, friends, and my home, it was important to me to be able to be better-rested and heal as much as I could before returning home to them. Technology made the extended stay more bearable and I was less homesick. My friends skyped with me (video chat) on the computer, and one of my cousins and another one of my best friends texted me encouraging words and verses every single day. I sent frequent late-night jumbled texts to my college girlfriends that were Ambien-influenced. I felt like I was high when I took that stuff! Although I still had numbness and tingling in my right hand and it was uncomfortable, I sent the occasional mass text to update friends and family. Best of all, I got to see my kids on a skype call too. The tube in my nose confused my kiddos a little bit and I could tell my appearance troubled them. Luke put his fingers in his mouth for self-soothe, and Natalie kept looking to Granny for reassurance. When I tried to talk, they couldn't understand me. It made my heart hurt a little. To put them at ease and be a little silly with them, I pretended my feeding tube was an elephant trunk and made a poor attempt of making elephant sounds. They both laughed and smiled, Luke took his fingers out of his mouth long enough to point at me laugh and say, "Mama's an elephant." They couldn't understand me, and I couldn't hold them, but it was so good to see my sweet babies. And it was incredibly reassuring to hear that they were being very good and cooperative for Granny. I wasn't going to want to leave Phoenix until I could properly attend to them.

The LORD made me mindful and aware that I was a pitiful patient in 2007. Although pain was intense and the medications at the time were partly at fault, I regretted being so self-absorbed and whiny after my 2007 bleed and surgery. In fact, when I'd had my bleed in December of 2011 and it had been decided that I'd have surgery again, I thanked God for the opportunity to respond differently. Even if I was miserable, I asked that God give me the strength to not make others miserable. And to not be irritable with others.

Whether I was using the whiteboard or broken speech, I made every effort to connect with the nurses that attended to me and to always be kind. I even made an effort to speak Spanish to my housekeeper. She was quite impressed how well I spoke her language, especially given that I'd had a brain bleed and brain surgery. Spanish seemed even a little easier to speak and roll off the tongue than English was at the time. I asked friends and family to continue to pray Colossians 4:2 over us. I wanted to be a witness to those around me and share Christ's message of salvation one way or another. "Help me be a light, LORD." Many of the nurses were definitely a blessing to me. I had two nurses I took a special liking to, and I was always delighted to see them. Tracy was one of my second-shift nurses and my favorite nurse. Even with my broken speech, I felt comfortable talking to her, she was funny, kind and took especially good care of me. I told her about my kids and she told me about hers, she read to me a time or two from the Bible before leaving the hospital at the end of her shift; and she took me on a few wheelchair walks inside and around the outside of the building. I loved Tracy.

Dawn, another one of my second-shift nurses, was also very friendly and kind. Being in the hospital day after day and not being able to drink much water, my skin and hair were getting nasty and dry. Dawn took extra time with me to pamper me and fix my hair. That felt good. Each night before falling asleep, I thanked the LORD for Tracy and Dawn and asked that He bless them and reward them for their selfless love and kindness. I had an immensely better experience with inpatient rehab in Phoenix than I'd had in Wichita. I was grateful that we stayed.

Also, when I wasn't being bothered with therapy, I spent time with Dad and Mike. Dad liked to talk to me and be with me but was uncomfortable when I cried. He kept telling me not to cry. I needed to cry and sometimes I didn't want to stop. I was frustrated with Dad for not letting me grieve, but he honestly took good care of me. He jumped up and swabbed my mouth each time it felt miserably dry and then jumped up again to do suction in my mouth when the water and drool pooled in my mouth. It was a bit of a vicious and annoying cycle to me, but Dad never complained. He was always asking me if there was anything he could do for me. Dad was around in the early weeks when I was more fatigued and sadder, and since he didn't want me to cry, there wasn't much he could do or that I wanted him to do. I could tell that Dad needed to be helpful, so I thought perhaps he could read to me. I had brought my kindle with me from home, thinking I might be able to do some reading. I was able to sit up in bed and read for a short while before exhausting my eyes and falling asleep. Dad offered to read aloud to me. The only book I had been reading was *The Phantom of the Opera*. It's a decent movie, but a long and boring book. I knew that Dad *really* loved me when he offered to read aloud to me from *The Phantom of the Opera* day after day. I had a hard time focusing and following the story, but I could tell it made Dad feel better like he was being more useful and helping me.

When Mike and I spent time together, he helped me eat dinner and on my down time we were restful and watched movies or our favorite show, *Psych*, together. One evening we were laughing out loud so much at a movie we were watching that my night nurse rushed in thinking maybe something was wrong. After losing my speech, I didn't laugh or cry quietly or gracefully. Loud bursts of noise came out of my mouth that sounded more like raspy barking rather than laughing. I'd bark, gasp for air and do it all over again. When he realized we were both laughing, he stopped to watch the movie with us for a while as he prepared my nightly meds. I dearly appreciated my time with my husband. He *never* treated me like an invalid. He helped care for me, but I was still his wife. I was valuable to him and still his companion. I thought we were actually better together at the hospital than we'd been at home. We did normal everyday activities together. We occasionally used the machines at the hospital to do our laundry. I even had my occupational therapist help me make cupcakes for Mike's birthday. Poor guy had to spend his birthday in the hospital, but he didn't care. We truly made the best of a trying situation. The hospital tried to as well.

The hospital had an activities director. He planned events on weekends for patients to attend as they were physically able. I tried to be more restful on the weekends, but attending outings was strongly encouraged to maintain mental health and get back out there in the real world. Per the request of another rehab patient, the activities director was taking a group to Target. I liked Target. Before I'd left for Phoenix, I'd made some trips to Target and bought some loose-fitting tees and sweat pants. Since then, Mike had bought me a few more tees and a sports bra to wear at the hospital. Apparently, Mike didn't like me going around the hospital without a bra on. He was trying to keep me modest; how sweet.

A trip to Target sounded perfect for me and tame. Maybe we'd find some more comfy clothes to buy for me; I would need to do laundry less often. I opted to go with the group, and Mike tagged along. I thought to myself, "Mama would be proud; I'm choosing to do a normal activity outside the hospital." Target was my first outing. I still had my nose tube in, my drool was better under control, so I didn't carry a washcloth with me anymore, but my mouth often gaped open and saliva still pooled in the corner of my mouth.

Although I hated it, I got used to the way I looked and acted at the hospital. Most everyone else at the hospital was in the same boat and understood. However, when I agreed to go to Target, I didn't consider the reactions I would get out in public from strangers. When we arrived, I wanted to crawl into a hole and die. Mike pushed me in a wheelchair and I stared down at the floor. I wouldn't dare make eye contact with anyone. Once in the Phoenix rehab hospital, I'd seen a man scooting around in a wheelchair who gave me a big broad smile. He was just being friendly, but when he smiled at me, I burst into tears. I pictured my face and how pathetic I must look, how pathetic I felt, and I felt frustrated I couldn't return his smile. My mouth just gaped open. I couldn't bear to see what people's reactions to me may have been in public. I still looked and felt pathetic and couldn't smile even if I wanted to.

Being broken and debilitated in this way was an eye-opening experience. How often have I seen someone in public who was in a wheelchair, mouth gaped open, drooling, couldn't talk well and had pity on them assuming they must also not be mentally intact? I didn't want anyone to make that assumption about me. I didn't want to see anyone look at me with pity. I was still smart, alert and understood everything. I would never make that assumption about someone else again simply because they were nonverbal and couldn't return a smile. The outing in public was not as enjoyable as I thought it was going to be. I was embarrassed and uncomfortable.

I avoided the pitiful looks from strangers while in public, and was relieved to get back to the hospital where my physical condition was much like everyone else's. My nurses and doctors at Barrow knew me and that I was a mess physically, but that I was mentally sound. However, I had one nurse that did treat me like I had the mentality of a child simply because I was nonverbal, and it infuriated me! She helped me to the restroom because my assigned nurse was otherwise preoccupied. When she came to my room, I pointed to the bathroom door and attempted to say, "Bathroom please." I suppose because of my jumbled speech, and weakness in my left extremities, she assumed I was slow to understand too. She talked in a singsong way as one would to a very small child. She left the bathroom a moment and I stood up ever so slightly to turn on the sink faucet and she ran in and said, "No, no don't do that or I'll have to turn on your bed alarm, Ok?" I rolled my eyes and wanted to flip her off; I refrained. She helped me back to bed, administered my afternoon medications through my nose tube, and I said, "Thank you." Before leaving my room, and I so desperately wanted her to leave my room and never come back, she knelt down and said, "Oh you are so welcome, sweetie." She patted my hand and said, "Is there anything else I can do for you?" (again talking to me like I was a small child.) I glared and said, "No." Even after she'd given me my anti-anxiety medication, I couldn't relax. I fumed long after she left. I am well educated, I have a degree in Psychology, I read and write for fun, I can do puzzles, I have two children of my own, and I'm married. Don't treat me like I'm stupid! When my assigned nurse finally came in, I wrote out what happened on my dry erase board. Once finished writing my story, I cleared the board and wrote in large letters, "I'm smart, Dammit!" Then I burst into tears. This was my fear realized. If I couldn't talk and couldn't speak clearly, people would assume I was stupid. It happened right there in the hospital, even though my chart and board in my room said that I was mostly nonverbal but intellect was intact and I could understand everything.

I had to get my speech back before returning to the real world, I just hated others hearing me talk. I hated to hear myself talk too, but I knew and thanked God that my intellect was still intact and didn't take that for granted. I felt more comfortable in my room talking to myself and so occasionally read out loud or read sentences Claire had created for me. It was boring, but a better alternative to reading through lists of words. My mouth fatigued quickly, so I didn't read out loud for long. I needed to save some of my mouth strength to eat. Two weeks into inpatient rehab and I was eating soft foods (lots of fish and ice cream) and getting close to eating more solid foods. Also, I didn't drool as much. I was slowly getting better, but I was still fairly quiet and relied on my whiteboard a lot to communicate to the staff and my family.

Early one morning, at the end of my second week, one of my therapists came in and said the staff had a meeting concerning each of their patients. She said my name came up several times and they were concerned I still wasn't talking. She said, "We're going to have to take your whiteboard away and make you talk." I looked at her wide-eyed, and she said, "That's right; no more whiteboard." So that was it; I *had* to talk! They allowed me to carry the whiteboard with me still over the next several days but I tried to use it much less. As I wrote words down, I tried to say them aloud too. Claire was impressed and pleased that I was taking that initiative. Eventually I wasn't relying on it at all. Mike carried it to each session still, however, just in case the therapist absolutely could not understand what I was trying to say. It was exhausting to talk so much, and I still didn't like the sound of my voice, but the staff was pleased that I was trying and I was improving. My tongue still felt so weird in my mouth. It was fat, felt numb and uncomfortable. Still when I tried to talk or eat, I bit my lip, tongue and cheek, frequently. I had to eat each of my sensible soft food meals very slowly so as not to choke. Sometimes it took me over an hour to eat a small simple meal. By the time I finally finished a meal, I was very tired and hungry again! Although eating was a challenge, I was very happy when I graduated from tube feed. I'm thankful it kept me from starving to death, but it was nasty stuff. It was also a very delightful day then when they removed the tube in my nose. I was taking my medication orally, drinking water and eating food. It felt much better to get that stupid thing out of my nose and throat, and I looked a lot better without it. No more elephant trunk. Once that stupid thing was out, I felt more like myself and less like a patient. I looked at myself in the mirror and smiled instead of crying. The first time I brushed my teeth and didn't have to pull my nose tube out of the way, was wonderful. I was starting to regain the ability to spit, instead of letting my toothpaste run out the side of my mouth and having to wipe it out. I was so excited when I could again spit. Such a small thing to take for granted.

Unfortunately, during one speech therapy session, I had a setback that really scared and discouraged me. I was reading aloud through a very boring list of words for Claire. I'd back up and repeat a word if I said it incorrectly or it was incomprehensible. Mike would often listen and say, "What was that word?" Claire would laugh as I sighed, and I'd say it again. Words with "th" and "s" were especially difficult to pronounce. Halfway through the list I stopped because I suddenly had trouble breathing. My head was swimming and I couldn't make out the words on the page. I felt like I was gasping for air, and when I tried to tell Claire and Mike that something was wrong, my speech came out in moans and groans again. In an instant I was back to my baseline before I'd started therapy. I bit my cheek and lost all control of the muscles in my mouth and throat. I completely lost it and sobbed. I had come so far in two weeks. What happened? I sounded like I did right after I'd had my bleed that debilitated my speech and swallow. My mouth drooped, and as I cried, I drooled out of the side of my mouth. Mike sat next to me on my bed, and I pulled at his shirt, saying "Help me, help me, help me!" It all came out in groans. Mike grabbed my whiteboard from across the room; I hadn't needed to use it in several days. I cried uncontrollably and shook as I wrote, "Help!" Claire and Mike stayed calm, fetched my nurse, and the nurse notified my doctor.

Within the next twenty to thirty minutes, they had equipment in my room to do an EEG to see if I'd had a seizure. Surely, I didn't have a bleed; Dr. Spetzler took those masses out entirely, didn't he? By the time the equipment for the EEG had arrived, my speech had returned to the way it was prior to the episode. They did an EEG, but it didn't show I'd had seizure activity. They didn't see any need to do an MRI, because it didn't last. A psychologist in the hospital that I'd seen a time or two before thought it might have been a panic attack. Well whatever it was, I prayed it would never happen again. It scared me. I thought I was going to have to start all over again. It did make me feel all the more grateful for how far I'd come in two weeks, though. Once I could safely swallow again, my nurse gave me an anti-anxiety med, and I slept off the trauma of that bizarre episode.

Thankfully, the episode did *not* reoccur and I continued to progress in my speech and swallowing. When the hospital staff had their next meeting, they agreed that I was nearly stable enough to return home. My discharge date was set for March 21st. Claire encouraged me to keep talking and keep eating. By my third week, I'd lost fourteen pounds and was continuing to lose weight. Claire said I needed to eat more at meals or they'd have to send me home with a feeding tube in my stomach. I ate a lot more ice cream because it was easy to eat and could help me gain back some weight. I took a few sips of Ensure at each meal and poured the rest down the drain, but I left the empty can on my tray to make it look like I'd drunk it. It was just enough to convince Claire and the dietitian that I could maintain my weight at home, eat enough and not have need for a tube feed.

I was not initially in a hurry to get home, because I wanted to get well first. But after being away from my babies and Mama for over three weeks, I wanted to go home. When Claire finally had me read a children's book aloud to get the practice I needed to read aloud to my kids, I did fairly well, although I had to take several sips of water between sentences. When I got to the very end of the book I sobbed. I really did miss Luke and Natalie very much. I was a little nervous to go home to them though. I wasn't 100% better yet. I still struggled to eat and my speech was still messy. I had no doubt that it was going to be hard to face people and reintegrate into the real world feeling even more broken and awkward than I did before.

Even though I hadn't been in fellowship, I heard from the LORD regularly and felt His presence ever with me while in the hospital. One morning I woke up in the hospital and my tongue and mouth had felt so much better. I had better control, and speaking was easier and much cleaner. I sat down to my breakfast, lifted my arm to heaven in praise and sang worship to God as loudly as I could. It was so refreshing! My morning nurse came into my room to give me my morning meds; she had tears in her eyes as she said, "We heard you singing in the hall; it sounded beautiful. You've made my day, sweet girl. Your neighboring patient was blessed by it too." I softly cried tears of joy when she left my room and I kept singing. By the time I began to cut my French toast into small bites to eat, I'd worn out my mouth and it was difficult to eat my breakfast. But I didn't care; it was well worth it to use my strength to sing praise to God instead.

Then the LORD reminded me of something He'd said to me at church several weeks before we left Wichita for my surgery. During worship one Sunday I'd felt a strong prompting from the LORD to approach our worship pastor and to volunteer to be on the worship team. I was so nervous to offer, but the prompting was so strong and clear that I felt if I didn't obey and respond, I would regret it. I approached our worship leader after church and said, "I think I'll need brain surgery soon, but I feel so strongly that the LORD wants me to serve on the worship team." Our worship leader was grateful and excited and said, "That's awesome. Thank you."

When I recalled this encounter with the LORD, I realized that in a way, He *did* give me a promise that I'd heal and that I'd get my speech back again to sing praise. "Thank You, Jesus; I love You LORD!" The morning that I was able to sing praise and worship God made me miss church. I wanted to get back to our church and again worship with my brothers and sisters in Christ. Mike and I decided while we were still at the hospital, we would create an atmosphere of church and hold a service on the rehab floor. The activities director thought it was a great idea and he made flyers for us that we taped to the walls of the rehab hall. On my last Sunday in the rehab hospital, we hosted a church service in the community room where patients could gather and spend time with their families away from their hospital rooms.

We weren't sure that anyone would come, but Mike and I put

together a short set of songs for worship, chose some scriptures to read and thought we'd take time to share and pray with one another. I was truly excited and hoped people would come. Mike and I set up for service. We waited for twenty-thirty minutes before three families finally joined us. There were some other families that had clearly missed community and their churches too. I got a little teary-eyed as we joined together in songs of praise to Jesus. An older gentleman hearing a familiar hymn started weeping as we sang. It was good for all of us to be together in church. We shared together, held hands and prayed together. One of the patients said repeatedly how thankful he was that we decided to do church at the hospital, that it gave him a renewed sense of strength and hope. His wife was very appreciative as well. I think it helped lift all of our spirits.

Just a few days later, I had a visit from Dr. Moon and Dr. Williams from Dr. Spetzler's team to wish me well and commend me on my diligence to work hard and were pleased with my progress in therapy. Dr. Moon smiled and said, "Keep up the good work." Dr. Williams was pleased to report that the most recent MRI scan showed that my head looked good, surgery was successful and they wished us safe travels home. I gave each doctor a full embrace and said, "Thank you." Those guys helped saved my life. It was a bittersweet departure. I likely wouldn't see any of my nurses or therapists again. I hugged each of them and thanked them too for investing in me, believing in me and taking such good care of me. It was an unforgettable, traumatic and challenging four weeks!

Journal entry while in the hospital—

God's closeness
LORD,

I realize I could not have possibly prepared myself for the

recovery of this surgery. Although it was a similar procedure and the same type of mass, it was in a different area of
the brain, so entirely different results. LORD, of course it's
hard to dismiss the frustrations with my body in the here
and now. However, I thank You that I'm not being
subjected to steroids now, I'm not entirely obsessed with
my ailing body. Instead, I'm focusing on my heart and
mind and making an effort to be aware of others. I pray
You continue to allow me to be an example of Your love
and Holy Spirit dwelling within me. I've prayed and
listened attentively, God, what do You want me to gain
from this? Stripping me of my ability to speak has
humbled me. My speech sounds dumb and slurred and I
didn't want to open my mouth at all; I fought it. I hated
sounding stupid. I wanted people to realize that I was
smart and treat me as such. Then I realized that my stillness and broken speech somehow shows a more childlike
quality in my faith. While here, I embrace the chance to
improve in these people's presence, my faith and praise
intact.

So, while humbling me, I've also gained a strong passion to
sing. It's why I approached our worship pastor at church
long before surgery. Of course, there was reason for Your
prompting. My heart is filled with joy and praise, and I'm
going to give back the gift of voice You've given me. I
know my progress is not only part of Your plan for me and
the unfolding of my victory, but is also being used as a
testimony to encourage the faith of the people around the
world who are praying for me.

One blessing I've repeatedly received during these physical
trials is an outpouring of love from the body of Christ and
more! I pray somehow my faith can be a witness and inspi-
ration to someone who doesn't yet know the love that You
have for each and every one of us alike. You know that I'm
pleased and delighted with what Your journey has entailed,

but as You know, I'm notorious for wanting more! It seems
not only was the healing You'd promised me for just my
body, but also for healing between Mike and myself.
He has been incredible, and I pray this never ceases. I
desire for us to draw closer to You together and separately.
I've actually enjoyed this time together away from work,
home and family. We have fought this battle together, head
on. It's been incredible to have Mike stand in for me, to be
strong for me when he needs to be. I'm anticipating
further healing and I can't wait to see what You have
ahead. I plead that what's ahead is more healing; no more
setbacks, no more surgeries. I love You Jesus. Even when
times are tough and I'm miserable, I trust You and as
Whitney Houston sang, "I look to You."

> Your daughter,
> Megan

P.S. Every Bible passage I've turned to this week speaks to
me in a new way. I realize there isn't anything in there that
doesn't apply. Oh, the beauty and mystery of Your word.
I've truly found my story embedded in Yours.

"Whenever I consider your heavens, the work of your fingers, the
moon and the stars, which you have set in place, what is mankind
that you are mindful of him, human beings that you care for
them?" (Psalm 8: 3-4).

"Are not two sparrows sold for a penny? Yet not one of them
will fall to the ground outside your Father's care. And even the
very hairs on your head are all numbered. So don't be afraid; you
are worth more than many sparrows" (Matthew 10: 29-30).

18

W hen I was officially discharged and free to leave the hospital, Mike took me to the extended-stay hotel where he'd been living for the last four weeks. Mike had bought our plane tickets home, but they were dated for three days later. We'd have to spend some time together in the hotel before going back home. By the end of the fourth week, I was desperately longing to see Luke and Natalie and Mama and Dad. I wanted to go back home! But, for three days, Mike and I were exclusively in charge of me and my care, and that frightened me.

In all the time we'd been in Phoenix, Mike was without a car. It was much too expensive to rent a car for four weeks. For the few days Mike's dad had been in Phoenix, Mike, Dad and Tim had the luxury of having a car to use to get around town as needed. But when Tim went back home just days later, Mike and Dad no longer had a car. They walked to and from the hospital, which was just across the street from their hotel, and they took buses and subways to get around town for their meals. Without a car, Mike and I would have to do the same. If we needed to get somewhere, we used our own two feet for much of our transportation.

When we arrived at Mike's room, I nearly cried. There was trash on the table and floor, there was a smell coming from the waste basket or sink (I couldn't tell which), the floor was filthy and in serious need of vacuuming, food that belonged in the pantry was left out on the counter and the sheets on the bed were dirty and rumpled. I felt like I'd walked into Mike's old bachelor pad. It was a far cry from my standard of a clean home. Mike said the hotel was alright and affordable but there were no housekeeping services, which made me wonder if it was really worth the expense at all to stay there. Had I known how bad it was, I would have encouraged Mike to ask for help with expense to stay at a nicer place where he'd get a little service. Once Tim and Dad had left and Mike was on his own, he spent very little time at the hotel. It served as a place for him to eat and sleep. The sheets on the bed were oily and dirty, and I felt uncomfortable laying on dirty sheets, but I was tired enough that it didn't matter and I was asleep within a few minutes after we'd arrived.

When I woke up hours later, Mike was sitting at the table playing his game on his computer and I noticed he'd taken time to pick up and take out the trash. I was incredibly hungry when I woke up. When we walked out of the hotel into the very bright outdoors, we spotted a Chinese buffet; we guessed it was roughly three blocks away. If we could clearly see it, we figured it must not be terribly far from where we were standing, so we started walking towards the restaurant. After having walked for two or three blocks, I realized the restaurant was farther from our hotel than we'd anticipated. I asked Mike to slow down and I rested on the curb and sat directly in the sun. I was sweating, feeling weak and ravenous. We had stopped to rest in front of a grocery store. Mike ran off toward the store and came back with a shopping cart. He said, "Climb in." I sighed and said, "We can't take that; it's stealing." Mike said, "No, we're just borrowing it, now get in!" I was reluctant to comply but went ahead and climbed in. Mike pushed me in the shopping cart the rest of the way to lunch. I closed my eyes and rested my head on my hand. I felt guilty for stealing the shopping cart and was sure we'd get in trouble, but was grateful Mike didn't "give a shit," and took it anyway.

We arrived at the restaurant, and the cool air from the air conditioner inside felt amazing. The restaurant was buzzing with people milling about getting their food from the buffet, talking to one another as they stood in line and chatting as they sat and ate their food. I hadn't been in public much since my bleed; the activity and stimulation of the busy restaurant was somewhat overwhelming and disorienting. Mike steadied me and carried my plate as we walked around the buffet trying to find something I could easily chew and not choke on. I steered clear of steak and chicken, it was much too warm to eat soup, and I didn't think I could eat any sort of lo mein or other dish that had a variety of food and textures to sort through and manipulate in my mouth. Claire said to stay away from that for a while. Up until the day I'd left, the hospital was still serving me simple soft foods at each meal. Mike and I finally decided that fried rice would be a safe option. I sat down with my bowl of fried rice and Mike sat across from me with his assortment of delicious Asian cuisine: Mongolian chicken, beef and broccoli, lo mein, egg rolls and desserts. His plate looked much more appealing than my boring bowl of fried rice, but I knew I couldn't chew and safely swallow any of the delicious foods on his plate yet. I chewed each spoonful of rice slowly and carefully as Mike shoveled in his food. Mike was finished with his first plate long before I was done with my rice and he went up for seconds. I was very hungry and impatient with my mouth and throat. I tried to eat a little faster, but as I did, I bit my cheek, my tongue and my lip many times. Even so, I kept trying but was done when I'd chomped down too hard and ground my teeth. I winced in pain and discomfort. I didn't even make it halfway through my bowl before I pushed it away. I was nowhere near full, but I was done trying. My mouth was tired and sore. I wasn't ready for fried rice or was simply too tired after having walked just part way to the restaurant. Especially since we had a lot more walking ahead, I'd try to eat softer, easier foods to chew, the remainder of our trip.

Mike had been restless the last three weeks and wanted to go on some outings; although I was tired much of the time and I'd preferred to rest at the hotel, Mike said he'd go with or without me. He needed to get out. I didn't feel comfortable being left all alone, so when Mike had the itch to get out and about, I went with him. I complained about my hair because my hair had gotten very dry and nasty in the hospital, so we walked to a nearby salon and I got a pixie cut. The hairdresser said it was a very flattering cut for me. Mike lied and said he liked it too. It was the shortest my hair had been since I was a very little girl. I preferred my hair long, and I knew Mike did too.

Although we took subways and buses part of the way, we also walked entirely too far to a disc golf course so Mike could play a round of disc golf. The journey to the course was exhausting; I couldn't also play disc golf with him in the blazing sun. So, I waited in a picnic area in the shade while Mike played. On the way back to the hotel, I fell asleep on the subway and woke up to a drool-covered shirt. I had been drooling in my sleep and drool was still hanging from my mouth; that was embarrassing! I slept a little more once we'd got back to the hotel, but when I awoke again, I suggested we celebrate Mike's birthday. We walked to a bar close by the hotel so Mike could sing karaoke (he *loves* karaoke). Even with my slurred speech, Mike coerced me to sing karaoke for the very first time. I told the crowd I'd recently lost my voice because of a "stroke," and admitted it was my first-time singing karaoke, "So, go easy on me." I must have sounded pretty awful, but the bar crowd cheered and whistled when I was finished singing my song dedicated to my husband, for his birthday. I still can't believe he persuaded me to do that when I had such messy speech, but it was fun, and I was oddly proud of myself. We chatted with some of the bar crowd as we listened to others sing and Mike awaited his turn. When people in the bar asked what brought us Kansans to Phoenix, Mike freely told them about my scary brain surgery and my traumatic brain history. I just nodded, listened and interjected a word or two. I cautiously had a few sips of a margarita Mike ordered for me, then I had Mike finish the rest. I put forth a great effort to party with Mike, but it wasn't long before Mike had to walk me back to the hotel when I felt I couldn't tolerate any more brain activity for the day. Just the hubbub of the bar scene was exhausting. I needed to lay down and rest. Mike, however, wanted to return to the bar, sing some more karaoke and continue celebrating his birthday. I asked him to please not leave me alone, but he said, "You'll be fine, get some sleep. I'll have my phone on me if you need me; I just need to blow off some steam."

I suppose part of me understood and I did want him to be able to celebrate his birthday and relax; I just felt very nervous about being left all alone. I had only been out of the hospital one day! What if something happened to me while he was gone? What if I sporadically had another seizure or bleed? He was all I had in Phoenix. I didn't have other family or friends and I no longer had a hospital staff looking out for me. Although I begged Mike not to leave, he returned to the bar that night without me.

I felt uneasy when he left but soon fell asleep. I woke up later in the night to my phone ringing on the side table next to me. I could see it was Mama but I couldn't wake myself up enough to answer it, and I couldn't talk; I was barely intelligible. I fell asleep again for a short while before I awoke again to use the bathroom. I still really couldn't speak very well, felt a little dizzy and my head was throbbing. I had pushed myself too hard that day. I looked to the other side of the bed; Mike still wasn't back. I glanced at the clock; it was one in the morning! I started to panic. Where was Mike? I called him, but he didn't answer his phone. I called him again, but he again didn't answer. I came back to bed, laid there awake feeling afraid as my face and tongue tingled. I kept glancing over at the clock as the minutes passed. My head continued to burn and throb as I lay awake. How could he leave me alone for so long? What if something happens in my brain while he's gone?

Mike returned to our room after two in the morning and was drunk! I was wide awake, head burning, feeling scared and angry! Mike was certainly more relaxed in his drunken stupor and he tried to be playful with me. But when I didn't respond positively to his playfulness, and I pushed him away, he knew I was truly upset, scared and in pain.

My body was rigid, I struggled to breathe and could barely choke out the words as I said, "You're all I have out here, Mike; you scared me!" He was inebriated and it was difficult to tell if he was truly sincere, but he seemed immediately remorseful. He kissed my aching head, said he was sorry for worrying me, fell into the bed and fell asleep. I wasn't worried about *him*, I was worried about *me*! Although Mike soundly slept, I had a difficult time falling back asleep. I had never seen Mike drunk before; how could he do that while I was exclusively reliant on him in Phoenix? I had no one else. He was so careless, and it broke my heart. We needed to get home, back to our family.

I longed for Mama's love and care. She would have never ever left me alone like that just four weeks out of massive brain surgery. I was incredibly eager to get home. My head pain grew as I laid awake that night. I took some pain medicine, thought of Mama, Luke and Natalie and seeing their sweet faces again very soon, and I cried myself to sleep.

Mike truly felt bad the next morning, and he let me sleep well past noon. It had been a rough night, and I didn't get sound rest. We were going to be much more restful that second day together outside the hospital. We went to get more ice cream. It was my fourth visit to a local ice cream shop to get mint chocolate chip ice cream. Honestly, I was getting tired of eating so much ice cream, but it was easy to eat, had plenty of calories and filled me up. After ice cream, we ventured out to Target to buy more clothes for me, we walked through other stores in the strip and bought me a swimsuit so I could swim in the hotel's pool. We walked to a restaurant to eat more seafood. I attempted to eat French fries, but when I realized I couldn't safely chew and swallow them yet, the restaurant gladly exchanged them for mashed potatoes. We swam in the pool and relaxed the rest of the evening.

I don't recall the events of our final day in Phoenix, and the events of those last three days all run together in my memory.

Mike tried to make the best of the situation, but those three final days Mike and I spent together in Phoenix outside of the hospital were generally not enjoyable for me. Even on our more restful day, I was nervous about my physical state the entire time. I felt anxious about not being monitored and cared for by a trained hospital staff. Mike and I were in an unfamiliar city, without a car, and all on our own. My meals were no longer brought to my room each day, so we walked and rode subways when we wanted to eat. My food palette was still limited to soft foods. Outside the hospital, we soon discovered that fish was the easiest, safest option, but it was also the most expensive. We were spending money that we didn't have to spare, and it was exhausting to need to walk to eat.

Mike dragged me around on the outings and it was good for me to be outside rather than in the dark dingy hotel room, but I was always worried we might be pushing me too hard. I would have loved to do even more before we returned to our kiddos. I wanted to be present and enjoy some alone time with my husband, but I simply wasn't well enough to enjoy a 3-day "vacation" with my hubby. I was still so tired. I needed to instead be back home in Wichita to rest and heal.

Our final night in the hotel, Mike left me alone in the room to sleep while he went out with his computer to play and sleep on the uncomfortable, scratchy hotel lobby chairs. We had an early flight and would need to leave the hotel in the middle of the night. Mike felt I'd get better rest without him laying next to me in bed. He selflessly put my needs first and allowed me to get uninterrupted sleep. At three in the morning, Mike came to get me and we made our way to the airport to fly home; at long last!

When we landed in Wichita I was nearly in tears. I was so excited to get to the house to see Luke and Natalie. My heart ached because I'd missed them so much. When we finally arrived home and I saw my babies, I embraced both of them and cried tears of joy. I squeezed them and kissed them and didn't want to let go. The kids seemed a little confused when we arrived and didn't know how to react; we'd been gone for four weeks! I also sounded funny and looked different. They each brought their toys and books to Mike and me to show us what they'd been doing with Granny while we were gone. It was so cute. Mama laughed and cried. We had been gone for a month, and I thought perhaps Luke and Natalie would be troubled by my extended absence, but they were well loved and cared for. It was a blessing that Mama was able to be with Luke and Natalie and a blessing that they behaved well for her. I'm forever grateful for Mama's care of my sweet babies. I felt the Holy Spirit had guarded my kids' hearts and minds, and took care of them. It was so good to be back home with my sweet kids.

Mama still primarily took care of my kids in the early morning and midafternoon which allowed me to have a time of rest at home, but I needed to quickly get back into a routine and continue healing at home. I needed to get strong enough to care for my kids again. Mama began driving me to therapy again across town. I met with a speech therapist in addition to my occupational and physical therapists. I'd come a long way and made tremendous progress with my chew, swallow and speech since my massive bleed, but I still had a lot of work to do. I loved my outpatient speech therapist in Wichita. Speech was hard and the most challenging of all the therapies, but she quickly became my friend and allowed me to talk about my heartaches and trials. She asked me about my kids, about Mike, and my interests. I did all the boring stuff too: read lists and sentences for her, but she also seemed genuinely interested in getting to know me. I grew very fond of her and looked forward to speech therapy. I attended all three therapies for several months, grew more confident in my speech and was able to eat a greater variety of food consistencies.

We lived with Mama and Dad and they were a huge help yet again. Mike was doing a bit better with living with Mama and Dad; however by September, Mike thought it was time to start looking for a house of our own. I was nervous and not sure if I could physically cope yet without Mama's help and if I could take care of my kids by myself. But I at least entertained the thought of moving into our own home and agreed to look at several different houses. There were some houses I hated and I didn't feel comfortable in some of the houses' neighborhoods. Unfortunately, the houses we were able to afford were not ideal. Ideally, I wanted a house in a good neighborhood with a backyard for the kids to play in. After having walked through over a dozen houses, we had nearly given up. But Mike came across a house listed online that was located within two miles of my parents' house, was in a great neighborhood, had a spacious backyard for the kids, three bedrooms, two bathrooms, a playroom for the kids, a kitchen and a dining room with a fireplace, and it was miraculously in our price range. It seemed too good to be true. Something had to be wrong with it. We did a walk through and fell in love with the house and the location. There was an elementary school right across the street from the house, so when the kids were ready to go to school they would be just across the street. It was perfect. It was a true blessing from the LORD, and too good to pass up. So, we made an offer and bought our first house in Wichita.

Mike was so much happier being in our own place and better established and grounded. He started a new job that he felt was a better fit and had greater potential for advancement and greater income. And I was pleasantly surprised how well I adjusted to being on my own with the kids. I mapped out a schedule for chores and we had lots of playtime in our big backyard. I took lots and lots of pictures of my kiddos as we played and as they grew. I missed my parents and got weary of doing all the chores, but because they lived so close and I still needed Mama's help getting to and from therapy appointments, we saw them a lot. To make a little income, in January of 2013, I signed back up to sell Mary Kay, and Mike and I bought me a car. Mama and I did Mary Kay together and I finally gained some independence back when I got my own car and could drive myself. I didn't drive to many public places alone with my kids because they still would run away from me; but it was nice to have the option to just go as I pleased.

By March, we took in two puppies which added responsibilities for me, and I celebrated my one-year anniversary since my massive brain surgery that had threatened my life. We celebrated by going out for cheeseburgers. I was doing quite well and so thankful for how far the LORD had brought me in a year. We were all thankful.

On March 23rd, 2013 I received a troubling phone call. I had a Mary Kay facial scheduled for early afternoon and Mama was supposed to bring the facial supplies over to my house since we shared demo product and facial supplies. When I saw on the caller ID that Mama was calling, I thought it was to talk about my facial. However, when I answered the phone, it was Dad on the other end. He said, "I'm taking your mom to the emergency room." "What? What's wrong with Mama?" Dad started to explain, but he didn't get much out before I heard Mama say, "Just give me the phone." Mama said, "Hi Meg." "Mama, what's going on; are you Ok?" Mama said, "I don't know. I woke up this morning feeling Ok, went downstairs to eat breakfast and drink my coffee but my coffee dribbled out my mouth, and I began losing feeling in my left hand." I knew my masses were hereditary; Ang had them too and either Dad or Mama had them. Sounded like Mama was having a brain bleed, and I knew she'd suspected that too. All I could say was, "Oh, Mama." She choked up and said, "I know." I could hear her crying when Dad then took the phone. He told me not to worry and said he'd keep me posted. "Oh, dear Jesus," I prayed, "Please be with my mama and help her."

The ER doctors took Mama's vitals and noted that she had high blood pressure. They speculated that she may have had a stroke provoked by high blood pressure. They sent her out to Wesley Hospital to have further testing to get to the root of the problem and to closely monitor her for a while. I went up to visit her in the hospital after tests were finished and she was able to rest.

I walked in on her watching a WSU basketball game. Mama loves watching WSU and KU basketball. I teased, "Mama, is that really very good for your blood pressure?" She laughed, "I'm only half paying attention." Mama's mouth drooped a little to one side as she talked and she said her hand still had some tingling and numbness, but her speech was perfectly clear, she was able to eat and said she was already feeling better. While I was visiting with Mama and Dad, a doctor came in to discuss the results of Mama's MRI. He said that Mama did have some bleeding on the brain likely to be the result of high blood pressure. As far as I knew, Mama hadn't much trouble with high blood pressure except that her job as a musician could be really stressful. She had been talking about retiring for a few years, but couldn't yet bring herself to do it. I said to the doctor, "Are you sure there was nothing else? My sister and I have cavernous malformations that are hereditary. Either my mom or dad have them. Are you sure it wasn't from a cavernous malformation?" He said, "If there was anything abnormal like that present in the scan, the lab would have said that." I pushed, "I don't think any of us are convinced that it was from high blood pressure. My mom wasn't even under any stress when it happened. Please look again." He again said, "They would have mentioned if there were other abnormalities present." I shook my head and just asked him to please have them look again to be absolutely sure. "Look at the scan closely and be on the lookout specifically for cavernous malformations." Later that night as I tried to fall asleep, I tossed and turned and prayed for Mama. If Mama did indeed have cavernous malformations and she was the one who passed them on, a lot of other relatives could be at risk for bleeds as well. I tried not to worry and fret about the unknown.

Early the next morning, Mama called me and said that a neurologist looked at her scan and paid her a visit in her hospital room. The neurologist gave her a different report than she'd received from the doctor the night before. The neurologist said that the MRI images showed that she in fact had four cavernous malformations in her brain like myself and Angie, and that her symptoms she'd had were as a result of one of the masses having bled. It's what Mama and I had known and feared from the start. Mama was the one who'd passed on the awful hemangiomas and she too had a bleed. I grieved for Mama and committed to praying for the entire Corman family: my aunt and uncles, my cousins and their children. Mama has five siblings, from which I have fifteen cousins, and there are many more children born to those cousins.

And yet, I felt a little angry that there were three out of four people in our own little family that had been afflicted with these awful cavernous malformations, and everyone else in the large family had no symptoms or knowledge of having them themselves. I didn't wish that any of my other family members had hemangiomas too, it just made me feel incredibly sad that Mama and my sister were in danger of devastating bleeds from these terrible things. Our little family had already suffered enough. *Mama* had already suffered enough!

Although it was hard for her to let go of it all at once, Mama decided to retire from playing the oboe and English horn given the fact that putting pressure on her brain from playing her instruments in the future could cause another bleed. Perhaps even a fatal bleed. She wasn't willing to take that risk. She went through a time of sadness at having to let go of her career so suddenly and because of a brain bleed, but I think we all considered it a blessing in disguise. She was losing the joy in playing and I observed it was causing her more fatigue and stress than it was worth. I was glad she was done with that part of her life. Mama sold her instruments, we threw her a retirement party and Mama began attending physical therapy at the rehabilitation hospital, as I had years ago. I teased her when she canceled or rescheduled appointments because her brain was just simply too tired to go. I said, "Hey, you never let me skip therapy, even when I was in terrible pain and thought my head might explode!" She laughed and said, "I know; sorry." Mama was getting a small taste of how I'd felt after a brain bleed: the fatigue, the disorientation, the pain, the mood swings, the loss. Mama grew more tearful after the bleed both as a result of brain damage and the emotional turmoil the bleed caused. Mama and I grew even closer after she'd experienced a bleed. She could relate to me on a different level and understand my suffering. Of all people, I hated that Mama had gone through it, but it was nice to have a greater level of compassion and understanding from my mama. Mama had always had a soft spot for me and selflessly cared for me, but I believe it softened any hardness she had in her to push me. I think she better understands and realizes that I was never being a wimp when it came to my frequent tears from pain and suffering.

Mama's bleed forced her to slow down for a while. Mama had already been someone I'd looked up to and had inspired my faith, but I observed that her faith grew and matured even more as she worked through her trial. I admired her even more for it. Mama felt a little empty without her music and missed her musician friends, but once the oboe was gone, she became more available to enjoy her family and let go of the stress that accompanied being a musician. As a musician, she had the pressure of practicing her instruments every day; she made her own reeds, often worked holidays and weekends and worked late nights. She was getting to a place in her life in which it was more challenging to keep up with the demands of being a working musician. Losing music as her comfort also allowed the LORD to take His rightful place as her sole source of comfort. Although it was a traumatic experience and I was sorry Mama was in danger of having more bleeds, it helped her to grow as a person and grow in her faith as it had myself.

I wondered once my sisters discovered that the hemangiomas were hereditary if it would factor in to whether they decided to birth children. Personally, had I known my masses were hereditary, I wouldn't have had children. Mama and many other people who know and love Luke and Natalie all say, "I'm glad you didn't know."

I don't know what the future holds for Luke and Natalie, if they will suffer brain bleeds or not, but I know this; God has a purpose for them and loves them. He veiled the awful truth from me for a time so that I was willing to have them. He wanted Luke and Natalie, He wanted me and He wanted Mama. He knew us and loved us before He knit us together in our mother's womb. Whatever God has in store for Luke and Natalie, I pray He equips us for and that it will be beautiful to be a part of. Through my adversity, I see my kids' faith struggle, but I also see it develop and mature. In my experience, what Satan intended for bad, God has used for good and to glorify Himself. I know that whatever Luke and Natalie or any of my other family members may struggle with, He can and will use the trial for good and for their benefit as well, if they invite Him in, and allow Him to.

"The moment we get tired in the waiting, God's Spirit is right alongside helping us along. If we don't know how or what to pray, it doesn't matter. He does our praying in and for us, making prayer out of our wordless sighs, our aching groans. He knows us far better than we know ourselves, knows our pregnant condition, and keeps us present before God. That's why we can be so sure that every detail in our lives of love for God is worked into something good" (Romans 8:26-28 MSG).

"So, we're not giving up. How could we! Even though on the outside it often looks like things are falling apart on us, on the inside, where God is making new life, not a day goes by without his unfolding grace. These hard times are small potatoes compared to the coming good times, the lavish celebration prepared for us. There's far more here than meets the eye. The things we see now are here today, gone tomorrow. But the things we can't see now will last forever" (2 Corinthians 4:16-18 MSG).

And I feel I must address something more before moving on. A verse I've heard many times misquoted to me and many others who suffer is "God only gives us as much as we can handle." Perhaps people mean to encourage and empower when they say this to people who hurt, but I believe it's counter-productive. People already struggle with the temptation to become embittered toward God and blame God for their pain and also question His love for them and His goodness. This phrase that many have adopted as scriptural and helpful is actually non-scriptural and can be destructive. The verse I believe many people are using and misquoting actually instead says,

"God is faithful; He will not let you be tempted beyond what you can bear. But when you are tempted, He will provide a way out so that you can endure it" (1 Corinthians 10:13).

We've allowed Satan to abuse scripture and to confuse and discourage when we add or take away from God's word. For our beloved friends and family who struggle, it's better to be still and quiet but present. Lavish love and offer prayers to God, who is the perfecter of our faith, for the people in pain who surround us.

FINAL WORDS

It's now been more than seven years since my last brain surgery and since I've had any other brain trauma; thank You LORD for the break! It's the longest break I've had yet. As my shoulder surgeon predicted, I did have need for another surgery. It was painful, but minor in the grand scheme of things; at least it wasn't brain surgery! At this point, my left side is still debilitated and I still have some weakness in my mouth and some damage to the part of my brain that processes language. Even now I tire out when I attend church or am at some sort of social event in which I listen to or engage in conversation. That damage was caused and remains as a result of the bleed in 2012; I didn't have that struggle before. Although my smile is still awkwardly crooked, I've had much improvement with my speech and can eat most food safely if I eat slowly, sometimes methodically, and take small bites. I've had some close calls and nearly choked on some tough meat when I've been tired and tried to rush. I've learned I now function best when I take a nap midafternoon every day and I've accepted and gotten used to my new routine. I can't have a fast-paced demanding life. I'm more mindful of my limitations and know when I need to give my brain and body breaks. If I ignore warning signs such as tingling and numbness in my face, disorientation, excessive fatigue or growing head pain, and I push through, I put myself at risk for a seizure, a migraine or perhaps even a bleed. I still have a piece of the mass that was resected in 2007 and since then, the piece has grown in size and doctors have spotted an additional small cavernous malformation on my brain stem. I live my life, as Dr. Spetzler prescribed, but I also take the precautions doctors have given me and listen to my body for guidance.

It's not always easy to slow down because I want to be able to keep up with my able-bodied friends and family and I want to do more with my time. But I've learned and allowed myself to be patient with me and my limitations. I desire to be here, alive and available to my husband and children for a long time. If I have to live at a slower pace to do so, so be it.

It's Ok that I can't always keep up; I'm Ok. It's in my weakness I'm made strong and as I relax into the place God has for me, I experience joy; *immense* joy! When I had sustained more brain damage, working was more difficult for me and financial provision was a concern. Our kids have needs as they grow, our house needs repairs, we need money for groceries, utilities, etc. There are always financial needs. Honestly, with the need for daily rest and breaks, my difficulty with processing speech and information, not being able to use both hands or withstand much physical strain, not to mention my frequent migraines, I would not be a very good employee. The future may look different for me, but at least for now, the LORD has instead called me to be available to my family and to take care of my health.

Although there's often been strife between Mike and me in the area of finances, I've been prayerful and seen the LORD provide for us over and over again. He provided a great job for Mike and equips Mike with the ability to do well and succeed. And as we have extra need, the LORD has provided feasible work for me, hand-me-down clothes for the kids, disability, financial aid, and He provides in many other unexpected ways. As we need it, He provides. It's our job to be good stewards of what He does provide and to be thankful for what we're given. I am *so* thankful. I'm thankful that Mike, Luke and Natalie are more often than not also patient with my limitations. Although I don't produce much income and I need to rest, my worth to my family is not based on what I can or can't do. I am valuable, appreciated and loved. My children have compassion on me in my weakness and my pain. I occasionally have such intense migraines that I lay nauseated on the bathroom floor by the toilet, and I cry in the dark. My son's little heart breaks for me when I hurt, and he cries too. My children lay their little hands on me when I hurt, and they pray for my relief; that warms my heart. And quite often God hears their prayers and provides at least enough relief for me to sleep. Daily the LORD is my physical strength and my song. I can't go on without Him! The love of my Father and my children keeps me going and fighting each day.

Although I see the blessing in my struggle, I still often feel the burden of being broken. I have nights I can't relax and sleep because my left arm is so tight and painful. And sometimes I feel I'm a burden to my husband. I buy into Satan's lies that I'm worthless and life isn't worth living in a broken body. In desperation, as I struggle to sleep, I lay prostrate on my living room floor, tears streaming down my face and cry, "LORD, just heal me now; please!" When time and time again He does not respond with a miraculous healing, I've wondered if it's just not His will that I be healed and whole here. Perhaps it's better for me that I remain broken.

I don't know when I'll be healed, if it's here on earth or not until heaven. I need to remind myself that the time and place is not important. For as I am weak, I truly rely on Christ to be my strength and I see the blessing in my weakness. In my suffering I've learned to be dependent on Christ in all things. Christ is truly in control. The LORD told me many years ago to stop planning for and anticipating my physical healing as if it's something I have to have to make my life complete. I had to repent of seeking after it.

The apostle Paul in the Bible accepted the thorn in his side and realized it was purely for his benefit that it remain there.

"In order to keep me from becoming conceited, I was given a thorn in my flesh, a messenger of Satan, to torment me. Three times I pleaded with the Lord to take it away from me. But he said to me, 'My grace is sufficient for you, for my power is made perfect in weakness.' Therefore, I will boast all the more about my weaknesses, so that Christ's power may rest on me" (2 Corinthians 12:7-9).

I wondered if it's what the LORD wanted me to do also: to accept my disabilities as a gift, a blessing and permanent.

Yet more recently, the LORD has asked me to not give up hope! I believe for a time that the LORD *did* call me to a time of acceptance and asked me to embrace my brokenness and weakness to allow Him to transform me through it. And yet now, I believe the LORD is asking me to act in faith, and believe that He can and *will* restore function! Twelve years have elapsed since my more devastating bleed, and I'm not sure how healing could come about now; but the LORD is asking me to trust Him, to obey Him, to allow Him to guide me and to surrender to His will. "LORD, I believe, but help me in my unbelief."

I thought once and for all Mike had come to a place of acceptance as I once had; that he thought it must not be God's will for me to be healed, or that he had simply given up asking. However, I discovered that Mike was still pleading to Christ for my healing. He was tired of seeing me suffer, and desired to see me restored to good health. When Mike told me this I was deeply touched and cried. "I didn't know you still cared." Just a year ago, while Mike was praying privately in his truck, the LORD brought to his mind some rehabilitation devices I'd tried in Phoenix five years prior. We had forgotten all about them. We felt the LORD leading us to revisit them, so, we called a Bioness representative to check out the devices a second time. The devices could potentially rehabilitate my left arm and leg. The devices are strapped on to the weakened arm or leg and low levels of electricity stimulate the inactive, dormant muscles to move. It potentially strengthens the muscles and retrains the brain to help the muscles function properly. Five years prior, the devices had been difficult to operate and we didn't see any value in them. But in five years' time the company had made advancements and improvements with their products, and they were easier to use. We saw real promise for the healing of my left arm and left leg from these devices. They were very expensive, but the amount of financial support we got from friends and family was truly amazing and humbling and we were able to obtain both the device for my arm *and* for my leg. It appeared that not only my husband, but many many other friends and family still cared about the condition of my arm and leg and were inspired to hope for healing too. I was deeply touched.

At first with each use of the Bioness devices, I easily wore out. My arm was especially angry when I tried the device with the representative from Bioness. That part of my brain had been "resting" and the stimulation to that part of the brain even for twenty minutes exhausted me. I was very tired the rest of the day and all the next day! Thankfully, I have built up an endurance to each device and use them both daily. The device for my leg especially has been life-changing. I wear it all day every day. I can walk faster and safer without a foot drop because the Bioness cuff gives me a jolt of electricity to lift my foot each time I move my knee; it's amazing! I've also been able to wear a greater variety of shoes. I easily tripped or my ankle would roll in anything other than a New Balance tennis shoe with a stiff support in the ankle prior to using the Bioness cuff. But now I can wear sandals, boots, slippers and even walk barefoot! My walk is much more fluid and doesn't feel as stiff, painful and rigid anymore. However, I still have a habit to break. Prior to the help of the Bioness, I couldn't lift my foot up as I walked. For many years I've compensated and lifted my left hip when I walk to help my foot clear the ground. I'm still trying to retrain my brain, break that pattern and habit that I don't need to do anymore!

The progress with the Bioness device for my arm is slower, probably because it was in worse shape; but since I've started using it more faithfully, the LORD has given me vivid dreams of playing the violin again. I see myself in the dream holding the violin under my chin, my left hand wrapped around the neck and my fingers slowly moving across the strings. And in the dream, I say aloud, "Ok LORD, this time I'm going to use this instrument for Your glory." I wake up from each dream with tears in my eyes. I've also had dreams of being able to put my hair in a ponytail, of me running, and starting to extend my fingers; all dreams of healing. I've had dreams of me *beginning* to heal and other dreams of being fully restored and healed! I don't know if these dreams will become a reality, but they seem to confirm and validate what I've heard from God: that I will indeed experience healing. I *love* it when God speaks to me in dreams!

God has clearly told me to not give up hope and to work hard with the promise that whatever happens, healing or not, He will richly bless the journey and be with me every step of the way.

Honestly, I've struggled, and I hesitate to act because I'm afraid what I may work hard to obtain again will also be taken again. As He speaks to me of healing, God has not given me any promise that I won't experience loss again. That makes me feel angry, scared and stubbornly resistant to act. Even so, the LORD is asking me to act in faith, to be obedient, and to move. As hard as that is to accept, and I will most certainly get impatient along the way, I must consistently and faithfully respond to His instruction aloud with a "Yes, LORD" and be ready for what's next.

Through my journey of pain and the testing of my faith, I've grown stronger, but my pain and suffering has also deeply challenged my marriage and the testing of Mike's faith. Just as nursing my infants had not come naturally and as easy as I thought it would be, marriage and loving one another didn't come as naturally and easy either. When Mike and I dove into marriage together, we took on challenge right from the start. As I predicted, Mike didn't seem to be up to the challenge neither mentally or spiritually to be wed to a disabled wife. We had many rough years at the start of our marriage, but through the testing of our love for one another and of our faith, we've grown together. As odd as it seems, I believe the transformation and softening of Mike's heart started in Phoenix in 2012 after my emergency brain surgery. He found a pure love for me that didn't come easily, but daily made a choice to love me unconditionally and put my needs first. We still have our spats and there's always room to grow, but I know with full confidence that Mike is my greatest advocate and support, will always choose to love me and fight for me.

His love and respect for our dear children has grown too and it's reciprocated. The day that Luke chose his dad's company over mine stung me a little, but it was good. Their bond continues to grow stronger as Mike *chooses* Luke. Luke and Natalie value, respect and trust that their dad has their best interest in mind and will always fight for them and never abandon them. I also have no doubt that if Luke or Natalie should suffer horrific consequences of cavernous malformation bleeds, he will be there right alongside them, encouraging, supporting and praying for them. I pray that God affords me the opportunity to be alongside them too.

I try not to feel afraid of or resist death, but often I have such bad migraines that I wonder if I'll wake the next morning. I often wonder if one of my masses will sporadically bleed and take my life. I wonder if I'll have a bleed or seizure while I'm driving that results in a fatal accident. I don't want to be fearful and dwell on these things, but when I experience a very intense migraine it's hard not to let my thoughts wander there. Mike and I have fought together through so much already. I feel he and I have earned the right and *deserve* to have a long life together. I don't want to leave my husband and kids before I feel "I'm ready." The thought of leaving them so suddenly grieves my heart and I can't stand the thought of any other woman filling the role I feel I've deserved and daily fight to maintain. Should the occasion of a sudden death occur, I have written my "goodbye" letters to Mike, Luke and Natalie. No one knows how, when and where the LORD will take us. I feel the blessing of living with such a serious and possible life-threatening condition, is that I'm always looking toward eternity and realize that this world is not my home and I don't want to squander what time the LORD gives me here.

No matter what happens in my future, healing or not, I'm truly thankful for my LORD and Savior, His wisdom, love, mercy, grace, compassion, the growth and guidance He's given me on my journey thus far and I'm truly thankful for my husband, my children, for dear Mama and Dad, our faithful loving church, our families and many friends. Truly among all the heartache there has also been an abundance of blessings; I see God's hand in all of it. I value and thank God for giving me perspective. I see what's truly important and that the eternal soul is of much greater value and worth than the temporal body here and now. Although sometimes I'd like God to lay out an outline of my life, tell me exactly what's going to happen when and why, I like and can appreciate that there's mystery to Christ; it keeps me in constant pursuit of Him. Everything will be revealed to me in time. For now, I only see in part, but I will see the whole picture once my body dies and my soul joins Him in heaven.

For now, we all painfully live in a broken world and will undoubtedly experience more hardships (although I hate the thought of that). "Thank You LORD that we have the availability of the Holy Spirit as our advocate and guide." When we are faced with something hard, we have a choice to make: blame God or embrace Him. God gives us a choice. He *wants* us to choose Him, but He doesn't *make* us choose Him. I do choose to embrace Him and I pray I always will, no matter what. I actually now *thank* God that He allowed my body to break because in so doing, He saved my soul, and my husband says it has saved his too.

I know there will be more trials ahead of us of all kinds. I ask that the LORD help us to stand strong together, fight for each other, and that He again will go before us and be with us always. In our brokenness we can come to Him over and over and over again. He never tires of hearing from us; that's good news. "Hear our cry oh LORD. Have mercy on us and forgive us again and again, love us, be ever near us and guide us. Amen." I love my hubby. As we put Christ at the forefront of our lives and turn to Him first nothing will beat "Team Wohler."

"Two are better than one, because they have a good reward for their labor; for if (when) they fall, the one will lift up the other. If two lie down together, then they have warmth. And though a man might prevail against him who is alone, two will withstand him. A threefold cord is not quickly broken" (Ecclesiastes 4: 9-12 AMPC).

"Wherever two or more are gathered in My name, there I AM in the midst of them" (Matthew 18:20).

"Humble yourselves, therefore, under God's mighty hand, that he may lift you up in due time. Cast all your anxiety on him because he cares for you" (1 Peter 5:6-7).

"We know in part and we prophesy in part, but when completeness comes, what is in part disappears. For now, we see only a reflection as in a mirror; then we shall see face to face. Now I know in part; then I shall know fully, even as I am fully known" (1 Corinthians 13: 9-10, 12).

In this crazy journey of the development of my faith through pain and trauma, I've had several songs that have ministered to my heart as I've struggled with my disabilities. "Need You Now" by Plumb was my anthem as I deeply desired healing, was tired of waiting for it and just wanted to be delivered from my affliction. Yet God seemed to just be giving me the strength I needed to keep going as I remained broken.

"Even If" by MercyMe became my anthem when I'd resolved to accept my disability. I knew God could take it from me, but even if He didn't I would still love Him and follow Him. But, my current anthem is "Move" by TobyMac because yes, my heart has been broken, my prayers for healing haven't been answered yet, but I'm no longer in a place of desperation *or* acceptance. I realize that God can and is still using me. The song inspires and encourages me to keep moving and walking with courage and confidence where the LORD leads. "LORD, I love and trust You and I am indeed ready for what's next." I'll lift my head and not despair. It's not over yet.

Dear Reader,

Thank you for taking the time to read my testimony. Writing my story has been a ten-year work in progress. I began jotting down notes and pieces of my story when my son Luke was born. Just in case I had a fatal bleed before my son had the chance to get to know me, I wanted him to know my story: the testament of my faith. I wrote casually as I remembered something that I thought might be interesting or important to note from my journey. When my daughter Natalie was born, I wrote with a greater sense of urgency. I sincerely wanted my children to know that although my journey has been very difficult, the growth I've experienced in Christ far outweighs the pain. Over the last several years I've had many distractions: two shoulder surgeries, two brain surgeries, therapy after surgeries, raising two small children and caring for my home. Only within the last two years have I begun to write more regularly and diligently. It was a huge undertaking, but a blessed and therapeutic journey. I had many people praying for me and encouraging me as I made my writing a priority. I initially wrote this story for my kids, but the LORD challenged me to publish and share far and wide; this both terrified me and excited me. I'm glad to finally present a finished product after ten long years. I hope you've been blessed and encouraged from my testimony as I have been.

Sincerely,
Megan

NOTES

Ch. 10

Philip Yancey, *Prayer: Does it Make Any Difference?* (Grand Rapids: Zondervan, 2006), 221 & 275.

Lynn Austin, *Faith of My Fathers* (Bethany House, 2006), 196.

Ch. 13

Warren W. Wiersbe, *Be Joyful: Even When Things Go Wrong, You Can Still Have Joy* (David Cook, 1974), 42.

Warren W. Wiersbe, *Be Mature: Growing up in Christ* (David Cook, 1978), 164.

Philip Yancey, *Where is God When it Hurts?* (Grand Rapids: Zondervan, 1990), 89.

Warren W. Wiersbe, *Be Confident: Live by Faith, Not by Sight* (David Cook, 1982), 152 & 153.

Philip Yancey, *Prayer: Does it Make Any Difference?* (Grand Rapids: Zondervan, 2006), 238.

Larry Crabb, *The Pressure's Off* (Colorado Springs: Waterbrook Press, 2002), 12.